Some Like It Cold

Arctic and Antarctic Expeditions

Neville Shulman

SUMMERSDALE

Summersdale Publishers Ltd
46 West Street
Chichester
West Sussex
PO19 1RP
UK

www.summersdale.com

Printed and bound in Great Britain.

Paperback   ISBN 1 84024 142 X
Hardback   ISBN 1 84024 201 9

Photographs supplied by Neville Shulman,
Andy Goldsworthy, Steve Pinfield and Ian Ford.

Some Like it Cold is dedicated to Ann Shulman,
mother, grandmother and great grandmother,
without whom I wouldn't have had the opportunities
to travel to the ends of the earth.

Not everything in Life is surreal.
Even living on the edge it's possible to be truly happy,
even if only for the briefest of moments.

CONTENTS

Foreword by Sir Ranulph Fiennes

Foreword by David Hempleman-Adams

Introduction by Sir Nicholas Serota

PART ONE – THE ARCTIC

PART TWO – THE ANTARCTIC

Sir Ranulph Fiennes

Fiennes has been described as 'the world's greatest living explorer'. He has led several expeditions across the polar regions, to the North and South Poles, and across the desert of Oman to find the legendary lost Arabian city of Ubar.

Of all the magical places in the world to visit the North Pole and the South Pole take a lot of beating. Neville Shulman is one of that still small group who has experienced standing at the Top of the World and then at the Bottom of the World. There are those of course who think the Arctic and the Antarctic are merely huge frozen wastes and themselves could never contemplate spending any time there. But, as Shulman succinctly puts it, Some Like it Cold.

Probably the best known of all the polar explorers are Roald Amundsen and Robert Scott who battled heroically and dramatically against each other in order to be the first to reach the South Pole. Amundsen arrived there in December 1911 and Scott a month later in January 1912, only then to die with all his team so tragically on their return journey. Stories of their exploits and those of the other great Arctic and Antarctic explorers are detailed in the chapters, The Men Who Dared and Ice Warriors.

In this fascinating book, Neville Shulman recounts two adventures; his travelling to the North Pole, following in the footsteps of the naturalist sculptor, Andy Goldsworthy and ten years on, his journey to the South Pole to fundraise for the Red Cross. There are also detailed chapters with fascinating information on these beautiful but remote ice regions, their extraordinary animal and bird life and of course the excitement of Shulman's personal journeys and his own battles to make it through to the end. Within the book he gently explains the philosophy he uses to help him overcome innumerable obstacles and couples this with the humour he includes in all his books. These are inspiring and reflective journeys which will undoubtedly encourage others to attempt to travel to both the North and the South Poles.

David Hempleman-Adams

Hempleman-Adams has climbed the highest mountains on each continent, the Seven Summits, and has also led expeditions to both Poles. Recently he achieved a series of world records by ballooning from Spitzbergen in Norway to within one degree of latitude of the North Pole.

Many of my own adventures have been in the Arctic and Antarctic regions and I know exactly what Neville Shulman means by calling his book *Some Like it Cold*. When you are trekking across huge tracts of fragmenting ice, fighting against intense, bitter winds and sub-zero conditions you couldn't really do it unless you had some sort of affinity with the immense cold that is all around you. I have been drawn again and again to travel to the polar regions and they are absolutely fascinating places, full of beauty, mystery and of course solitude. I was certainly fortunate to become the first man to walk solo and unsupported to the North Magnetic Pole and also the first Briton to walk alone and unaided to the South Pole. My latest adventure in ballooning all the way to the North Pole region, although fraught with danger, was yet full of excitement and I know very well that I want to return.

Neville Shulman tells wonderful stories of his own adventures in reaching first the North Pole and then the South Pole and there is very much to admire within his own tremendous determination and absolute commitment. The fact that he undertakes his journeys primarily to raise funds for charity only serves to enhance his own personal endeavours and efforts.

Neville Shulman has provided a great deal of comprehensive background information on the Arctic and the Antarctic as well as intriguing and provocative references to the many explorers that have travelled before us. As he lucidly explains, his own Zen philosophy undoubtedly helped him to cope with the many trials and tribulations that face anyone venturing into these completely frozen and dangerous territories. I realise, like myself, he is completely hooked and also will always remember the exciting times he had travelling in the ice footsteps of so many of our great polar explorers.

Introduction

Sir Nicholas Serota

Serota is one of the leading art experts in the United Kingdom and is the director of Tate Britain (formerly the Tate Gallery) and was instrumental in establishing Tate Modern. Each year he heads up the committee choosing the Turner Prize for modern art created by the Patrons of New Art.

When we were approached by Andy Goldsworthy, that most innovative and creative of naturalist artists, to ask the Patrons of New Art if they would like to participate in his expedition to the North Pole, I doubted very much if anyone would really be willing to join him. Of course, I had reckoned without our member Neville Shulman, who continues to amaze all his friends by the extraordinary explorations he undertakes to faraway, remote and often dangerous destinations. He is a real adventurer and obviously loves to test his mettle in sometimes life-threatening situations, whether on a mountain or in a jungle or even combining both testing habitats within one expedition.

At the time, I knew the Arctic planning and arrangements were fraught with difficulties and on a number of occasions we doubted whether Andy would actually be able to take off himself. We were also concerned whether the two Patrons of New Art, who indeed were the only two to volunteer, would be able to travel out and meet up with Andy either in the Arctic or more particularly at the North

Pole itself. It is a tribute to their determination and enterprise that they were somehow able to make it through and eventually all meet at the Pole. Andy has brought back some remarkable photographs of the powerful sculptures he was able to create there as well as earlier at Grise Fiord, the Inuit village.

In *Some Like it Cold* Neville Shulman tells the story of the Andy Goldsworthy expedition as well as of a subsequent expedition through Antarctica to reach the South Pole. He has also written about the adventures of previous polar explorers, both in the Arctic and Antarctic and of course the heroic struggles between those who were so determined to be the first to arrive at the North Pole and then a few years later at the South Pole. Shulman also provides a great deal of interesting information and background on both polar regions and is able very effectively to portray both the beauty and the glory that is undoubtedly to be found there.

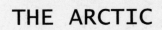

THE ARCTIC

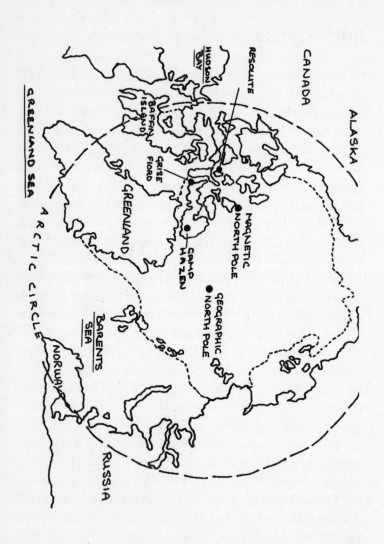

Chapter One

North Pole Invitation

'Who wants to go to the North Pole?' There are about fifty members of the Patrons of New Art in the downstairs meeting room of the Tate Gallery, London's vibrant Museum of Modern Art, most presumably drawn there out of curiosity rather than a spirit of adventure. When Nicholas Serota, the Director of the Tate, called the Patrons together, I had very little knowledge about what he was going to propose and even less of a concept of what would then be involved. But it had been one of my childhood dreams to travel to those glorious but intangible two Poles, the North and the South; as an adult I still dream.

Nick explains that Andy Goldsworthy, the naturalist sculptor, has conceived an exciting, new art project, 'Touching North', and there is an opportunity for some of us to be part of it. Andy creates his works as being at one with the elements of nature, sculpting with leaves, twigs, rocks, wood and often incorporating the poetic vibrancy of water. By working with ephemeral and impermanent structures he tries to stimulate an awareness of the specialness of nature, the environment around us and how we all should relate to it. Andy would certainly understand what is implied in the evocative Zen koan, 'What is the colour of wind?' One koan can take years before being truly understood but afterwards it can be the key to unlock the secret of many. 'When the many are reduced to one, to what is the one reduced?' When you are at last one with any koan you are truly seeing into one's own private nature.

Andy was originally born in Cheshire but now lives in Penpont, a remote northern part of Scotland, where he often works sculpting ice and snow. He has also created ice sculptures in many other parts of the world, particularly Japan. (Many years after the polar expedition he embarked on a project to create gigantic winter snowballs and then transport them into the heart of London in the middle of summer.) Nick informs the Patrons that Andy has now conceived a special and unique art project and he is looking for a few hardy, some might say foolhardy, souls, to be a part of his highly innovative project. Andy will travel deep into the Arctic and stay in the tiny Canadian hamlet of Grise Fiord during March and April working with the native Inuit of the region, learning their ice cutting techniques and creating a series of ice sculptures that would harmonise with the awesome Arctic landscape. Then he plans to fly on to reach the North Pole itself, to work at the Pole for four days where he hopes to create a large and spectacular polar sculpture. It will be a difficult and complicated adventure as he will be travelling in a light aircraft between Inuit villages and working in extremely cold temperatures of possibly less than -20 °C. The weather and travel conditions will be unpredictable not to mention hazardous and potentially dangerous.

'Would some of the Patrons of New Art like to follow in the footsteps of Andy, so becoming a part of his unique art conception and meet him at the North Pole on Monday 24 April?'

Automatically and flippantly I immediately respond, 'In the morning or the evening?' But inside, my heart is beating very fast. What an amazing and wonderful chance, an incredible opportunity to achieve one of my dreams at last!

north pole invitation

We are shown some pictures of the Arctic regions through which we will have to travel and told that there could be no guarantees we would arrive in time to meet up with Andy or even eventually reach the North Pole. But we just *might* make it! I am completely fired up by what I've just heard and the magnificence of the idea and it really seems, despite the many problems that are likely to occur, something not to be missed. The writer Ursula Le Guin summed up the essence of all travel with her words, 'It is good to have an end to journey toward but it is the journey that matters, in the end.'

'Who would like to go?' About twenty of the Patrons provisionally volunteer and, even though at that moment I'm not certain if I can make the time, I am the first among them. Previously I had read avidly about the early explorers and their expeditions to the polar regions but had never really imagined I would ever have the chance to travel there myself. Now that I could, I must.

The group quickly splits into two, those who plan to go and those who don't, the latter mostly drift away. Goldsworthy will travel out in mid-March and base himself in the high Arctic island of Ellesmere, in the community of Grise Fiord. There he will create his first Arctic sculptures. He will be joined a few weeks later by the photo-journalist Julian Calder who will document the expedition. Then, if the weather conditions permit, the plan is for Goldsworthy and Calder to travel to the North Pole on 20 April to establish a camp for four days, allowing Andy to sculpt his final polar work of art there. We will set out some weeks after him, travelling through the Arctic, staying in the same places that Andy has previously stayed in and hopefully joining up with him at the North Pole on 24 April.

The aim is for us to arrive on his very last day in order to witness the work he has created and to become a living part of this glorious art experience.

Andy's own philosophy is expressed in a poetic and Zen-like way in the few simplistic words: 'I want to follow North to its source, to try to come to terms with it, in the same way I work with a leaf under the tree from which it fell.' There is a direct correlation between the way Goldsworthy works and haiku, the very short form of poetry that is said to 'catch life as it flows'. It has been described as the final flower of all Eastern culture (Dr R. H. Blyth). Haiku is not Zen but Zen may be haiku in its most minimalist form. The Zen poet Buson was a past master at exploring and capturing one exquisite moment, 'The butterfly – resting upon the temple bell; Asleep.' No wonder the Japanese find Goldsworthy's work so inspirational.

Those of us who have put our names down start meeting over the next few weeks, learning about the logistics and costs of travelling to the Arctic; there are no easy options. It is going to be expensive and arduous. However, the more obstacles that are raised the more determined I become to see it through, no matter what. If the others are going I will also. Then strange things start to occur; odd accidents, family and business complications, unmissable engagements that prevent most of the others from continuing. One by one they drop out. It is very worrying particularly as we learn more about the dangers of travelling to that remote and frozen region. Various fears and concerns are expressed more openly by friends and colleagues. There is also the real possibility that even after going all that way we will be prevented, for one reason or another, from finally standing at the Pole. Perhaps I am taking on more than I can cope with! But I can't pass up such a terrific opportunity. When would it occur again? I must commit and continue. It is definitely a Zen moment in time.

Eventually the group is whittled down to just two of us from the Patrons who are able and willing to travel to the Arctic and join up with Andy. Penny Govett, a feisty art collector who heads the arranging of the Patrons' art events, and myself. When we realise that we are the only ones, and that all the others have dropped out for a myriad of reasons, we arrange to meet in order to take a long, cool and hard look at each other. The unspoken thoughts in both our minds are surely: 'Do we want to spend so much intensive time together, can we get along during such a tough trip, will we complement each other or end up hating each other's company?' They are unanswerable questions, only time will tell. But in the end the lure of the Arctic, the call of the wild, wins through and our overwhelming desire is a streetcar to our North Pole destination. There are, in fact, to be two others going with us on the expedition; Fabian Carlsson, the Norwegian owner of the gallery handling Andy Goldsworthy as an artist, and Erik Mustad, a Swede and an old friend of Fabian. Erik lives and works between Norway and Switzerland and will join up with the three of us in Montreal.

The trip is being co-ordinated by James Bustard for the Fabian Carlsson Gallery and Anne Berthoud, another gallery owner and keen supporter of Andy's work. Over the next few weeks all of us meet several times to confirm the travel arrangements, to decide on suitable equipment and the gear we need to take with us, but above all to lend moral support and encouragement to each other as the departure date looms ever nearer. We intend to take only the minimum baggage and leave behind whatever is not really essential. We need to travel light, indeed preferably with hand luggage only. We will be flying mostly in small aeroplanes where weight will be a major consideration. As a kind of homage to the Arctic adventure I design a T-shirt with the logo: 'Monday at the North Pole 24 April'. The die is cast – we can't waste the T-shirts, we definitely have to go now and must reach the Pole on that date. The only trouble is that the weather will be beyond our control and it will eventually decide whether we, or indeed Andy, will make it to the North Pole for 24 April.

Fabian Carlsson is initially very ebullient but then starts to become rather despondent as the plans and arrangements begin to change. Particularly as he has done his costings on the basis of a much larger group and as people drop out the costs start to soar. Still, he is a man of his word; he has made a commitment to Andy and he refuses to cancel. Also, as a London gallery owner with plenty of media publicity organised, Fabian doesn't want to lose face and the potentially substantial sales of the Arctic cibachrome photographs. I become somewhat worried however that he might be cutting corners on the back-up and safety arrangements in the Arctic.

Furthermore, there is an even bigger concern from Fabian's point of view; the Arctic region where we will be mostly based is an alcohol-free zone and the Inuit are, officially at any rate, forbidden to sell spirits and drinks. For a Norwegian, particularly someone like Fabian, this is a totally unacceptable position and he decides to jettison much of his personal clothing and equipment in order to carry with him a good supply of whisky and brandy for the whole trip. Erik Mustad, Fabian's drinking companion from old, is also told to stock up likewise. Throughout the Arctic, you could always tell when Fabian was approaching as there would be plenty of bottle-clinking noises to advise us of his imminent presence.

Andy Goldsworthy sets off, some four weeks before us, and soon it will be our turn. It's not easy to prepare for a trip to the Arctic; there are no longer any polar bears in England. Even London's Regent's Park Zoo doesn't have them any more. After seeing their awe-inspiring, intensely wild but natural habitat I am certainly very pleased about that. When starting my own family there used to be a small, much-loved polar bear cub in London Zoo called Brumas. Sadly he is no more. Although in some ways perhaps it is just as well, as the tiny area that was allotted to the polar bears in the zoo could never compensate for the vastness of the Arctic and the freedom it allows, no matter how many fish the keepers might throw their way.

I know the journeys and our time in the extreme cold will be onerous and exhausting, so at least I must keep as fit as possible. Therefore in the run-up to setting off, I decide to run and run. Most nights, all the way up to Highgate and around the surrounding Hampstead hills, building up my stamina as much as possible. I also do regular weight training sessions, paying particular attention to the ankles and knees. In the bitter cold I know how easy it would be to wrench a leg muscle and I must prepare myself for anything I might encounter within the frozen ice lands.

Also I need to learn more about the Arctic, its remoteness and its animals, as well as more about those that have journeyed and explored there and endeavoured to reach the North Pole. Soon, hopefully, it will be my time.

Japan's most important early poet, Matsuo Basho, always advised of the necessity of combining the spiritual rudiments of Zen together with Tao, 'Learn the rules well and then forget them. If you want to learn about the pine go to the pine, about bamboo go to the bamboo. Poetry arises by itself when you and the object have become one.' Basho could find the meaning of the universe in the smallest detail. Perhaps I would find something within the vast Arctic.

Chapter Two

The Men Who Dared

The ancient Greeks gave the name *Arctos*, the Bear, to a group of very bright stars in the northern sky. The point around which these stars were thought to revolve was named the Arctic Pole, eventually to be known as the North Pole. The Greek explorer, Pytheas, made the first recorded voyage crossing the Arctic Circle. He had heard that somewhere to the north could be found a strange and mysterious archipelago known as Thule (pronounced too-lee). No one could find Thule despite numerous voyages and it always seemed to be further north, no matter how far explorers travelled. The name was eventually changed to Ultima Thule – 'the land furthest north'. Thule also became the name given to the natives of the region who were the forerunners of the Inuit. The Inuit shaman, Qillaq (subsequently known as Qitdlarssuaq, meaning the great Qillaq) also wanted to be the first one to find and reach the land furthest north and in the mid 1800s tried several times but failed to find the way through. The quest to find Ultima Thule subsequently became the quest to reach the Geographic North Pole (90 °N – where all directions are south) and it was this goal above all which the polar explorers sought.

The Magnetic North Pole is situated much more southerly; presently set on the south-west of Ellef Ringnes Island and is the point from which the Earth's magnetic field radiates. It is also the point to which all compass needles are trained and lies at latitude 78 °N. It is in constant lateral movement and has shifted several hundred kilometres northwards from the point where first discovered in 1831 by the British explorer Admiral Sir James Clark Ross. A magnetic compass can't work within a few hundred kilometres of the Magnetic North Pole. There is a third Arctic Pole, relatively obscure and unknown and described as the Pole of Relative Inaccessibility. It is the furthest point from land in all directions and lies at 50 °N, 160 °W. Not many people know that!

Britain had for centuries been one of the supreme maritime powers; France, Spain, Portugal and Holland its major maritime rivals. They constantly competed with one another to achieve a breakthrough in finding new sea routes. However, Sir Francis Drake and centuries later my particular hero, Lord Horatio Nelson, proved that there were few who could match the adventurous and extraordinary exploits of the British sailor. Curiously Nelson was a young midshipman on HMS *Carcass* in 1773, on its exploratory expedition led by Captain Phipps in an attempt to find a route to the North Pole.

Daring Elizabethan seafarers like Martin Frobisher and Henry Hudson, in heavy competition with men from other nations, had long sought to find the North-West Passage which it was believed would provide a very lucrative shortcut through to China and the Spice Islands. It was a golden age of ocean adventure. Bringing back the cargo of just one heavily-laden ship could make the owner rich. Successive British governments considered that, above all, finding this route would establish Britain's trading supremacy in the world.

Frobisher eventually sailed his ship into the bay subsequently named after him in 1576, initially believing he had actually discovered the North-West Passage to Cathay. He also brought back rocks from the Baffin Island area that mistakenly convinced the court of Elizabeth I that there was gold in abundance to be mined there. This turned out to be a very costly mistake indeed. Henry Hudson sailed into the straits and the bay named after him in 1610, unfortunately his voyage ended in mutiny and his untimely death. Hudson had promised his crew a way through to the Pacific Ocean but sailed them into another bay where the ship was quickly trapped within the ice. In a forerunner of the Captain Bligh incident, Hudson and his young son were cast adrift in a small boat, but unlike Bligh's survival, they were never seen again. William Baffin was the nearest to finding the passage as the entrance actually lay through Baffin Bay. Unfortunately for Baffin he didn't realise this and assumed it to be a dead end and a closed bay. It was to be several centuries later before the route through was discovered, and again only out of tragedy. So many seafarers had tried to find this elusive passage that inevitably it became no longer a trading necessity but national pride which would drive men on to sail deeper and deeper into the Arctic wastes, no one even being certain if it really existed.

The maps of the Arctic region mostly showed vast tracts marked 'parts unknown' and it was not until the beginning of the nineteenth century that real interest in further exploration was awakened. The French Revolution of 1789 and the Napoleonic wars that followed had occupied the attentions of the countries of Europe but after the Treaty of Paris in 1815 the Royal Navy suddenly had a surplus of men and ships. Opportunities to utilise some of them were urgently needed.

A respected whaling captain, William Scoresby, experienced in sailing far into the Arctic waters, reported unusual thawing of the Arctic seas around Greenland. He recommended that it was an ideal time again to attempt to explore the Arctic and to find a way to sail through. It was indeed an opportune moment. The Second Secretary of the Admiralty, John Barrow, became enthused by the idea and in 1818 authorised two separate expeditions led respectively by Captain David Buchan and Commander John Ross. Buchan's expedition was considered a failure and he had to return, but Ross was initially more successful; he met a tribe of Inuit (then known as Eskimos) who had never seen white men or ships of such size before. They called the ships 'creatures with wings.' Ross thought he saw a range of mountains that he smartly named the Croker Mountains after the First Secretary of the Admiralty. Unhappily, this did him no good as no one else believed him and several of his officers disputed his claims. Ross returned in total disgrace. New commands were given to William Edward Parry who had been second-in-command to Ross and to John Franklin who had been second-in-command to Buchan.

Although both of these expeditions were only partly successful, this time each Commander came back to hero's welcomes, although with very different accounts and achievements. Parry and his ship had been stuck in the ice for over nine months before breaking loose and then being forced to return home. Franklin and his men had been given up for lost only to return three years later having barely survived. They had been reduced to eating their boots, straps and animal hides until rescued by friendly Inuit. Thereafter John Franklin was always known as 'the man who ate his boots'.

Both Parry and Franklin went on to mount further expeditions with varying degrees of success. Still they were famed and honoured by a society that loved to hear of their close encounters with starvation and death in the remote Arctic wilderness. John Ross was given another opportunity to redeem his reputation when Felix Booth, the creator of Booth's gin, financed an expedition. Presumably bountiful supplies were taken on board the ship – a paddle steamer called *Victory*. Possibly Booth was able to write off the costs to research and development or even to publicity and promotion.

Victory was entrapped in the ice off Prince William Inlet for three winters and eventually had to be abandoned. Ross and his men escaped across the ice to Fury Beach and, after being trapped for another year, used boats abandoned there by Parry seven years earlier to sail on to Baffin Bay and then to return. The amazing stories of his adventures and escapes fully restored his reputation. He was welcomed back this time with great honour and was subsequently knighted. In fact, it was his nephew, James Clark Ross, who during this voyage determined the location of the Magnetic North Pole on the Boothia Peninsula.

In order to encourage further seafaring adventurers, the British Admiralty had offered a reward of 20,000 guineas to the first person to find a way through to the North-West Passage. Sir John Franklin, supposedly at the end of his career as a sailor and explorer, applied for one further chance. He had fought alongside Lord Nelson at the battle of Trafalgar and his earlier expeditions had helped survey

1,760 km of the northern Canadian coastline. He had also been governor of Tasmania but returned after a bitter dispute with the colonial secretary there. He was now 58 and initially thought too old to be given such a dangerous mission. However, he was, after considerable lobbying, given the opportunity to mount a final expedition to try and locate the North-West Passage. He was given command of two massive ships, the aptly named HMS *Terror* (345 tonnes) and HMS *Erebus* (380 tonnes). Franklin would command and sail the *Erebus* and Captain Crozier would command the *Terror*, although still under Franklin's supreme command of the overall total of 129 men. They set out in 1845 and carried supplies estimated to last them three and a half years! They never returned and not one sailor was ever found alive.

There were several search expeditions sent out to look for them, including some sent by the indomitable Lady Franklin who refused for many years to accept that her husband had perished. She even consulted clairvoyants who predicted where the sailors could be found, or at least their remains, but no one would take those predictions seriously. She never gave up and continually badgered everyone of importance to allow further expeditions to continue the search; including such notables as the Prime Minister, the Emperor of France, the Tsar of Russia and the President of the United States. After a further rescue expedition was also lost in 1852, the Admiralty authorised one final attempt to look for the two lost crews.

Francis McClintock led this search party but only the rescue expedition was found, although one of its leaders, Robert McClure, actually discovered the entrance to the North-West Passage. Unfortunately however, he didn't navigate it but walked for most of its length. John Rae, an officer of the Hudson's Bay Company, while surveying the coast of Boothia Peninsula, finally came back with the news everyone had been dreading. Local native traders had provided clues about the fate of Franklin and his men and the mystery of what had become of them. It seemed that they had been trapped in the ice with their boats for some considerable time and had eventually succumbed to lead poisoning from seepage of their canned supplies. There was additional evidence, although never officially accepted, that possibly driven mad by the poisoning, some of Franklin's sailors had resorted to cannibalism. This would have been unthinkable in Victorian society, particularly by those who would not really understand the enormous deprivation experienced by such heroic adventurers and how desperate they would have become. Jane Franklin naturally refused to accept that terrible accusation as fact, as did her friend, the author Charles Dickens, who philosophised, 'The men who learn endurance are they who call the whole world brother.' However as recently as 1992 some of the crew's skeletons have been discovered which showed cuts made by knives consistent with cutting flesh.

Over several years some ravaged corpses and skeletons were discovered and in 1857 Lady Franklin financed a further search expedition, again under the command of Francis McClintock. His ship, *The Fox*, first sailed to Baffin Bay, where it was iced in for the first winter and then sailed to Bellot Strait. Contact was made with the Inuit tribe that Rae had met who confirmed again the story of the deaths of Franklin's men. McClintock's lieutenant, Robert Hobson, whilst exploring the coast of King William Island, then made a startling discovery. In a cairn, Hobson found the only written record of what had befallen Franklin and his men. On a standard Navy form were two messages. The first was dated 28 May 1847 and stated that the ships *Erebus* and *Terror* had survived two winters without serious mishap. It ended with the two simple words – 'All well.' With stark and despairing words, the second, added in the margin, told a very different story. It was dated 25 April 1848. '*Erebus* and *Terror* were deserted on 22 April. Sir John Franklin died 11 June 1847. Deaths to this date 9 officers and 15 men.' There is no further record of anyone having subsequently survived. The epitaph of Sir John Franklin was written at his wife's request by the poet laureate of the day, Lord Alfred Tennyson and placed in Westminster Abbey. The British Government and most others, appalled at the terrible loss of life suffered by this and many other expeditions, lost their previously keen desire to explore further for several decades. Even today there is a continuing fascination in Franklin's expeditions; the Royal Canadian Mounted Police are currently sending out a 20 metre patrol boat in an effort to locate the remains of *Erebus* and *Terror*. This is part of a 35,000 km adventure of rediscovery, retracing the voyage of the police schooner that first circumnavigated North America through the North-West Passage.

Subsequent to Franklin's time there have been many polar explorations to and through these frozen lands and some incredible exploits. Having experienced myself, though not to the same degree, the powerful emotional pull of the North Pole, I could appreciate and understand the 'Arctic Fever' that has gripped so many through the centuries. The immense desire to make the long and arduous journey across wastes of ice and snow that always threaten to overwhelm and to reach the end goal, no matter at what cost to yourself and your sanity, can only be understood by someone who has been similarly gripped or who has attempted to travel there. The Arctic is a desolate place.

In 1888, the Norwegian explorer and zoologist, Fridtjof Nansen, made the first crossing of the Greenland ice-cap with his sledge teams. His exploits earned him the nickname 'Nansen of the North'. He was an inspiration to generations of young enthusiasts who wanted to emulate his exploits in polar travel. The polar explorers of those times had the same glamorous images as the space explorers were to have in the 1960s. None was more enthralled than Robert Edwin Peary who went on to become a US Navy civil engineer. Peary's father had died when the boy was just three and his mother overly protected him and spent her time trying to make his life easier. In that she indisputably failed. Perhaps in retaliation to her coddling Peary developed a reputation as a hard man and was dedicated to making his own mark in the field of polar exploration. Despite numerous setbacks and injuries on his many expeditions he would never give up and he certainly showed the Zen spirit at all times. When several frost-bitten toes were crudely cut away to avoid the onset of gangrene, he wrote on his hut wall a Latin quotation from Seneca, *Inveniam viam aut faciam* – 'I shall find a way or make one'. They were the words chosen to represent him in death as well as life and inscribed on his monument at Arlington National Cemetery in Washington. He is reported to have said, 'A few toes aren't much to give to achieve the Pole.'

Yet controversy still remains over the claim by Commander Robert Peary that on 6 April 1909, he was the first man to reach the North Pole. It took him and his team five months to return before he could make the historic announcement on 6 September 1909. His famous despatch simply stated, 'Pole reached. *Roosevelt* safe. Peary.' *Roosevelt* was the steamer he had sailed out on initially and anchored at Cape Sheridan before setting out with his dog teams. Another telegram to the *Associated Press* read, 'Stars and Stripes nailed North Pole. Peary.' There are as many researches and reports supporting Peary's claim as there are opposing it. Whatever the truth of the matter, Peary was undoubtedly an intrepid explorer to whom tremendous respect and admiration is due for taking on this frightening and overwhelming wilderness of utmost hostility.

His polar expedition had set out in late 1908 with fifty-nine Inuit and just seven members of the original exploring team. Peary eventually said goodbye to the last of four support teams on 1 April 1909. Making the final trek with Peary were four Inuit and Matthew Henson, an African-American descended from former slaves. Henson accompanied Peary on eight Arctic expeditions and had saved his life more than once. There was undoubtedly a special bond existing between the two of them. On this last stretch they had cut the expedition size to five sledges and forty dogs. In his diary Peary wrote, 'The Pole at last! The prize of three centuries, my dream and ambition for twenty-three years.' For well over fifty days the men and their dog teams had fought their way across the ice from the last point of land to the North Pole and back, a total distance of 1,530 km.

It is stated, maybe Peary felt he owed it to him, that Henson was the one who actually planted the US flag at the Pole, thereby becoming the first Afro-American to reach there. Peary was only fifty-two and Henson forty-two. Peary and Henson had worked together and planned this moment for some eighteen years. All his life Peary had been driven by his dream of making it to the Pole and as a young boy he often used to quote from the poet, Henry Wadsworth Longfellow, 'And the thoughts of youth are long, long thoughts.'

Matthew Henson's dark skin helped considerably in the Arctic as the Inuit were able to identify with him and were therefore willing to lend support of manpower, dogpower and equipment. They were also very impressed with the tremendous skill and ability of Matthew Henson as a dynamic dog-sledge driver. He had learned their language and they called him, *Miy Paluk*. During earlier expeditions both Peary and Henson were known to have taken Inuit mistresses; on the 1905 expedition they installed two on board ship, respectively Alequasina and Aqattannuau. Henson's son was called Annaukaq. The exciting discovery of a tribe of dark-skinned Inuit, living at the edge of the polar ice fields, has led researchers to believe that they may be descendants of Matthew Henson. He only died in 1955 at the age of eighty-eight. Two years earlier President Eisenhower had finally bestowed on him a medal to honour his major polar contribution. Due to his many and varied abilities Henson had been selected ahead of five white men but contemporary accounts more or less relegated him to the role of valet.

There is also evidence that Peary himself fathered children by the natives, as did other explorers. This could account as to why some Inuit are exceptionally white. In some ways these actions may have been very beneficial to the Inuit by introducing outside genes. Otherwise they could have become dangerously inbred and might not have survived, certainly in the numbers that they have. In that same year of 1909, Captain Bernier – himself an Arctic Mariner who had also attempted to devise plans for reaching the North Pole – proclaimed Canada's sovereignty over the entire archipelago from the mainland of Canada to the North Pole. Peary died on 20 February 1920 from pernicious anaemia, having by then become a rear admiral and is mostly referred to in current references as Admiral Peary.

Dr Frederick Cook, a surgeon, who had been on expeditions previously with Peary, claimed he had beaten Peary to the North Pole and reached it a year earlier on 21 April 1908. He lacked any real proof but argued his case until he died in 1940, although his claim had been by then almost totally discredited. Even his own Eskimo companions contradicted his claims in 1909, although under intense interrogation by Peary and his men; additionally, no one could understand how he and his men had survived in the Arctic for a year when they had provisions for only a few months. An earlier assertion pertaining to his claim to have climbed Mount McKinley had also been discredited. Cook was an enigma. A man of personal charisma as opposed to Peary's stoicism, he made friends easily and initially persuaded many to his cause. He had even tended Peary when he had broken his leg. He had also impressed Roald Amundsen as a young man when both had served on the ship *Belgica* in an early Belgian expedition to Antarctica. Amundsen expressed his initial thoughts of Cook as, 'the one man of unfaltering courage, unfailing hope, endless cheerfulness and unwearied kindness.' Cook earlier received numerous honours, including the Gold

Medal of the Royal Belgian Academy, the Silver Medal of the Royal Geographical Society of Belgium and also became the President of the Explorers Club.

Cook's story is proof of the adage, you can fool some of the people some of the time, but not all of the people all of the time. Amundsen was bitterly disappointed at the revelation and found it hard to take. 'Whatever Cook may have done or not done, the Cook who did them was not the Dr Cook I knew as a young man. Some physical misfortune must have overtaken him to change his personality, for which he was not responsible.' Possibly it was the call of the wild, the lure of the Arctic, the desperate dream to reach the North Pole first; they can all unhinge a man. Robert Scott was also to experience that terrible desperation when finally reaching the South Pole in January 1912.

Another somewhat controversial polar figure is Rear Admiral Richard Byrd, although highly regarded at the time and mostly since. He claimed to be the first man to fly over the North Pole, achieving that record on 9 May 1926 at 9.02 a.m. He called it 'the dream of our lifetime.' Pilot Richard Byrd took off from King's Bay, Spitsbergen, Norway, along with Floyd Bennett. They flew a tri-motor Fokker aircraft, the *Josephine Ford*, and made the flight to the Pole and back, a distance of 2,445 km, in about fifteen and a half hours. They returned to the United States to a hero's welcome and both were awarded Congressional Medals of Honour.

Almost immediately some disputed their claim and stated that the aircraft lacked the speed to make it to the North Pole and back in less than 16 hours. There were also some doubts about Byrd's navigational abilities to reach the Pole and concerns expressed that he hadn't dropped the bundle of US flags at the Pole as he had originally stated he would. As recently as 1996 Dennis Rawlins, an astronomy professor at the University of Maryland, who specialises in examining polar explorers' navigational records to assess their claims, announced that Byrd's claim was false. According to Rawlins an erased sextant reading belonging to Byrd showed a different figure to the one submitted to the US Navy and asserted his aircraft couldn't have come closer than 150 miles to the Pole. However, other experts have subsequently repudiated Rawlins' assertions. The debate continues.

Three days after Byrd's reported flight over the Pole, the Italian, General Nobile and Roald Amundsen flew over the North Pole in the airship *Norge* on 12 May 1926. They dropped Norwegian, Italian and American flags, together with a large wooden cross given to Nobile especially for that purpose by Pope Pius XI. If Byrd's claim were incorrect then Amundsen would be the first person whose claims to have reached both Poles are undisputed. However, the honour, if not the full glory, would also have to be shared with his colleague Oscar Wisting, who accompanied him on board the *Norge* and who had been on the expedition to the South Pole. Amundsen never entered into the Byrd controversy and was content with having been awarded more polar honours than anyone else in history, before and since. Possibly some were not too happy to allow an Italian and the famous Norwegian another great polar honour and preferred it awarded to an American. William Molett, himself a polar navigator, declared himself satisfied that Byrd could certainly have achieved the flight to the Pole and back. Some of his several arguments are, that in reaching the Pole, Byrd's plane would have used up half its fuel making the plane considerably lighter and therefore allowing it to fly faster, as well as his having a tail wind to aid him. In addition, the plane's greater height would have also allowed it to fly faster.

All these polar claims and counter-claims are similar to the many arguments that rage about whether Shakespeare really wrote all the plays attributed to him. Some antagonists work themselves into such a frenzy of accusation that they resemble a Shakespeare anti-hero, rather like Richard III. If only Shakespeare had known what was going to occur, so many centuries later, he would have written a play about it, undoubtedly a comedy. 'There is nothing either good or bad but thinking makes it so.' Many are utterly convinced that the name of the playwright himself is actually a clue that he is not the author. Spear shaker is meant to indicate that the name is a *nom de plume*, shielding the real identity. Among those who are said to be the author are the writer Francis Bacon who went on to become Lord Chancellor, the playwright Christopher Marlowe, the fifth Earl of Rutland (Roger Manners) and even several Royal patrons. The most important thing is that the plays exist and succeeding generations continue to benefit from their magnificent prose. What does it really matter if the truth will always be shrouded in 'secrece and mystere'. So it is with the North Pole, it exists and has been reached, who was there first now becomes academic.

Shakespeare has rightly been acclaimed and voted as the man of the second millennium. The name is sufficiently a shining symbol of the supreme literacy of a language that can be so passionately and poignantly expressed. One of his lines could have served many an Arctic explorer battling through the frozen wastes, 'To fear the worst oft cures the worse.' We owe so much to all those early explorers who fought to create the trail, so that those of us coming afterwards would also benefit.

There are many other polar heroes who have also carried out extraordinary feats. One of the greats is undoubtedly Wally Herbert. In 1969 Herbert led an expedition to complete the first surface crossing of the Arctic Ocean a total of 6,115 km. It took him 16 months to reach the North Pole, after trekking across some of the most treacherous, frozen waters in the world. Of course Herbert wasn't the first man to walk across water! However, luck and timing conspired against him. A few weeks later, before Herbert could return to the United Kingdom, Neil Armstrong became the first man to step on to the moon. His 'one small step for mankind' immediately pushed Herbert's own colossal achievement off the front pages and so he became just a footnote in the history of exploration.

The Inuit themselves were not so impressed by space exploration; their ancestors had been visiting the moon for thousands of years; all they had to do was think of the moon to be transported there. When any eclipse occurred they would simply stare at the moon or the sun, and blow at the sky to banish whatever was making the sky ill. The fact that the eclipse would quickly end was proof to them that they were right in their action. Their simplicity of belief and understanding means they are never shocked or fazed by anything. They are always great survivors and believe in total reincarnation.

However, Herbert deserves to be remembered for a host of Arctic and Antarctic achievements and adventures;

outwitting huge, aggressive polar bears, surviving temperatures of -50 °C, mapping over 60,000 square kilometres of Antarctic wilderness, making so many explorations that an Arctic island was named after him. Even Prince Charles has described him as, 'a man of such heroic proportions that his country should have him stuffed and put on permanent display.' Sir Ranulph Fiennes has stated Herbert to be, 'the greatest living polar explorer of our time.' You can't receive better testimony than that. After being neglected for so many years, he was finally knighted in the millennium honours lists.

When Erling Kagge and Borge Ousland skied together to the North Pole in 1990 it was generally accepted that the two Norwegians had actually obtained the record of being first to reach the Pole across the Arctic ice without outside help. However, some controversy arose, and still exists, about their attempt. They had a third team member who was injured and had to be airlifted out and thus his initial contribution in carrying part of the equipment caused the argument that they had 'outside help'. Kagge then went on to be the first individual to ski unaided to the South Pole in 1993 and Ousland became the first to ski unaided to the North Pole in 1994.

Of course Ranulph Fiennes himself has as great a claim to the title of 'greatest living explorer' (as Prince Charles declared him) as anyone does. Apart from desert explorations and discoveries he has trekked, marched and forced himself through the snowy wastes on so many heroic occasions. He attempted to be the first, together with his colleague, Dr Mike Stroud, to walk without any outside support from northern Siberia to the North Pole. This meant they would have to walk for over 800 km, at the rate of a marathon a day. The attempt was scheduled to last only 45 days, as anything longer would require them to drag more food and fuel supplies necessitating a much greater energy output than planned, which in turn would have meant carrying even more food. It was a very fine scientific calculation but leaving really no margin for error. At one stage Fiennes went snow blind and Stroud's ski fastenings, which were meant to be totally unbreakable, broke and had to be abandoned. Despite those and many more mishaps they only narrowly failed, defeated by a combination of sickness, pain and bad luck. But still a triumph in anyone's terms. Fiennes received the Polar Medal in 1987 together with the bar for both Arctic and Antarctic exploration and in 1995 he was awarded a second clasp. In the millennium year 2000, he attempted completely on his own, to become the first Briton to walk to the North Pole totally unaided. This very brave attempt only failed when he suffered severe frostbite, losing the tips of several fingers. In May 2000 two Royal Marines, Alan Chambers and Charlie Paton went on together to become the first Britons to accomplish this extraordinary feat by trekking 1,126 km for 70 days. More men have walked on the moon than have walked unaided to the North Pole.

Robert Swan was the first man to walk to both Poles. His team's journey through the Arctic took 55 days, but was years in the planning. He and his team finally arrived at the North Pole on 14 May 1989. Over a number of years I have been lucky enough to get to know Robert and to share some polar experiences with him. He's one of life's real adventurers and uses his achievements to inspire others, particularly children. In some ways he was born out of his time but perhaps all modern explorers share that in common. They relate back to the great adventurers of past centuries who battled against the odds to discover new territories and the routes to reach them. Robert was to write in his diaries when feeling close to despair and failure, 'Sometimes amidst all this ice rubble and black spots of open water it would seem to me impossible for a human being to survive.' But his determination, strength and courage won through and he made it to the end.

Only a certain breed of men and women would ever dare to journey through the Arctic and confront the toughest and rawest weather conditions imaginable. Apart from their Zen-like 'fierce tenacity of purpose', they all share one abiding characteristic – enormous respect for Nature. Now I am to follow in the footsteps of courageous travellers such as these, explorers of the highest calibre. How lucky I am; I can't wait.

Chapter Three

Arctica – Catching the Cold

Let's flash back 90 million years or so. Then the Arctic was probably as warm as Florida is today, during a period possibly lasting for 6 million years. Creatures, a cross somewhere between a crocodile and lizard, nearly three metres long, called champsosaurs, roamed across that balmy and steamy landscape. Remains of these creatures have been found which show they possessed a long snout and razor-sharp teeth. They ate fish and even small dinosaurs and were thought to have been excellent swimmers. Also fossil trees have been discovered, 1,600 km further north than any trees now living. The hot temperatures of those times were provided by gases released by large numbers of volcanoes. It is possible and even probable that in the Earth's future this may occur again. Global warming on a massive scale is taking place in the Arctic as well as the Antarctic regions and the polar ice is calculated to be one third thinner than it was only twenty years ago.

Although what is often called the 'greenhouse effect', due to the warming of the Earth's climate, is more noticeable in the Antarctic than anywhere else, it is markedly occurring in the Arctic. This is because its ozone layers have also considerably thinned. In the Antarctic there is a gigantic hole in the ozone layer which is probably getting bigger each year. The ozone may be incapable of repairing itself for many tens of years even if the correct remedial actions are finally taken by those countries mostly at fault. Although to a lesser degree, there has also been substantial thinning of the Arctic polar cap (presently covering in total about 5 million square kilometres). The depletion of the ozone layers and melting of parts of the two ice-caps is likely to have incalculable effects on the whole of the world.

If only a tiny percentage of additional fresh water continues to flow into the North Atlantic from melting glaciers, then the northwards flow of the Gulf Stream would cause temperatures in the affected European areas to drop dramatically, perhaps by 10 °C and many countries, Britain included, would experience months of ice and extreme cold. It would then be too late to do something about it when the first polar bears saunter up the Thames to Westminster and dispassionately take their frozen seats in parliament. It is a terrible irony that after 500 years of seafarers trying vainly to find a way through, global warming has finally opened up the legendary North-West Passage and enabled ships to cut up to 8,000 km off sea voyages between Europe and Asia.

Research over the period 1978–98 showed a downward trend in the ice of the Arctic of 37,000 square kilometres each year. That's an area larger than the size of Wales, and over the whole period an area greater than the State of Texas, approximately five per cent of the total area. This statistic is interesting on several levels; good news perhaps for whales who have more water to swim in and catch fish, bad news for polar bears who have reduced ice hunting grounds. The line at which the warm Atlantic waters meet the cold polar waters has moved about 100 km north over this same period.

It is important to remember that just 15,000 years ago, between 30 and 50 per cent of the world was covered in snow and ice. The most recent Ice Age began about 2 to 3 million years ago but no one can tell if it is actually over. There are numerous, long glaciations regularly occurring which cause further freezing intermingled with lengthy periods of interglacial warming. No one can actually be certain whether the world is getting progressively warmer or colder as these events can only be judged over some millions of years. The uncontrolled polluting actions of most nations have caused extra global warming to occur in recent years but whether that warming will continue and for how long can not be definitively stated. Whatever the eventual outcome, we should make certain that we ourselves are not upsetting the sensitive balance of the natural forces and disturbing and therefore unleashing the awesome power delicately balanced at both the polar regions.

The Arctic region is characterised by one of the most extreme environments on the planet, with limited sunlight, intensely cold temperatures and a very short growing season. Its sea ice, snow cover, glaciers, permafrost, tundra, boreal forests and peatlands all react sensitively to variations in temperature, sunlight, heat, chemistry of the ocean and the atmosphere above. The tundra is known as 'the land of little sticks,' due to the tiny, dwarfed willow trees that grow there. There is permafrost just below the surface.

There is a Zen folk saying, 'Snow disappears into the sea. What silence!' However, the irresistible force of moving ice has the totally opposite effect and can initially create an overwhelming sound and fury, as if the whole world is crashing down around you. Then will come utter silence – until the next time that is! An extraordinary fact is that snowflakes falling on water emit a piercing sound, too high-pitched for human ears, but which can disturb aquatic creatures and may also disrupt their sonar. The flake landing on the water deposits the tiniest bubble of air just below the surface and the bubble has to adjust its volume by oscillating which in turn causes the very tiny sound.

Within the Arctic the power of the ice is immense. Ice in all its forms has the colossal force necessary to wreak havoc on the environment. Huge blocks of towering ice transform into icebergs as soon as they enter the ocean. The creation of an iceberg needs only two things: an ocean and a large advancing glacier. As the tip of the glacier slides forward pieces break off and drop into the ocean. They start to float away and are called icebergs. Those the size of houses are called 'bergy bits'. Some may be the size of small islands. 'Growlers' are green ice sections which float almost entirely under the water and are extremely dangerous, particularly to small ships. The part of the iceberg concealed under the water is usually four to five times bigger than above. Although 90 per cent of icebergs are formed in the Antarctic those in the Arctic can be just as destructive. Of course the most famous disaster caused by hitting an iceberg was the sinking of the ocean liner *Titanic* on its maiden voyage from Southampton, England to New York in April 1912.

A glacier is created by layers of deep snow falling faster than they are able to melt and then compacting to form ice. This mass is then pressured forward so it slowly moves across the ice beneath it. Most glaciers, once created, continue to exist for centuries and are slowly edging forward. Glaciers cover 10 per cent of the Earth's surface and surprisingly contain about 75 per cent of its fresh water in this frozen form. This frozen power carves huge tunnels and caves into the ice going down hundreds of metres. At that depth the ice is so densely packed together it will only reflect the colour blue. However, in the area where it is relatively arid and there is little precipitation, as in much of the Arctic, glaciers do not occur. The whole region is a surprisingly dry place, receiving less moisture than many desert areas.

Another phenomenon of this strange, frozen world is the 'aurora borealis' translated as 'Northern Lights'. In the past the aurora borealis was the subject of legends, stories and mysteries for all mankind. The Inuit believed that they were the torches of spirits guiding souls to the land of ultimate happiness where no one would want for anything. Other native peoples thought they were the cooking fires of the Inuit who were boiling huge mounds of whale blubber. Even today people believe it will bring good luck if a child is conceived whilst the aurora dances overhead and honeymoon tours, particularly from Japan, are organised with that end result in mind.

The aurora itself is conceived 150 million km away on the boiling surface of the sun. The gigantic explosions occurring there send irregular emissions of charged particles – electrons and protons – showering towards the Earth at some 3 million km/h. The effect caused is termed a 'solar wind' and the power generated can reach the equivalent of one billion watts. These discharges collide with the Earth's magnetosphere (generated by the molten metals within the Earth's interior) where most are deflected away into outer space. Some get through and these interact with gases to produce these extraordinary lights mostly blue, green and red, forming one of the most spectacular displays it is possible to behold. The aurora takes many forms and shapes and in the Arctic region they usually occur between

60 ° and 70 °N. They occur in eleven year cycles resulting from equivalent high sunspot activity. The aurora borealis is matched by a mirror phenomenon within the Southern hemisphere where it is known as the aurora australis. These are just two of the many absolutely breathtaking natural wonders to be found within this amazing world we are so fortunate to inhabit.

Who knows what other hidden mysteries and treasures there are to unlock and uncover within these colossal Arctic ice wastes? In Siberia recently, for the very first time, the body of a woolly mammoth has been exhumed some 20,000 years after it perished. Named Zharkov, after the family who found it, the mammoth is undergoing extensive examinations and tests in order to find out as much detailed information as possible about this enormous, two-tusked animal that lived in the distant past. The mammoth is male, more than three metres high, up to eight tonnes in weight and judging by the tusk rings was nearly fifty years old. This is truly information frozen in time. With the rapid advancement in gene technology scientists are taking DNA samples from various parts of the mammoth and although it is unlikely to be successful initially, they hope eventually to try and recreate this prehistoric creature, possibly by injecting its DNA into another living colossus, probably the African elephant. The last mammoth died out only as recently as 4,000 years ago but no one is certain why this actually occurred. Now answers to some mammoth questions may be possible.

There is a caveat in unlocking some of the Arctic's mysteries. There could be deadly, prehistoric viruses, lying dormant for centuries but still capable of being revived. Recently researchers have found a bug, usually found in tomato plants but fortunately not harmful to human beings, buried within certain ice packs. This raises the literally chilling prospect of ancient strains of potentially deadly diseases such as polio, smallpox, even kinds of flu being allowed back into the Earth's air, perhaps even transmitted to modern civilisation through the scientists and explorers who have first released them. This rather frightening possibility is also being brought nearer by global warming which could cause these viruses to emerge naturally as the ancient ice melts.

The Earth's axis is tilted 23.5 degrees from the plane of the Earth's orbit. Because of this tilt, if you are at a location 23.5 degrees from the North Pole on 21 June, the summer solstice, the sun will not completely set. Similarly if you are at a location 23.5 degrees from the North Pole on 21 December, the winter solstice, the sun will not completely rise. This special but invisible location zone of 23.5 degrees from the North Pole (latitude of 66.5 °N) is known as the Arctic Circle. As the Earth's axis is wobbling slightly the tilt is constantly changing and therefore the Arctic Circle is constantly moving. The summer solstice (also known as Midsummer's day) is the day of the year when the midday sun appears to be highest in the sky. The winter solstice is the day when the midday sun appears to be lowest.

Of course it is completely the reverse in the Southern hemisphere. The period when the sun does not rise above the horizon, north of the Arctic Circle is called the Polar Night. The North Pole has effectively the shortest calendar of anywhere in the Arctic. Just two days, although they are effectively six months long. During half the year the sun circles the sky, low on the horizon, its long, glowing rays dappling across the ice. The North Pole is approximately

arctica – catching the cold

725 km from the northern tip of Greenland, the world's largest island.

The Arctic Ocean is the smallest of the world's five oceans. It is just six per cent of the size of the Pacific, the largest. It has an undersea range of mountains, the Lomonosov Ridge – approximately 3,000m high but no part actually rising above the water. In winter the ocean is almost completely covered by ice. This freezing doesn't occur in any of the other oceans, including the Southern Ocean, which surrounds the Antarctic. The ice melts partly in summer at the edges but three-quarters of it remains frozen. The ice moves and drifts, freezing and fracturing in a never-ending cycle.

The ocean floor is 4,085 metres beneath the surface. Even still, there is life down there. These include protozoans, worms of a kind, even clams and the extraordinary sea spider (pycnogonid). This latter creature is not actually a spider but does look like one. Each pycnogonid has five or six pairs of legs carrying its tiny body and they continually scurry across the bottom of the ocean looking for any kind of food. These creatures are actually discovered at great depths in all oceans and are usually fairly drab in colour but can occasionally be a very bright red. What they find and eat must be something still unknown to science and very much tinier than they are.

Another strange sea creature that lives throughout the cold polar waters is the amphipod known as the 'piranha of the north'. They hunt and eat anything and will swarm over a dead or dying animal and quickly strip it to its bones. There are stories of Inuit who have drowned and when pulled from the icy waters have resembled characters from a horror film. The clothes were left untouched but every bit of flesh had been eaten. Amphipods are shaped like humpback shrimps and are themselves nutritious and in turn have been eaten, obviously as a meal of last resort, by members of lost expeditions who otherwise would have starved.

As parts of the Arctic are officially classified as desert, due to the tiny amount of rainfall that occurs, it is not really surprising that there are also oases found there. They are known as polynyas, the Russian word for an area of open water that is surrounded by sea ice. There are a few dozen, varying in size from perhaps 90 metres in diameter up to the largest, North Water, with a diameter of approximately 104,000 km. North Water is at the upper end of Baffin Bay and is larger than Canada's Lake Superior. As well as polynyas, which are non-linear openings in the ice, there are also water channels called leads, which have linear openings. There are major leads around the perimeter of Hudson Bay and James Bay and along the southern coast of Baffin Island. Probably the most important lead rims the entire Arctic Ocean and has been called 'the arctic ring of life'.

Polynyas and leads are vital within polar wildlife. Some of the early Thule native settlements were built around the polynyas and remains of them can still be seen. These days it is possible to see seals and walruses on the surrounding ice lounging around them, with the tracks of polar bears and arctic silver foxes criss-crossing the ice in all directions. By winter, most seabirds and ducks have fled south. Perhaps a few whales are still battleship cruising and spouting around. The strong winds skimming off the new ice as it forms, coupled with the strong currents, usually prevent these waters freezing over and closing. On the rare occasion when they do close, the results for the wildlife can prove disastrous.

The bird with probably the most endurance is the Arctic tern. It summers in both the Arctic and the Antarctic but always returns to nest in the north. It flies between both polar regions every year, to avoid the winter completely, a total journey of 40,000 km. This calculates to the Arctic tern spending eight months of its life flying and most of that in daylight.

As spring returns to the Arctic, around May, all kinds of whales start arriving as well as millions of seabirds and waterfowl of which many will nest in the ocean cliffs well before the sea ice finally melts. If the polynyas were to remain frozen over, there would be no opportunities for the birds to catch fish and they would starve to death on the ice. Those that breed would lose their chicks. There would be a knock-on effect to the other polar creatures and indeed the seals and bears would also suffer.

The Arctic is a sea of floating and moving ice. The total area of sea ice is between 10 million and 12.5 million square kilometres. In order to find your way to the Pole you have to read the bearings, make the calculations and plan to arrive exactly at 90 °N in order to be at the precise spot. Of course an ordinary compass is not much use in the vicinity of the North Pole, as all directions face south. That's part of the strange magic you are likely to encounter if you can reach that exquisite point on the globe. The North Pole, unlike the South Pole, is not a fixed place that can be specifically visited by travellers to the Arctic; it always has to be found by precise measurement. There's no post or marker that can be touched that lets you know immediately you've found the Arctic's G-spot. You may be aroused but the Arctic won't be.

The Arctic's natural and immense resources have been exploited to an extent ever since man first arrived here, following the retreating ice masses after the last glacial period some 15,000 years ago. Initially interest was only in the pursuit of animals and fish for food, then subsequently trapping for furs became important, and after that mining and more recently defence.

At the height of the appropriately named 'Cold War', particularly with the aggressive stand-off stances of the USA and the USSR, there were in excess of 75 nuclear submarines patrolling around or under the Arctic ice, all bristling with weapons of mass destruction. At present, and hopefully in the future, it seems this threat has been brought to an end. Of course all countries denied that their subs carried any nuclear weapons and claimed they were there only to carry out research. These secrets weren't too well-kept, as each opposing nation actually needed the other side to know that it could retaliate immediately if any attack action were to be taken. This was known as a sub-zero stand-off. Russia is currently selling off its submarines to industrial concerns who will then be able to ship goods on routes below the Arctic ice, thereby saving thousands of kilometres on normal journeys. The commercial possibilities of transport below the ice seem almost limitless. Perhaps licences and routes could be put out to tender in the way telephone and airwave licences have been sold off, the receipts could easily mount up to billions of pounds. These vast sums could then be used for the benefit of the Arctic itself and its adjoining territories.

Fortunately the Arctic (and also the Antarctic) has come to be recognised as a completely unique area of the world, requiring constant scientific consideration and research. The power of this remote place can only be described as awesome and if this region were ever to be misused it could cause damage on a scale too massive to even contemplate. We just cannot afford to neglect or abuse an area which would destabilise every territory in the Northern hemisphere, with the consequent same dire results in the South if, for whatever reason, it unleashed its colossal power.

Chapter Four

Inuit of the Arctic

As a rule Inuit have shorter, thicker bodies than their European counterparts. Therefore they lose less heat through their limbs. They also have more blood vessels in their hands and feet, which means they can use them in much colder temperatures, sometimes as low as -40 °C. Their eyelids and cheeks are also fleshier to protect against the extreme cold. Inuit object to being called Eskimos. It is a Cree Indian expression with the meaning, 'Eaters of raw meat,' and quite naturally is considered derogatory. Many people in their ignorance still try to use 'Eskimo' as a general description but it should never be used any more. 'Squaw' is another Indian word which has a deeply offensive meaning, and hopefully will also be dropped. Places using Squaw in their names should also have them renamed. It's a word that has been featured mistakenly in many old Western cowboy films, presumably it wasn't then realised that it indicated a woman of ill-repute and is very offensive. The Province of British Columbia has taken the major step of wiping 'squaw' off the face of the map by renaming eleven creeks, rivers, lakes and mountains. 'Inuit' has the straightforward meaning, 'The People.'

The usual Inuit word for white people is *qallunaat* meaning, 'high brows'. Sometimes they also call white people *kabloona* meaning, 'pale face'. Another word, although hardly used nowadays is *arnasiutiit* – 'stealers of our women'. Hopefully the latter description is a word that has faded into the historic past. The language of the Inuit is Inuktitut. This means 'in the manner of the Inuit' or 'the way an Inuk does things.' If you add titut to any word it also has the same meaning. So Englishtitut can mean 'the way an Englishman does things.'

There are seven dialects and seventeen sub-dialects and two writing systems. It's quite a heritage which the elders are doing their best to preserve and protect. The area known as Baffin, which includes Baffin Bay and Baffin Island where the Inuit capital Iqualuit is based, is their main homeland. The Inuit settlements are mostly dotted along the coasts, comprising anything between 100 persons to perhaps 1,000. No one is absolutely certain how they first came across to the Arctic. They were there before the Vikings and the great seafaring travellers who crossed oceans and dangerous waters in search of new lands to settle or conquer. It is thought that they initially migrated eastwards from Alaska, they travelled on foot, by sledge and by boat to reach Baffin Island and the other surrounding areas, some 3,000 years ago. Legend handed down tells that they were called Tuniit, Dorset and Thule. The Thule are the direct ancestors of the Inuit.

They lived in igloos or semi-subterranean oval houses built into the ground or ice. These had whalebone rafters covered with skins, mostly seal. They used slate tools and weapons. For heating, their lamps were set within stone with moss wickers. They were nomads depending on the winter and summer seasons as to where they would base themselves. The Inuit are a peaceful people and have never tried to conquer other nations but have only wanted to co-exist within nature and to live off the land as well as the ice. They say the land owns them, rather than man owning the land as many other cultures think. Inuit treat everything as well as everybody with respect. It's fundamental to their way of life. They are hunters only by necessity, as they can not farm or sow and therefore must hunt those animals which also live in the tundras and snowy wastelands, as they do themselves.

The Inuit have always travelled and carried their few possessions on sledges (*komatiks*) pulled by husky dogs or in their boats built with animal skins (*umiaks*). They have also built their boats (*kayaks*) for faster travel and hunting and used whatever materials were to hand, mostly bone, skin or wood. *Kayaks* were used to hunt whale and seal, and polar bears were tracked on foot or with the *komatiks*. *Umiak* is their word for a boat made of walrus skin. The Inuk man and Inuk woman always work as a family team, he hunting, she preparing the food and making their clothes. She uses a crescent shaped knife called the *ulu* for practically every task. She might send out her man to hunt, wearing bearskin trousers, sealskin boots and a caribou parka with the hood framed by wolverine fur. You can't get much closer to Arctic nature than that.

This is a society where child abuse is totally or virtually unknown, as it would be like attacking a grandparent or ancestor. The creator of Peter Pan, J. M. Barrie, particularly understood how often childhood could be a portal through which to understand more. He said, 'I'm not young enough to know everything.' Possibly he deliberately chose the name Pan, the mystical, half-man, half-animal, to symbolise the boy who was to remain forever young. Barrie needed to conjure up an image of someone with a natural spirit, linked but apart. There is one essential piece of wisdom which hopefully is always carried by all explorers, to lean on in times of crisis 'Don't panic!' However, I wonder how many of them realise panic is derived from the meaning, 'fearing the sight of Pan'!

The Inuit have always had a comprehensive understanding of the way the animals of the Arctic live. They have never hunted purely for pleasure. They probably do not understand the violent nature of the big game hunters who come to the North, to kill the polar bears, seals or other creatures of this immense ice region. The Inuit do not like to waste anything and will use the entire animal for a myriad of purposes. Food is the primary one but also for clothing, tent coverings, weapons, needles and heating. They believe every animal, as well as every object, has a soul and should be respected. Ivaluardjuk, the Inuk hunter, has stated, 'The greatest peril of life lies in the fact that human food consists entirely of souls.'

One of the Inuit beliefs is that the spirit of an animal could be chosen to be the spiritual guardian (*tornaq*) of an individual. *Tupilak* is their name for an Inuk ghost or spirit. After Sedna, the ocean's legendary goddess, held to be the supreme of all beings, the most powerful spirit, is that of the polar bear. The spirits of bears and man are considered to be primarily interchangeable. They share so many traits; standing upright if necessary, walking on hind legs, sitting or leaning in a similar manner. They also eat similar foods. Above all, the bear is so powerful that they must be respected at all times. In Inuit legend the bears are thought to live inside houses as humans but don their bearskins when they go outside! The Inuit respect nature in all its forms so are well able to understand more than most the work of Andy Goldsworthy and the way his work pays homage to the environment in all its seasons and guises.

The seasons have always dictated how the Inuit live and their lifestyle. In the spring, particularly after the bleakness and darkness of winter, there would be the good seal hunting. It is a period of especial rejoicing and the start of easier times. In the summer families could fish together, the father, the mother and all the children, clustered around one of several fish holes in the ice, trying to catch the Arctic char which had travelled in from the furthest seas and waters. The autumn and winter are always the most difficult and dangerous times as there is only a short time to hunt for the muskox and caribou. Inuit will try to lure them into an ambush inside the stone cairns they have built. How successful they are will determine if they will have sufficient food to see them through until spring.

The Inuit have perfected their carving and design skills over the centuries, passing their wonderful ideas and techniques from generation to generation. The master carver is always honoured and respected in the community and some exquisite carvings from ancient times are still in existence. In fact, the ability to carve is part of their survival as they need to create skin scrapers, harness equipment, snow goggles and needles to carry out their ordinary daily routines and duties. This is in addition to the ceremonial masks, amulets, combs, pipes and toys for their cherished children. The Inuit carve in bone, granite and other hard stones, ivory, soapstone and sometimes marry these with precious metals. Often the carvings and sculptures tend to be naturalistic and also depict narratives; animals in realistic hunting scenes as well as legends and stories are favourite subjects. The predominately grey stones are often blackened and polished, then incised. Carvers view each stone as a challenge, working against it and fashioning intricate, delicate and dramatic pieces with tremendous flair. Elegant and humorous animals are very popular subjects. Each carver works differently and usually has a speciality which marks him out from another. Inuit believe the animal is already in the stone; in order to release it all they have to do is carve away those parts around it. That's certainly a Zen way of expressing it. Once it was the prerogative of the male only to be the carver but now the Inuit also recognises the skill of the female artist. Both men and women work as designers using cloth, material and sealskin to create traditional and more modern clothing items, including *kamiks*, parkas and tablecloths.

All the Inuit skills and arts are celebrated every spring in April in an event called Toonik Tyme with contests in seal hunting, igloo building, parades and of course sumptuous feasting. The Inuit culture takes many forms. They especially like drum dancing; combining music, dancing and story telling. They will celebrate all their important events, national, community and family in this way. Birth, marriage, hunting, the changes in the seasons and other special happenings.

Throat singing is a traditional Inuit musical style. Two women face each other, creating deep, resonant sounds from within the throat, using special and well-practised breathing techniques. The women are interpreting and expounding concepts of nature like the Northern Lights, the forces of wind and the wildness of the sea. The only other people to practise throat singing are the Mongolians, primarily the men, who live in a land-locked country between Russia and China, possibly as far removed in terrain and locale from the Arctic as it is possible to be. Strangely enough the Inuit and the Mongolians have very similar physical features and also share their laid-back temperaments.

Originally the Inuit had their own forms of law and regulation, usually arising out of family and peer pressures. However, there were no specified punishments for crimes and each act was decided on its own merits or lack of them. Inuit leaders were chosen because of their accepted abilities and prior knowledge, particularly their skills as hunters, the highest accolades within the community. However, they still did not have specific powers and therefore no one was obliged to follow their decisions. Naturally this could lead to all kinds of confrontations and in order to calm things down the families concerned would meet inside large igloos or dance houses to participate in ceremonial music events as a way of settling disputes and creating harmony between them.

One way of dealing with a problem was to shame or embarrass the individual concerned. As an example, if someone was not pulling his or her weight in carrying out certain duties, then others would go over and do them instead, hopefully shaming that person by this procedure. The focus of Inuit law was not primarily to punish the individual or offender or even to provide what was perceived as justice, but more to ensure that the community remained in a state of harmony and equilibrium. Eventually the old ways have come to be considered unsatisfactory in these modern times and they have agreed to accept the dictates of the rule of law. However, traditional life has not been abandoned, but has just adapted to the modern and new ways.

When the Inuit kiss they do not consider it rubbing noses in the way others try to express it, but as an act of love, emotion, compassion and romance. As it is said in the words of one of the more succinct love songs, 'It's not what you do it's the way that you do it.' Inuit don't need an elaborate way of life. They live close to nature. They understand the essence of ice, snow, the cold and know how to relate to them. Henry Thoreau, the American philosopher, who lived for two years in a bare log cabin, might very well have had the Inuit in mind when he stated, 'Our life is frittered away by detail – simplify, simplify.'

One of the myths that has grown up around the Inuit is that they have 200 words or more for the word snow. This is just not so. The Inuit think of each snow form or description as very different to any other, so that light falling snow (*qannialaaq*), wet falling snow (*masak*), snow packed hard like ice (*annniugaviniq*), drifting snow (*natiruviaq*) and so on, are totally different concepts and must be described as such and distinguished one from another. There are just two snow root derivatives; *qanniq*, meaning snow in the air or snowflakes and *aput*, meaning snow on the ground. Every other description of snow stands alone and should be considered as an entirely separate word. As the American Broadway star, Miss Ethel Merman (almost) once said, 'There's snow business like snow business, there's snow business I know.' Perhaps one of the myths that should be buried in the mists of time. An Inuit joke is to describe their four seasons as Winter, Still Winter, Not Winter and Almost Winter. I think that says it all.

Chapter Five

Outward Bound

Our Arctic exploits start at Heathrow Airport. I am driven there by James Bustard the project director. Perhaps he wants to make certain I actually make the flight in time or don't suffer from last minute jitters and decide not to go. If he but knew. I wouldn't give up this chance for all the tea in China, or more appropriately, all the ice in the Arctic. James looks rather wistful and suddenly I have the idea that he is thinking that if one of us is a no-show or has to pull out for any reason, he would be there ready to step forward and make up the team number. I wonder if he has his passport with him, just in case. This time it is a case of unlucky Jim. Although I am feeling somewhat apprehensive and nervous there is no way I would give up such an exciting opportunity and the chance of such a glorious adventure. I hug him goodbye and he wishes us well and a safe journey. I remind him of something I heard from a Chinese friend. She had told me that one thing she had learned about life from her country's history, is that the journey itself is the reward – and it's a long process. It is a philosophy that fits in with my own and it is particularly apposite now. Who knows what the next few days will bring and what we will see and experience?

There are just the two of us setting out from Heathrow, Penny Govett and myself; we plan to meet Fabian Carlsson and Erik Mustad *en route*. Both Penny and I are wearing the T-shirts I had printed with the slogan, which now seems very optimistic – 'Monday at the North Pole 24 April'. The challenge, and part of the excitement, is to reach the North Pole in the shortest time, without allowing any margin for mishaps, errors of judgement, aeroplane delays or other difficulties. However, the weather conditions are notoriously unpredictable in the Arctic, as indeed in the Antarctic, so we will need more than our share of good luck to arrive at our agreed rendezvous on time.

We book into Air Canada and I am asked to check in my bulky hand luggage as it is twice the allowed weight. However, my pleadings and explanations on the purpose of the expedition finally win through and I am permitted to proceed as far as the final gate, for a final decision. Arriving at the gate we say goodbye to James; the next time we meet we will all know whether we were successful or not. He is obviously regretting he isn't going with us. I cover my outsize bag with my coat and I am allowed through. I am also carrying something very special. A secret not yet to be revealed to anyone. I am determined that it will make the journey with me, all the way to and through the Arctic, until that momentous moment when, hopefully, I will meet Andy Goldsworthy at the North Pole. What a moment that will be! The thought and pleasure spur me on. The American poet, Robert Frost, lends some words to lean on, 'We dance around in a ring and suppose, but the Secret sits in the middle and knows.' I snuggle in my seat, thinking of what it will be like to stand at the North Pole. I dream of the Arctic, polar bears, husky dogs and never-ending expanses of snow and ice most of the way over.

The flight, which takes off just after 1 p.m., is relatively uneventful and we arrive at Montreal Mirabel Airport at around 3.30 p.m. local time. We take a taxi to the Four

Seasons Hotel and excitedly meet up with the two other members of our group, the Norwegian and the Swede, Fabian Carlsson and Erik Mustad. They are old friends and insist we must all toast each other several times over. It's obviously a portent of things to come! We stagger to our rooms to freshen up and arrange to go out for dinner at 7 p.m. (12 p.m. London time). We meet first in the lobby from where we adjourn to the bar and have more drinks in the hotel. Then we taxi to a Greek restaurant, Milos, which had been recommended to me. The food is excellent and we gorge ourselves on oysters, clams and lobster, followed by strawberries, all the time accompanied by huge quantities of beer and wine. We arrive back at the hotel at 11 p.m. (London time 4 a.m.) and for Penny Govett and I it is time to call it a night (or day) but Erik and Fabian decide to go out drinking on their own. I tell them the Swedish joke (it could easily have been Norwegian) about two Swedes meeting in a bar to drink. They steadily (although subsequently unsteadily) drink their way through most of the evening when one eventually lifts a glass to toast the other and says, 'Cheers'. The other angrily responds, 'I thought we were drinking, not talking.' Erik and Fabian laugh but seem somewhat puzzled and Penny and I leave them to it.

Next morning, after breakfast, we eagerly meet downstairs at 8 a.m. ready to set off. Now everyone including Erik is wearing the 'Monday at the North Pole' T-shirts. It takes about one and a half hours to reach Montreal Dorval airport. Fabian has already restocked by buying quantities of champagne, whisky, *foie gras*, cheeses and chocolate. The plane, a Boeing 737, is fairly empty so we spread out in different rows and have plenty of room. Fabian and Erik work their way through the drinks menu.

Kilometre after kilometre of ice, snow and utter stillness. Nothing to be seen, no people, no animals, no habitation, human or otherwise. I study the map issued by Canada's North-West Territories called the Explorer's Map. It shows the area over which we are flying and beyond. There are wonderfully evocative Inuit names given to some of the places and towns. Frobisher Bay has become Iqaluit, 'Place of Fish'. Some of the British names still left include Prince Charles Island, Melville Peninsula, Somerset Island, and Devon Island. Cornwallis Island is where Resolute is situated which is our final destination before setting off for the North Pole. The Explorer's Map also shows the Magnetic North Pole which I am drawn towards but must resist; the actual North Pole is our destination! We are cruising at over 8,900 metres, higher than Mount Everest and are told that at our intermediate stop, at Iqaluit Airport will be a comfortable −4 °C.

Iqaluit, 'Gateway to the Canadian Arctic', is on Baffin Island, the fifth largest island in the world, with a land mass larger than any European country, other than France. Its total population is around 10,000. A third of the entire Inuit population are based in Iqaluit. It's sometimes described as 'The Last Chance Saloon'; a place where people come from the cities and towns of Canada to rebuild their lives, perhaps to find themselves or as often to lose themselves, and their previous identities and existence. It also provides the lure of living right on the edge of the great wilderness beyond, being able to escape into the great outdoors, a place of no pretence and complete starkness. There's nothing else but no man's land from now on. The final frontier perhaps, a place to find a destiny of a kind, a place for those pioneers who have nowhere else left.

Flight time from Montreal to Iqaluit is three hours. We are still over 2,900 km from the North Pole. It's a long way to go and I pray we will make it. The airport building is bright yellow, very small and really just a staging post. We only have a 30 minute stopover to explore. Sir Ranulph Fiennes, the Arctic and Antarctic adventurer, had told me that the Inuit carvings in the co-op shop there are particularly good so I make a quick dash to see what they have. I am almost spoilt for choice; quickly deciding on a small, grey, granite man, hooded against the fierce winds, made by a local artist, Elisapee Ishulutak, and a beautifully sculpted head of a woman, green and mottled colours by Jimmy Kumajuk.

Everyone else thinks I am quite mad to lumber myself with carrying such heavy objects at the beginning of our time in the Arctic and I should have waited until we had travelled on or bought them on the way back. However, I have learned by experience that you must never wait for a later time, in travelling and in buying, as in so many other things in life. It's also part of my Zen philosophy of not waiting until the time is absolutely right, as it may never be. In Zen you must never be impatient but that doesn't mean you have to be patient. Sometimes you just have to go for it! In China in 1979, on one of the first Western journeys into that extraordinary country since the Communist takeover, I saw some fascinating antique carvings at the first gallery we came to across the border in Canton and didn't buy them, assuming we would see more of the same later on. But we never did! I still rue to this day the decision to put off acquiring such wonderful and unique objects. Now whenever I see something I really like I go for it and never wait. It's a good philosophy to follow in many courses of action.

Now we board for the next flight to Resolute Bay, usually just referred to as Resolute. It is named after HMS *Resolute*, one of the ships sent to look for the missing expedition of Sir John Franklin. The flight will take about two hours and we adjust our watches back one hour, making it six hours behind Britain. Though Inuit have travelled this region and camped around Resolute Bay for hundreds of years; it is also a place steeped in European history as a staging post for many of the great Arctic explorations.

This time the plane is completely full. It's a 1,500 km flight, north of course. Luckily I am seated next to Bill Thorpe the head warden of Ellesmere Park – 37,775 square kilometres, a park the size of Switzerland – situated at the tip of Ellesmere Island. There are two other wardens with him and the three of them have to patrol the Park without any further assistance. Of course the nearest tree is 2,000 km away. As we fly over, Bill points out various rocky peaks, called nunataks, poking up through the ice sheet, which can be up to 900 metres thick in places. The ice sheet creates valley glaciers up to 80 km long. Some might say that here the Ice Age never left. We fly practically the entire length of Baffin Island and then across the Parry Channel to Barrow Strait in order to reach Resolute which is located on the south coast of Cornwallis Island, almost 75 °N. It is indeed the gateway to the High Arctic region.

Bill tells me that there used to be a T-shirt with the logo: 'Resolute is not the end of the world but you can see it from here.' The Geographic North Pole is 1,700 km away but the Magnetic North Pole is only 500 km from here.

Chapter Six

Grise Lightning

Resolute Bay has a total population of approximately 200 people, of which 80 per cent are Inuit. The first Inuit families only arrived here in 1953 and there is still some controversy as to whether they were moved here to reside because game was plentiful or to establish Canadian sovereignty. What is incontrovertible is that the Inuit themselves were not consulted in the decision making and were moved from place to place without any consideration for their own wishes. The Inuit name for the bay is Qausuittuq which means either 'Never a day passes', or 'The place with no dawn'. It's the bleakest of places and many wryly comment that the real spelling of Resolute is Desolate. The airport is hardly more than a shack and the place seems like a frontier post of the old Wild West times. There are also plenty of odd characters buzzing around, mostly bearded, and clothed in all kinds of strange garb. Some in ski-gear. My much-travelled and well-worn Russian hat looks very much in place.

We meet up with Mike McDowell, an Arctic guide sent to assist us. From him we learn that the weather conditions at Grise Fiord, our next Arctic stop, are so bad that Andy Goldsworthy has been snowed in there for five days and has been unable to fly on to Camp Hazen and from there to the North Pole. This has put his plans to sculpt at the North Pole on ice, so to speak, and may mean he will not get there at all. That would be a catastrophe for all of us. The only chance is for Andy to fly back to Resolute where we are and then take our plane to Camp Hazen, from there he can make the flight to the Pole. We would then use Andy's incoming plane, the only one available, to journey on to Grise Fiord. If that all goes according to plan, although out here things rarely do, we must be prepared to respond rapidly to any changes in the very unsettled weather conditions and be ready to move like greased lightning.

It's going to be very much a case of touch and go and we are learning fast how precarious the flying arrangements are in this part of the world and how dependent we all are on the weather. There are continual and intensive radio communications going on between the two Inuit towns, trying to establish when and if flights can take-off and land. If Andy doesn't make it to the North Pole then we wouldn't either. To come all this way and not get there would be pretty disastrous for us, but even more so for Andy who has spent a month in this region preparing for his ultimate goal. We can only hope Andy will make it and so will we.

Bezal Jesudason turns up. He is originally from Goa and runs the local equipment store, Ranulph Fiennes had told me to look out for him and to pass on his regards. He told me Bezal would be a great help to our expedition and so it turns out. His store is called High Arctic International Explorer Services Ltd and has everything you could possibly need. I feel like saying, 'We'll take the lot', but of course Bezal knows just what we will need on our journey further north and hopefully, eventually to the North Pole itself. We must assume we will somehow make it and prepare accordingly.

Bezal provides me with a heavy, padded, down jacket, a pair of down trousers, an over-jacket, high boots, very thick gloves (two pairs) and a padded hat. I put them all on and immediately seem to resemble a polar bear. I hope it isn't the hunting season, although I soon find out it is!

Bezal is providing the clothes and kits for all the other expedition teams travelling at this time, including a Japanese team totalling about 20 explorers. Bezal has the monopoly in Resolute and good luck to him in that, if he is prepared to spend the season here at these constantly sub-zero temperatures. He invites us back to his home for tea and we meet his wife Terry. They have no children and possibly the cold has something to do with it but I don't enquire any further.

We are also given sleeping bags and then return to the airport offices of Ken Borek hopefully to await the aircraft from Grise Fiord. As we should have expected by now it is delayed, one and a half hours, and we sit around drinking plenty of coffee, eating biscuits and huge quantities of chocolate. People keep coming and going, practically indistinguishable from one another in their bundled-up, heavy clothing, huge mittens and knee-length snow boots.

I decide to take a walk outside and wander around. The wind whips across my face and the intense cold easily finds its way inside my hood and down the back of my neck. The area seems deserted apart from one small building which must contain the vital generators and from which smoke is gushing upwards to mix into the misty skyline. There are no obvious signs or names on any buildings, so it would be easy for a stranger to get lost and I return fairly quickly to the comparative airport warmth.

The Grise Fiord aircraft finally arrives and we are told Andy is on board and is immediately transferring to our plane which has been prepared to fly him on to Hazen and the Pole. We resist the temptation to try and meet him now as it might spoil the excitement of actually meeting up with him at the North Pole itself. Assuming we make it! That was always our plan and we decide we must stick with it. It feels strange to be so close and still not rushing out to greet him. We are told he is in 'resolute spirits' and the plane has been refuelled and will depart momentarily.

Eventually our Ken Borek aircraft, a Twin Otter (the one Andy arrived on) is also refuelled and ready for take-off. The four of us clamber on board, together with our bulky kit, sleeping bags, cameras and equipment – and our dreams. There are no other passengers. The Twin Otter normally seats ten persons, so we have some extra room to stretch out a little more. The flight takes approximately one and a half hours and we fly across vast expanses of uninterrupted whiteness. We cross the Wellington Channel, over Devon Island and then into Jones Sound. At times we are flying very low, possibly not more than 300 metres off the ice.

We reach the edge of Ellesmere Island and fly even lower, perhaps down to 70 metres, in between the mountain ridges. It is breathtaking but also pretty frightening as a strong wind could perhaps force the aircraft into a mountainside. It is clear how critical the weather is in deciding whether it is possible to fly on or not. We pass over some extraordinary rock formations, really majestic shapes, and all the time our excitement is mounting. We are getting closer and closer. Grise Fiord is just 1,500 km from the Pole. I tie my coat tighter. It's a heavy but safe landing as the aircraft crunches down on the ice.

Grise Fiord has a population of approximately 150 people and it seems as if a third have turned out to welcome us. Only 5 per cent are non-Inuit. In fact, it is not so cold by Arctic standards and of course we are wrapped up warm in our numerous layers of clothing. Our luggage is loaded on to a van that immediately takes off. We look around but there is no vehicle for us and we set off to walk in to the village, about 400 metres away. Suddenly several ski-doos (snowmobiles) roar up to offer us lifts. I climb on the back of one that is being driven by Pam, the cook at the lodge. Pam takes off at a very fast pace and I hang on for dear life, the wind blowing so fiercely that it drives back my hood. To keep out the bitter cold I need to haul it back with one hand and use the other to hold on with all my might.

Grise Fiord is the most northerly Inuit community in the North-West Territories of Canada. It is located on the southern coast of Ellesmere Island, on Jones Sound, north of Devon and Baffin Islands, 1,050 km north of the Arctic Circle. In the summer there are 77 consecutive days when the sun does not set. Bare rock mountains tower abruptly just beyond the narrow strip of beach area at the fiord entrance. The views around here are stunningly beautiful. The island is also rich in prehistoric Inuit sites. However, subsequently in historic times no Inuit lived here and only in fairly recent times have small communities begun to re-establish themselves.

Grise Fiord was named by the Norwegian explorer Otto Sverdrup, who charted the south and east coasts of Ellesmere Island from 1899 to 1903. In Norwegian the name means 'pig fiord' and to Sverdrup the sound of the walrus had reminded him of pigs grunting. Its Inuit name is Aujuittuq which means 'the place that never melts' infinitely preferable. The Inuit established a co-operative there in the late 1960s and a school was built. Nearby is

Goose Fiord, more delicately named, where Sverdrup was marooned for an extra year when the ice didn't break up. This is game-rich territory, particularly white fox, polar bear and the extraordinary looking muskox, the creature that seems to have wandered out of its time.

Chapter Seven

The Hairy Muskox

The muskox (known as *Oomingmak* meaning 'the animal with skin like a beard') is definitely a relic of the last ice age. There have been muskoxen in the Arctic for over 7,000 years and its ancestors originated on the tundras of north-central Asia about one million years before that. The woolly mammoth, the large-horned bison and the small horse all became extinct and only the muskox has survived. Muskoxen do not live in the extreme northern temperatures as they would starve, and only inhabit the areas where the tundras can provide something to eat; they must migrate south as the colder weathers approach. The muskox has a peculiar beauty all of its own. To me it is very reminiscent of the equally hairy yak, particularly the ones I have encountered in Bhutan in the Himalayas, although they are more closely related to the takin which is another very odd-looking, furry Bhutanese creature.

When a herd of muskoxen is challenged the adults retreat into a defensive ring against their attackers, like the wagons circling against an Indian attack in the Wild West. They usually move somewhat slowly, as a way of conserving heat and energy in the winter and possibly to avoid overheating in the summer. When necessary they can run and climb with tremendous agility. If forced to defend or attack they will head charge and it's better not to be in their way. It is estimated that a head-on charge is equivalent to a car driving into a wall at 27 km/h. In case you ever need to know this, one tip, a muskox prepares to charge by lowering its head down and pressing its nose against its knee, to release a musky-smelling liquid from a gland near its nose. But don't waste time smelling, start running fast. You are within a great wilderness and as such may roam free but always remember the muskox may charge.

The multi-layered fur coat, between seven and ten centimetres thick, though coarse and stiff on the outside includes an ultra-soft undercoat called *qiviut* which is shed in summer. This fleece is lighter, warmer and rarer than the finest wools. The fur covers the whole of their bodies including the udders, which is possibly why they mostly breed only one calf every other year. Their horns are broad and flattened close to the skull. Boss is the name given to the muskox horn.

The muskoxen tend to eat from the valley floors, where the snow cover is relatively thick, rather than on the windswept slopes where the grasses may be already exposed. This is because at the valley floor the vegetation is lusher and more nutritious. They either use their noses to push aside soft snow or work with paw and chin to break through the thicker ice crust. They will move from area to area, to find new eating grounds, as if they know instinctively that they must not over-use any particular place. They eat a wide variety of plants and grasses but have a particular liking for willow that tends to grow near rivers, which is why they are often sighted near water. The muskoxen don't however, merely contend with attack or adversity they seem positively to thrive on it. In winter and sub-zero conditions, faced with the prospect of starvation rations, they respond by immediately reducing their food intake and demands. It's a Zen-like discipline. If there is less to eat the answer is to eat less. They can reprogram their digestive systems to receive the maximum benefit from every mouthful of food. They reduce their bodily activities to conserve energy. Their liver and kidneys can reduce in weight almost by half. Within Zen, oxen of whatever kind have always had a symbolic place in many illustrations, usually drawn in a series to the important Zen number of ten. They illustrate stories that show the way that life unfolds explaining that people and animals are symbiotic. They reveal the concept of the infinite, explaining that nothing can ever reach to the end and therefore no one can know it. The sky is often painted azure, a colour that is reflective of the pure and clear mind.

Muskox cows can produce a calf annually but often several years can go by without any calves being born. This is usually a direct result of their sensitivity to the harsh environment. It is certainly appealing to understand these shaggy, woolly giants are, underneath all that outer, massive covering, sensitive creatures. They are also playful animals. It's again rather nice to accept that, even living in these very tough conditions, the adults as well as the calves play just for the pleasure of it. It has been established that the pregnant cows at the end of the winter still have high percentages of bone marrow fat which again illustrates their adaptation to the Arctic winters.

Muskoxen are prime survivors, given half a chance, but they can't fight off the over-zealous hunter and that's why they need protection and kills must be limited. They have already been wiped out in this region once and have only survived by re-stocking from Greenland. However, they are still right at the edge of survival. Otherwise they could go the way of the American bison. Unfortunately some people now think that's just a place to wash their hands.

Chapter Eight

Huskies Don't Lose Their Voices

We are staying in the Grise Fiord Lodge, a co-operative hotel, a small two-storey building with nine bedrooms, each containing two or three bunks, accommodating 24 guests altogether. There are very few people at the end of the season so I am allocated a room to myself and gratefully choose the top bunk. As we were delayed, dinner has been kept for us and just requires reheating. First we finish off the caviar, pâté and *foie gras* that Fabian has brought with him, washed down with lashings of champagne.

The North-West Territories are meant to be primarily an alcohol-free zone; the Government of Canada has forbidden the sale of any kind of alcoholic drinks, including beer, to help protect the Inuit populations in this vast and mostly inhospitable region. Otherwise, it is believed that with little to occupy them, they would succumb even more to drink problems and the whole Inuit infrastructure out here, delicately balanced as it is, would crumble. So no alcohol is sold but it seems that it can still be smuggled in without too many problems, although officially, during December and the first week of January you cannot drink, let alone sell, alcohol. Fortunately, no one raises any objections to our drinking and I know that Fabian was well aware of the ban, which is why he brought so much with him. I am surprised he had room for any kit at all.

It's been a long day so I turn in fairly early but as usual Fabian and Erik decide to have a few more celebratory drinks. The setting and their committed imbibing reminds me of the fabulous short film starring W. C. Fields titled *The Fatal Glass Of Beer*. It's also set in the snowy wastes and every time Fields tries to leave his trapper's hut he opens the door and an unseen hand throws a bucketful of snow in his face. In the film Fields has a son whose downfall has been brought about by drinking that first 'fatal glass of beer'. Of course, the film is just a scenario to allow Fields to show off his uniquely famous comic skills and parodies. Fields himself was no stranger to the alcoholic beverage and he undoubtedly would have been welcomed with open arms by Fabian and Erik. Fields was also famous for declaring that he would rather be living in Philadelphia than dead, but only just. I wonder what he would have said about living in Resolute. It is very blowy outside so I decide not to go for a midnight stroll, even though it is incredibly bright as the Arctic is enjoying 24 hours daylight at this time of year.

I return to my room, undress and try to sleep. The rooms are heated, overheated, and I have stripped down as far as possible and only use a single sheet covering. It still proves impossible to sleep, as all night the husky dogs continually howl. There's the apposite joke about why the prairie dogs howl all night long – there are no trees in the prairie, just cacti! Here there are no trees, nor cacti, nor anything, so there must be another reason.

I look out of my window and can see the dogs on the ice, chained to a central iron post. It looks decidedly barbaric. I subsequently learn that this is the usual practice. Huskies are tethered every night to a post, with metal chains to prevent them chewing through the leather or sisal ropes and for whatever reason they always continue to howl all night long. The barking and howling intensifies in extreme cold conditions and can carry up to 20 km. Possibly this is why the Inuit villages are always more than that distance away from each other. Presumably the villagers become immune to the hideous noise but we are only here for a few days and the racket is definitely not sleep-inducing. The dogs are fed by being tossed chunks of raw seal meat and this together with the natural dog waste creates a stench around the area which also drifts in all directions. The actuality is certainly not the romantic image that most of us will remember from the early films of the Arctic and the Antarctic, when we would see teams of huskies racing across the snowy wastes with the sledge leaders calling out, 'Mush, mush,' to encourage them to run faster.

The greatest and toughest husky race in the world takes place every year out of Anchorage in Alaska. It's called the *Iditerod* and was started in 1975 to commemorate the sled mercy dash of 1925. Apparently a doctor was desperate for serum to counter an outbreak of diphtheria that threatened to wipe out the town of Nome on the Bering Straits. Teams of huskies brought the serum there in 100 km relays. There is a statue of one of the lead dogs, Balto, in New York's Central Park.

The race is a solitary endurance test over a distance of more than 1,700 km. Each husky team of sixteen dogs will pull a load of around 180 kg and a contestant must finish with at least five dogs remaining. Those huskies that become too tired are left at stations along the way and contestants are forbidden to maltreat any. Two important commands are 'gee' meaning right and 'haw' meaning left. Hopefully a contestant, as well as the husky, will know his right from his left, otherwise they might end up going around in arctic circles!

Also out on the ice are a number of children playing. Inuit children are allowed to do primarily whatever they want and many therefore stay out very late to play and explore. The Inuit believe that people's spirits live on after death and transfer into their children. At birth, a child often is given the names of those that have passed on, a respected grandfather, a loved grandmother. They are then considered to have the souls of their grandparents and ancestors, so must be treated with absolute reverence. They are not punished for anything they might do, even if they disobey an instruction or request. As can be imagined this obviously leads to all kinds of social difficulties. The children are often very noisy. I spend a very fretful night, what with the bright, intense light, the smells and the sounds of the dogs and the children as well as the anticipation of what tomorrow will bring. But that matters little, after all I am in the Arctic, living with the furthest northern human community that exists!

We all breakfast early and there we meet Looty Pijamini. He is of course an Inuk (the singular of Inuit) and has been working with Andy Goldsworthy over the last month, helping him build his initial Arctic sculptures. They are set around the point, about 8 km from here and we are very anxious to see them. Looty can only take us now as he will need to take off the next day, as it is his last chance to hunt for polar bear. He is to set off with a tourist hunter who has purchased Looty's permit to hunt one polar bear each season. All the Inuit have this right. It seems that Looty has not shot a bear for eight years as he sells off his right each year to bring in additional income to his family. Looty's huskies died last year from flu so he is trying to build up a new team and has five puppies to train.

On one side wall there is a large poster of a polar bear rearing on its two hind paws, probably in the attack position. A beautiful and magnificent animal and rightfully the symbol of the Arctic all over the world. There are some interesting, bare facts listed on the poster, but I need to learn much more about this incredible creature.

Chapter Nine

The Great White Polar Bear

The polar bear (*Ursus Maritimus*, translating as the sea bear) is the world's largest and most powerful carnivore. The Inuit call him Nanuq or Nanook. It is rightly considered to be the most intelligent of all the Arctic's creatures. If you encounter one, better beware and decide your line of defence or attack immediately, as the white polar bear can react and act very quickly indeed. Without a gun no human is capable of besting a polar bear. All you can do is run and try to escape, but its speed across the ice is deceptively fast and it has great stamina and tenacity and rarely will you escape unless it decides not to pursue you.

The adult male can weigh over 650 kg and reach a height resting on its four paws of more than a metre at its shoulder. The females average less than half the male's weight and have narrower skulls but are still as deadly. Polar bears have a small black snout which vividly stands out against the whiteness of their fur. (Brown bears are only one third of the size of polar bears and they often have a small white patch on their chests and are mostly vegetarian).

An adult polar bear can easily kill a full-grown seal, weighing 150 kg, with one single blow. As autumn approaches and the big freeze occurs it is particularly lean and hungry and impatient to hunt after the months of forced summer fasting. It can smell a seal several kilometres downwind. The polar bears are also strong and powerful swimmers, have huge feet and partly-webbed paws. They have even been seen swimming some 80 km from the nearest land or ice floe. Polar bears don't slip on the ice, even at speed, as they have pads on the feet covered with small, soft papillae like coarse sandpaper, which increases the friction with the ice while small depressions in the sole act as suction cups.

Polar bears are meat eaters and have the fierce and very sharp teeth (42 in total) necessary for tearing at their victims as well as shearing them and clipping them. The one creature that is relatively unafraid of the bear is the Arctic Fox. It often follows in the wake of Nanook to feed on the scraps left from its hunting. Apart from their more normal prey of fish, seal and walrus, bears will attack anything. There are many instances when they have damaged whales so much that they have been able to drag them out of the water on to the ice to eat them. They are extremely cunning and have been known to stalk their prey in a variety of disguises including pretending to be a large piece of floating ice, sliding forward very slowly on their chests. If they sight a quarry they freeze instantly, sometimes for ten minutes whilst they plan how to get close enough to attack. They are able to move so slowly that it is not possible to see any actual movement.

Like the Inuit themselves they will wait patiently at a seal's ice breathing hole for it to appear, before suddenly and speedily swiping one massive paw to stun the seal and then swiftly sinking their jaws into it. Some seals will clamber out of their holes to rest and breathe more easily and then a bear may strike at incredible speed. Instinctively understanding this, it is rare for two seals to come out at the same time, as one would impede the other when trying to dive back through the hole to escape. Bears will also swim underneath the ice and water to attack, just raising the tips of their black snouts to breathe occasionally. There is a story, possibly apocryphal, that some bears when moving forward to attack hold one paw over their snout to avoid the blackness giving their intentions away. They do not drink water; they get all the liquid they need from the animals they eat.

A strange fact is that polar bears are left-handed, presumably it's not usually that relevant as a blow from either paw is just as damaging. How this can be definitively known I'm not really certain as obviously not all polar bears can have been checked. Surely there must be one bear out there who uses his or her right hand! In boxing terminology a left-handed boxer is called a southpaw, whereas, given the fact that polar bears only live in the northern Arctic and never in the southern Antarctic, this seems somewhat of a misnomer.

A bear, usually to preserve energy, can sleep in any position. It spends about a quarter of its time sleeping and particularly likes to sleep after eating. However, meals can be a few days apart or even a few months. That is why its main preoccupation is to keep its body at the right temperature and to store sufficient energy, in readiness to claim its next meal. The bear's fur is unlike that of any other mammal. There are two thick layers of dense, white wool with shiny and strong guard hairs. They help to recycle the bear's body heat back to the skin. These hairs are hollow and stay stiff even when wet so they don't matt and the bear can therefore shake off water before it freezes.

Strange as it may seem, although their fur is white to help in camouflaging them against the snow, their skin underneath is black, this absorbs the heat from the sun and assists them in contending with intense cold temperatures. It is why most people in hot countries prefer to wear white robes or lightly-coloured clothes, rather than black or dark ones. It's possibly why the huge, black furry hat worn by British guardsmen, sometimes called a Busby, is more usually known as a bearskin.

Polar bears do not hibernate though they may curl up to avoid a storm or to wait out the approach of prey or a change in temperature. When pregnant, a female bear can reduce her heartbeat and breathing considerably. In mid-winter she will live within a den she has dug and usually gives birth to two tiny cubs, occasionally three or four. Because they keep their cubs for about two and a half years, on average only about one-third of females are available for reproduction each year. The mother bear produces the richest milk of all animals in the world and has four nipples to nurse her young.

The cubs develop rapidly and can hear and see within a month. Weeks later they can walk and smell. In a few months they will leave the den and accompany their mother as she forages and hunts for food. This is their learning period when they must come to understand the ways of hunting.

Strangely, different to practically all other animals, female bears do not seem able to distinguish their own cubs from any others. There are too many cases of cubs from other families being raised by another mother for it to be a coincidence. Scientists have been able to confirm this odd quirk of nature by DNA testing on bears they have examined. The most plausible explanation is that cubs had become mixed up when two families happen to meet and as there are relatively few polar bear families there is very little necessity to recognise instinctively one's own cubs.

The collective noun for a group of bears is a 'sloth', which might be indicative of their apparent lack of concern about family relationships.

After two to three years the family breaks up and the cubs are on their own, in reality cubs no longer. They might stay in pairs for a short while but quickly become solitary hunters. A bear can often live for up to 30 years. Although well-adapted to the intense cold they do not have a natural, internal cooling system so will always seek cool areas rather than loll on the ice. Female bears are at greater risk due to natural hazards but the greatest danger to polar bears is man.

In 1976 the International Agreement on the Conservation of Polar Bears was established. This was designed to limit hunting by establishing hunting quotas. Russia and Norway stopped hunting altogether, the United States and Denmark only allow subsistence hunting, whereas Canada permits greater hunting opportunities and allow sports hunters to hunt (this really means shoot) bears under a settlement's quota. The fee is very high and is usually divided amongst people in the community. A fortunate further restriction is that no use of motorised vehicles such as ski-doos is allowed. The hunt must use dog teams. If successful the hide may be kept by the hunter but fortunately the United States does not permit the import of hides.

There is another major factor which is diminishing the bear population. As the Arctic is warming up so the ice melts earlier and freezes again later. This leaves less time for the female to sit out their long pregnancy and have her cubs in the spring. There is now also the danger from more toxic material accumulating as pesticides and other chemicals evaporate from further south and then condense out in the cold Arctic air. This gets into the fish and bears eating them can overdose on mercury and industrial chemical substances. We all bear a responsibility to safeguard this wonderful and untameable creature.

Chapter Ten

The Hunter, the Artist and the Ski-doo Riders

We now meet Looty's hunter, Luis Rivera Siaca, coming from Puerto Rico, himself a huge bear of a man, about two metres tall. (He tells us later he weighs around 128 kg.) He's very bearded, has big shaggy hair and is wearing an enormous pair of Bean, grey worsted trousers, very good quality and obviously expensive. This is topped with a red wind-cheater and gigantic red braces. Naturally he has a gold medallion hanging from his neck.

Luis tells us he is in fact Sicilian and lives and runs his own building company in Puerto Rico. As if to emphasise his Sicilian background he insists upon showing us his guns and knives. He is only here to hunt for polar bear and has two hunting rifles with him; one a Remington, the other a Webley. They are both hand-made, custom built and sighted for accuracy. Both the guns are loaded and Luis delights in showing us how they work and unloads and loads them several times. One seems very much a sniper's weapon and I decide that this is definitely not a man to have an argument with. He doesn't look like he takes any prisoners. His knives are equally as impressive and as deadly. All are handcrafted works of art, costing over 1,000 dollars each Luis proudly tells us.

The Sicilian has been here over a week waiting for the opportunity to go hunting again. With a previous guide, he was out hunting when they were trapped by a sudden, ferocious storm and had to sit it out in the hunter's hut for five days till it subsided. When a blizzard occurs, everything, man, animal, ski-doo, aeroplane must stop and wait till it abates. You need to shelter in a hut or your tent, build an igloo or dig an ice hole. Otherwise you are likely to freeze to death. To qualify as a blizzard an Arctic storm must be -12 °C with winds blowing at speeds in excess of 40 km/h. Additionally visibility must be reduced to 1 km. (The terrifying white-out condition occurs when visibility drops to less than 10 metres.) These conditions also have to last for three to six hours.

I think Luis' five days certainly qualify as a white-out – I wouldn't like to come across him in a black-out! He said he stopped himself going mad by reading six books. Although he doesn't look like the kind of man who reads, he certainly does look like the kind of man with whom one doesn't argue about such matters. He hadn't been able to get a bear during that time. Today he is going out with another guide/hunter, Larry, who has also sold him his bear permit. There's a silence as we all digest this information. I think most of us hope his luck remains the same.

I tell a bear joke which Luis thinks is uproariously funny, although I really mean it to illustrate our inner feelings. 'A hunter meets a gorgeous woman in a bar in one of the remote inland towns and after a while she invites him home with her. She shows him around and he sees that the apartment is full of toy bears, neatly piled on three shelves. There are small ones on the bottom shelf, medium-sized ones on the middle shelf and large ones on the top shelf. The next morning the hunter asks her, "Well, how was it?" She replies, "You can take any prize from the bottom shelf."' Fortunately, at that moment our guide Looty reappears and brings with him the complete head of a muskox with highly polished horns, that he has 'found'. Erik is also a hunter back in Norway, where he lives for part of the year and buys it from him to take home with him.

Looty has organised ski-doos for us and I am given my own to drive. What a terrific thrill! Fabian also has his own. Looty takes Penny on pillion, with a sledge tied on to the back for Erik to recline on like a Roman Emperor. However, he subsequently realises that he is breathing in the fumes from Looty's ski-doo and that isn't too pleasant. We set off round the point to find Goldsworthy's first set of Arctic sculptures.

What an incredible sight! Although already slightly damaged by the fierce winds they are still utterly magnificent. He is certainly wonderfully imaginative and creative! They are especially impressive within the plateau setting that Andy has chosen. One is a long line of thin very flat shapes, twenty in number, stretching across like a defensive ice wall from a long-ago destroyed castle; another a conical, bulbous pillar, resembling a giant spinning wheel, over three metres high; another consists of four hollow surrounds, one metre high, possibly built for the four of us and we each stand in one as a tribute to Andy. There are many different shapes of all sizes, balanced to the surrounding mountains, like monuments to a lost civilisation and another world. There is also a series of steps seemingly leading nowhere or perhaps to wherever you choose. There are over thirty sculptures in total. They stand in splendid isolation almost like a tribute to the mountains around us. We can only marvel.

I wonder what the Inuit's thoughts are of this strange Englishman who has travelled so far and in such difficult conditions to sculpt here. Particularly as the sculptures last such fleeting moments, as the winds and the sun quickly reclaim them to the ice and the land. Nature itself often creates incredibly beautiful snow and ice shapes and sculptures, but of course, they occur purely by chance, formed through the power of the elements and not by design or intent. The philosophy of the Inuit is all around us, everywhere in this rocky and evocative white landscape. The Inuit believe that all things have souls, the very rocks and stones, as well as animate objects. A way to understand this is to realise that everything has a relationship to everything else, to the whole world. It is not such a leap to accept it and then you can appreciate and help to protect the environment as well as individuals and animals.

Looty attempts to show us how to build an igloo. You have to finish it from within, actually trapping yourself inside before cutting out an exit. The traditional igloos were built using skins over whalebones. Now just solid snow is used. Snow is easier to cut than ice. Once the walls are finished a door and a short entrance tunnel are then added. The cracks are then stuffed with loose snow for extra insulation and firmness. An igloo can be any size but usually is just sufficient for the needs of one or two hunters or the family using it. That way the inside will heat up faster. It is estimated that four people will raise the inside temperature by 10 °C. Two tips: the air vent should be placed just over half a metre from the floor at a downward angle to prevent heat escaping; the inside temperature can be raised by burning a few candles.

It is very hard work and the wall part of mine that I laboriously complete is very lopsided and almost immediately topples over. But as always I've learned something by my lack of success. The Zen teachings take that to a higher level by expressing, 'The barn has burnt down, good, now I can see the moon.' Looty explains that in a white-out or in a blizzard, you might have to shelter for days, even weeks and an igloo will save your life. A person can live without food for weeks, without water for days but in very bad conditions one can only survive for a few hours without shelter. Igloos are usually temporary and are not intended to be permanent homes. A skilled hunter using his snow knife can fashion one in less than an hour. He could easily add a window using pieces of clear ice or even the stretched intestine of a seal.

We breathe and drink in the inspirational and heady atmosphere for a long time but eventually time starts to exert its own pressure and we must return. We drive back on the ski-doos and I am exhilarated by the thrill of driving at speed along these seemingly endless plateaux amidst such natural monuments to creation. At times we race each other but mostly it is just the joy of harmonising within this beautiful land. We are back at the co-operative hotel in time to see the final preparations for Luis before he takes off on his hunting trip (I really want to call him Big Louis from Detroit but feel he may not appreciate it, so just address him as Big Al and he seems to like that). Larry isn't ready yet but the huskies are anxious to move and are making more of a din than usual. I'm told it will be a half hour yet so decide to stroll through the village.

It doesn't take long. There are only a small number of houses and various wooden shacks, put up without an eye for design or harmony. There are plenty of ugly oil drums scattered around and it's clear that the main priority here is wind and cold protection. Out of season it must indeed be desolate and barren and certainly not a place to spend the usual holidays. However, some people do spend their lives here and never travel away. It makes me think of Siberia and similar frozen territories and the hardy and resilient peoples that also live in such inhospitable places. But to them it's home and they survive in their own way. Many people in the past have visited Britain and wondered how we put up with our weather. To us it's not so bad and we are not fazed by it, so presumably similarly are the Inuit and the Siberians. Of course a benefit of global warming to us in Britain has been the increase in temperatures over recent years. In London we now rarely have more than a few days snow each year, whereas in the past we regularly had snow for several weeks. Some of the Inuit houses have several polar bear skins stretched on racks outside, being prepared for sale. The bear's head is first removed for cleaning, then replaced at the end of the process. A very ignoble end to one of the most magnificent animals of the world.

I hurry back and Larry is finally ready. He has replaced two harnesses he wasn't happy with and has the one huge sledge (called a *komatik*) piled high with provisions, their tent, extra clothes and of course Luis's deadly guns. The sledge is about four metres long. Larry chooses his dogs for this trip in rotation, harnessing the leader first before tying on the others. Those left behind scream and howl even more intensely in protest. Surprisingly one of the dogs taken has only three legs but I'm told is a first class bird dog and is still fast enough to keep up. Larry's wife uses a long whip to try and keep the dogs in order but they still tangle themselves up in all kinds of ways and have to be continually sorted out. Generously she lets me try the whip the cord of which must be over six metres long. It has a metal attachment at the end, primarily to help the balance but it must also sting fiercely when it strikes the skin.

Luis is resplendent in a wrap around red jump suit, large, flashy French glasses, and his hunting knife prominent on his right hip. He takes the high front position and waves majestically at us. I wave back but still hope he is unsuccessful. Larry leans forward, cracking his whip and the huskies strain against the harnesses and ropes and start off at a very fast pace towards the north-east. Looty tells me, much to my delight, that Larry has an unsuccessful record as a hunter and it is likely they will return in two or three days without having killed a bear. Shortly another hunter sets off in their general direction hoping to meet up later to see if they need any help. We can now set off ourselves to explore and try to find some animals. But our shooting is with camera only.

We set off in our ski-doos towards the west with the intention of looking for animal tracks. I am the last in line, which enables me to lag behind, then put on bursts of speed to catch up. It is so exhilarating and really great fun. I enjoy the wonderful sense of absolute freedom in this vast land of snow and ice. It's absolutely magical. We travel in this manner for many kilometres and I wouldn't miss this for anything. Sometimes we pass through huge tracts of totally flat terrain, other times we cross rougher areas of rock and stone, often covered in all kinds of lichens. A couple of times my ski-doo gets stuck in a snowdrift on the rocks and I have to get off to pull it free and then restart the engine. At times I am so far behind that I wonder if they would find me if I couldn't restart the ski-doo but I always just manage it. At a stop for water, I ask Looty whether sometimes he finds it difficult to know the way. His eyes twinkling, he tells me, 'Inuit never get lost but occasionally the path wanders.'

We have reached a completely wide open area of white wasteland which seems to stretch on forever. We are as remote from any kind of civilisation as it seems possible to be. Sometimes the mists close in so that we are like ghost riders, other times the air is so clear we can allow tremendous distances to occur between our ski-doos without losing sight of eachother. Suddenly three massive snow mounds loom up in front of us, looking like ancient burial sites and we stop to circle and admire. They are a freak of nature and although they look as if they have been there from time immemorial, Looty assures us that they were only formed recently and will not last long. Here the forces of the elements can create and destroy their own sculptures in days or even hours.

We find the bodies of two dead seals and Looty thinks they were left there by some hunters for food for their huskies at a later date. I wonder how they would know where to find them but I guess that's part of their hunting and guiding skills. We come across a few seal holes, just a centimetre or two across, made by the seals for breathing when they are swimming under the ice for long stretches. There are about 1,000 seals around and they like to breathe every four to five minutes although can stay submerged for much longer periods. In the Arctic there are six different species and they live in various regions usually with their own kind. The six are – bearded, spotted, ribbon, harp, hooded and ringed.

Each female will give birth to just one pup out on the ice in the early spring. The pups need to grow the protective, insulating layer of blubber as fast as possible if they are going to survive in the freezing waters. Two breeds have particularly fast-growing pups, the hooded and the harp and therefore they are found the furthest north. The harp pups, called yellowcoats, grow from 10 kg at birth to 34 kg within 12 days; incredibly, the hooded pups, called bluebacks, weigh 42 kg within just 4 days. The mothers have very fat-rich milk to speed this process. During this feeding the mother is considerably weakened and loses about a quarter of her normal body weight. That's the main reason why a seal will only have one pup. Seals are slippery creatures physically and mentally and are difficult to catch. Polar bears are reckoned to have only a 5 per cent success rate in hunting them. The seals have short claws on the ends of their flippers which enable them to obtain a very sure grip on the ice. They can glide effortlessly and dive to depths of 500 metres where they can remain for up to 28 minutes. When the Inuit find a seal hole they usually mark it and stake it out to try and catch the seal. The usual way is to stand back about 10 cm from the hole to avoid being seen and when the seal swims to the hole to breathe, shoot to one side. Then cut the ice away to see if the seal was killed and the body is still there. We wait for a while but fortunately no seal appears and we drive off again.

Looty tells us some stories about the animals of the Arctic. It's important not to over-romanticise, as here the law of survival is paramount – for man and animal. The polar bears are fierce creatures and need to hunt as well to survive. If they can catch even a whale they will do so and they are always looking out for such an opportunity. Looty tells about a recent occasion when a group of beluga whales were trapped by shifting ice and every time they surfaced the bears were waiting by the ice hole and tearing off pieces.

The bears would also jump on top of them to weaken and damage them. Some of the whales were eventually so weakened the bears could pull them out of the water. A few of the Inuit had tried to help by punching extra holes in the ice to allow the whales to surface elsewhere and give them a greater chance of avoiding the bears. When the ice eventually broke up in that area as the warmer weather approached, the remaining whales were able to escape. There was very little else anyone could do, as it is always necessary to let nature take its own course. It is certainly something to ponder about and to remember how important it is to not interfere in the laws of nature.

We reach a magnificent blue ice formation that is a truly spectacular sight and stop to try and climb it. But it is sheer ice and without an ice axe to cut into it and create foot and hand holds it proves impossible. We travel on for several kilometres, stopping when we want, eating our sandwiches, drinking our tea, coffee, brandy sometimes, but mostly just to marvel at the incredible beauty of it all. We are all in great spirits and start swapping stories. Changing the setting to fit in, I tell the story of the huge polar bear that stomps into the furthest bar, in the last town, on the edge of the North-West Territories. The barman and the customers are quite literally frozen to silence by his sudden appearance. The bear goes straight up to the counter and leans his massive arms aggressively right over it, his hot breath spouting out like fire. 'I . . . want . . . the largest . . . glass . . . of beer . . . you . . . have.' The terrified barman finally stammers back, 'OK, but, but, why the big pause?' Looty gets it right away but Fabian takes a moment or two. They shouldn't have encouraged me and I can't resist one more; a three-legged dog shuffles into a Territories bar, reminiscent of the old Wild West cowboy saloons. He barks out, 'I'm looking for the man who shot my paw.' It's definitely time to move on.

We climb back on our ski-doos. Just as we are moving off we hear, rather than see, a sudden flurry as a creature dives hastily through a water hole. Looty who is more sharp-eyed, becomes very excited and declares it was a walrus, which is fairly uncommon to find around here. It would be a really rare treat if we could see one. He gets off his ski-doo to inspect the hole but after a few minutes finally decides it would not be beneficial to wait around as it's unlikely to return for several hours. What a great pity! I would love to have seen one in the flesh, so to speak, but instead content myself with finding out more about this odd and comical-looking creature.

<u>Arctic:</u>
Polar bear footprints

Polar bear stalking its seal prey

The team of huskies setting off from Grise Fiord

Neville Shulman about to ski-doo across the Arctic whiteness

The Arctic ice starting to crack up

Andy Goldsworthy's Snow Spires, Grise Fiord

An extraordinary translucent Goldsworthy zig zag ice design

The desolate and rugged Arctic stretching out before us

The Arctic sun never sets at this time of year

Rendez-vous at Hazen to switch twin otters on last leg to North Pole

Camp Hazen, the isolated and remote North Pole outpost

NORTH POLE

NEW YORK
5,461 Km

LONDON
4,292 Km

ROME
5,439 Km

MOSCOW
4,348 Km

SOUTH POLE
20,000 Km

North Pole signpost, all routes leading south

Goldsworthy and two team members outside their tiny North Pole tent

Andy Goldsworthy's majestic and powerful four voids built at the North Pole

Chapter Eleven

I Am the Walrus

More than its close relative the seal, the walrus (*odobenus rosmanus*, to give it the full Latin name) is a strange-looking creature but is absolutely fascinating to observe. In fact *odobenidae* means 'those that walk with their teeth.' The popular and pretty accurate image is of a very large, ungainly sea animal with bright, glaring eyes, a bulbous nose and an unkempt, straggly, huge swatch of whiskers. Those very human-looking bristles, splaying in all directions, have led many a novelist comparatively to describe a character as 'wearing a large walrus-like moustache'. They can often bristle out to a length of over 10 cm. The heavily-built walrus is one of the contributing, special factors which has helped to exemplify what sets this extraordinary Arctic apart, a place of mystery and excitement. Possibly for a similar reason, Lewis Carroll included in his *Alice Through the Looking Glass*, the story of the walrus inviting some oysters for tea, only for them to discover they are the tea. 'The time has come, the walrus said, To talk of many things: Of shoes – and ships – and sealing wax – Of cabbages – and kings – And why the sea is boiling hot – And whether pigs have wings. But answer came there none – And this was scarcely odd because they'd eaten every one.' In fact walruses do eat shellfish, particularly clams and mussels. They prefer to dive for their food in shallows of about 55 metres but can often go down to 90 metres. John Lennon and Paul McCartney were also intrigued by this unusually quaint creature and called one of their surreal, more strangely-worded songs – 'I Am the Walrus.' Did they mean – we are the walruses? Then who was the egg man? Probably Ringo at least was the one who egged them on. At one time in his acting career, having grown a long straggly moustache, he was certainly able to give more than a passable walrus imitation.

Walruses are pinnipeds, like seals and sea lions. *Pinni* meaning wing or fin and *pedis* meaning foot. Walruses are the largest pinnipeds and live in shallow water near land or the ice floes. There are two types, Pacific and Atlantic. The bulls weigh more than the polar bears, up to one tonne or more, and can grow up to three and a half metres. You can tell their age by the number of rings in a cross-section of their teeth, although you shouldn't try this whilst they are alive or at least not darted to put to sleep for research purposes. As a rule they don't attack humans but in defence are extremely fierce. One blow from a powerful fin will make you see double the amount of stars in the Arctic sky. They have, on occasion, even tusked a boat that they thought was being used to hunt them. They can move so surprisingly fast on land that they can catch up with a man and can actually walk on all four fins in a more elegant way than the lumbering seal. These could be the main reasons why the walrus is also called the sea horse.

The tusks of walruses are in fact upper canine teeth. They are made of ivory harder than that of the elephant and can grow to one and a half metres in the bull and half that in the cow. The longer the tusk the more important ranking they have in their own group. The bulls use their tusks to fight each other, particularly during the mating season, in order to earn the right to mate with their chosen female cow. The courtship of the bull and cow walrus is an extraordinary long and elaborate process between two heavyweights of the Arctic. First the male seduces with growls, barks and whistles. Then the two tenderly rub their whiskers together before laboriously getting down to the serious business at hand. A lot of grunting goes on. It's definitely what is known as a labour of love.

Matings usually take place from late April up to early June. Gestation takes over a year. Only one pup is born every alternate year and the birth takes place on an ice floe where the cow feels the safest. The cow is highly protective of her pup and will attack any one that tries to harm it. If the pup is actually killed then the cow is driven into a frenzy of revenge. The pup is born with short silver-grey hair and weighs around 50 kg. It is able to swim immediately but will closely follow its mother for the first few weeks. The cow and the pup stay together for up to two years before it is considered adult enough to go off on its own. Both bulls and cows will use their tusks as ice picks to haul themselves rather laboriously out of the sea to clamber on to the ice as well as using them to break the ice to create breathing holes. The tusks are also great for digging for clams which are mostly swallowed whole but sometimes are broken open. No shells have ever been found in the stomach so they must be able to crunch them into the tiniest of fragments. They also swallow pebbles and stones which are probably used to crush the shells and aid digestion.

Walruses are gregarious and sociable creatures and during the summer will usually lie around in packed, noisy groups, mostly males together, unless it's time for mating. Possibly they realise that no creature is ordinarily inclined to seek out their company. Herding together is also a protection against the few predators they face, mostly polar bears and killer whales, apart from man that is. They love to sunbathe if they can and grunt to each other; the phrase 'chewing the fat' could have been invented for the walrus. Like many other polar creatures they have a thick layer of blubber under their skins so they don't feel the cold from the wind or the water. Their skin is very wrinkly which also acts as armour in protecting the walrus from predators or when in combat with another walrus. They can sleep when floating, as they have inflatable air sacs in their throats that fill up to keep them buoyant, so they rather comically bob up and down with their heads just above the water. They change colour from pink/cinnamon-brown to a lighter colour when swimming in colder waters, because their blood vessels become smaller. They have a blood circulatory system, so when they get hot their blood is pumped to the blubber and skin enabling it to become cooled by the air or water, and when they are cold they reduce the blood flow to the skin and blubber to save on heat.

Walruses use their whiskers, which are highly sensitive, to feel around to find their food. Then they blow or snort to loosen the food or move it into position to eat. Their tusks can get in the way so they have to manoeuvre carefully. Mostly they eat invertebrates, living on the sea bottom; shrimps, crabs, snails, worms. They migrate in the spring and autumn, alerted by the advance or retreat of the ice floes, following their food opportunities. In some special cases bulls have been known to grow up to two tonnes. That's a lot of bull.

Chapter Twelve

Trouble With Harry

Perhaps nearly sighting the walrus makes me become too excited. I start speeding over the huge ice bumps, sometimes lifting off as the pressure kicks in; my own polar regions are taking the strain. I start zooming with the ski-doo in long sweeping loops, feeling the power of the ice beneath me, letting the engine aggressively race away. Suddenly I am amongst the rocks and my safety manoeuvres are in vain. I cannot avoid one rocky section and crash the ski-doo into it and it flips over. I am not really hurt, shaken but not stirred, but the undertrack is torn and the ski-doo needs a repair before it can be used again.

I am in disgrace, in the dog house, or is it the bear house? We have been driving away from the settlement for about four hours which means that it will take about four hours to return. Of course it is still broad daylight so we can stay out as long as we like. But we do need to head back, otherwise they might send out a search party if we miss dinner altogether. We shouldn't be lulled into forgetting we are in the wilderness, far removed from civilisation as we know it.

Looty spots another ski-doo in the distance and sets off in pursuit to try and enlist help. He returns alone, looking rather dispirited. It was another hunter who is out to catch snow rabbits and has arranged to stay out all night and therefore can't help us. Somehow Looty gets my ski-doo working but he needs to drive it as it's playing up and is liable to be temperamental on the long drive back. Now it's only fair that Fabian and Erik have a ski-doo each, so Penny and I agree to share the sledge. It's not comfortable but I cannot of course complain, it's my fault. The winds build up and we try to keep as low as possible to avoid them. We arrive back at about 10.30 p.m. The children are still out playing as usual. Looty estimates the damage to the ski-doo will cost about 340 Canadian dollars and I pay this to him. He insists on signing a receipt, though I have to write it for him.

Again dinner has been left for us pre-cooked and just needs heating. Another group of travellers has arrived, mostly Americans and they are really full of high spirits in more ways than one and we have an enjoyable time exchanging stories. One of the party, Sidney Hendricks, produces his own stamp marker with the words, 'Pole Expedition, April in Arctic' and we all stamp it into our passports. Sidney produces a bottle of a famous French wine, Chateau Lafite 1868, which he always carries with him for charity and that he intends to take to the North Pole. The wooden casket has been signed by various people, including Neil Armstrong, the first man on the moon and Sidney insists I also sign it. I was awarded an honorary colonelship by the Governor of Tennessee for my work in the Arts, so feel the special occasion warrants my signing as Colonel Neville Shulman. Seeing this Sidney forces me to salute everyone in turn; I should have kept my big mouth shut. Still, it's another small step for Shul*man*.

We all continue to drink and celebrate for several hours before turning in, the brightness of the skyline still causing confusion to all our internal time clocks. The chief pilot of the Ken Borek air fleet, Harry Hansen, is also staying in the Lodge with us and joins in our celebrations. He tells us that in the morning he will be going off early to Resolute Bay, but will fly back later to pick us up and then fly us on to Camp Hazen, in case Grise Fiord gets snowed in as happened previously. He is sure this will be OK and we are happy to rely on his assurance.

I'm pleased to still have my room to myself and just in case I lock the door from the inside. It's very hot so I strip down to my long johns and try to sleep. The light outside is still too bright so I put on some eyeshades and this helps. I doze and then fall asleep, only to wake suddenly with the need to visit the toilet. Probably too much wine. Still half asleep I climb down from my bunk and stumble to the door. I pull the catch back and step outside and the door starts to close behind me. Too late I realise the catch is still on and the door closes shut and locks before I can do anything to prevent it. The first thing is to visit the toilet (or to use the polite American description – the bathroom), then I'll think about my predicament. When I return I try every way I can to open the door but it's impossible. I roam through the building to find the owner but she obviously stays elsewhere each night and presumably only comes back to make breakfast in the morning. All the downstairs rooms are locked and there aren't any free bedrooms. I deliberate about what to do but in the end there seems to be no real choice but to disturb someone. It should be more useful to choose someone who knows the Lodge but it turns out to be another big mistake. I enter the bedroom where the pilot, Harry Hansen, is bunking with his co-pilot. There is only the one double bunk in their room. Hesitantly I wake Harry and explain the position and ask if he knows where I can find a key to unlock my room. He is totally unsympathetic and tells me to shove off in no uncertain terms, that there isn't a key available and that I must wait till Pam returns in the morning. He is rightly very irate at being woken in this way. I hope he doesn't realise who has done so and I quickly leave the room.

I don't wish to disturb Fabian or Erik or anyone else as I would probably receive the same reaction and they couldn't help anyhow, so I must somehow survive until the morning. I'm now feeling very cold and I look around for some covering, anything at all. All I can find is a cover for the armchair on the landing. I snuggle inside the armchair, trying to keep myself covered as best I can. I'm not very successful and spend some very uncomfortable hours until the morning. I keep looking at my watch but time goes very slowly indeed.

Eventually I hear the front door being opened and rush down to explain to Pam what has happened. She is highly amused and says it has happened before but that doesn't make me feel any better. It doesn't seem worth trying to sleep any more so I shave and shower and get dressed for breakfast, I am the first but soon everyone comes down. I hope nothing is going to be said but Harry is in a foul mood and loudly complains about 'the idiot' that woke him in the middle of the night. Everyone is completely sympathetic to his complaint and I quickly realise how important pilots are out here and how everyone treats them almost like gods. They are certainly the kings of the territory, as they must decide when and if to fly and must be the final arbiter on whether the weather conditions are suitable and safe. I remember how Andy Goldsworthy was trapped here for many days because of bad weather and again it would have been his pilot who would have decided whether it was OK to fly out. I don't think it politic to ask who it was.

However, the day is as clear and bright as yesterday and Harry seems finally to relent. He says there is no real problem and he will fly back to Resolute to drop off some items, refuel and come back for us in about four hours. Harry waves a cheery goodbye and sets off; none of us have an inkling of what is to happen later. Sidney the American has absolutely no recollection of last night and I learn he had spent several more hours drinking downstairs after I had left. Some people think it must have been him that disturbed the pilot, even he is not sure, but I confess it was me and everyone has a good laugh at my expense.

There's plenty of time before Harry is due back and I set out for a walk and another tour of the village. It's totally deserted, no one to be seen. Presumably the children are still sleeping after their long hours playing out on the ice. It seems that there is nothing for any of the inhabitants to do and therefore they only come outdoors when there is something going on. I knock on a few doors and ask for Larry's house, the hunter out with Luis. I am directed to it and it is no different from any other. One of his children answers the door and tells me his mother is also away, cross-country skiing. Without either of them being there I don't want to intrude and leave to wander some more around the village or the town, although both are overstatements really. It's really just a hamlet and it seems worthwhile to knock at a few doors to introduce myself. When will I ever pass this way again?

One Inuk I meet is particularly hospitable and invites me in for tea. He has been here all his life and remembers when it was very different and much harder, without any comforts. It still seems pretty difficult now, so I can guess it must have been a very tough life indeed in past times. He tells me that nowadays most Inuit bury their dead in the ground, although the permafrost, just under the surface of the ground, is so hard that often they need to use blow torches and even heavy construction equipment to break through. Previously the traditional way was to wrap up the bodies and leave them to the elements. With a wry smile he tells me; 'Long ago we used to put our houses below ground and our dead above ground. Then the white man came and told us to put our houses above ground and our dead below ground. We've never been warm since.' He's a delightful character and reluctantly I leave his home as I want to explore some more.

I ask at some other houses if there are any carvers in the village and eventually am directed to one particular house. The owner doesn't speak very much English but he also invites me in and offers me more tea. Through the translation of one of his children I ask if he has any carvings to sell. After some hesitation he brings out two carvings of a polar bear and a seal. He feels they are not worth selling but to me they are very evocative and full of artistry and I persuade him to sell them to me. He asks very little and I pay more, hopefully a fairer price. He also has two more major pieces, very heavy sculptures in rough black and grey stone, an Eskimo and a larger seal. I would love to buy them as well but they are too heavy to carry on our flights, where weight is always a consideration and of course here we need to carry our own bags. Anyhow I already have the pieces I bought on the way in at Iqualuit Airport. Reluctantly I refuse and say goodbye to the family and the father is happy to accept some chocolate I have with me for the children. In return he shows me a tiny wooden sledge he has built for his son and offers to build one for me. I tell him that we expect to leave in two hours and he tells me to come back in one hour. I also call in to see Looty but his son tells me he is sleeping, possibly preparing himself for his hunting after we leave, as he will not then sleep for several days.

I return to the co-operative and show everyone the things I have bought. Then Cecil the owner of the lodge comes to see us with bad news. He has had a message from Resolute, presumably on behalf of Harry Hansen, that the airport there is closed and the pilot cannot take-off to pick us up and take us on to Camp Hazen. He will telephone through if there is any change. We wait around and the hours pass but still no news comes through. Everyone starts to speculate and decides that it's because of me and my waking Harry in the night, that he's not coming and I cannot easily argue against that. Fabian is particularly morose and starts (or continues) drinking. He is the leader of our expedition so it's really up to him to contact Resolute directly and chase up our aircraft and I have to let him handle it. He promises he will keep phoning through but he's in a bad mood and continues to blame me. Erik and Penny don't say anything, after all it's Fabian's show, but I feel they probably think the same.

In the circumstances I decide to go out again and wander around for a while before returning to the house of my carver. He has the sledge ready and I buy it. His son has a different toy sledge and I ask if I can buy that as well. The carver says it belongs to his son so only he can sell it. It's a gracious way of putting it and I ask the son if he is willing to sell his toy. He's very keen and I presume his father will easily make him another one. On the way back, half-hidden in the snow, I find the skull of a muskox and wonder if I could or should take it back with me to London. It reminds me of a visit, many years ago now, to Much Hadham, the home of the internationally acclaimed sculptor Henry Moore. He had all kinds of skulls lying around in his spacious studios and used them to create some of the powerful sculptures for which he is so famous. I decide to take it with me and to ask Looty or Cecil whether I can keep it.

I return again to the lodge but as I had expected there is still no news and Fabian has obviously been drinking steadily since I left and is in an even worse mood, openly blaming me for the no-show of Harry. I think he is probably right so feel pretty guilty. It's getting late, even though the light is of course as bright as ever and I ask Fabian to try again. I then learn that he hasn't telephoned at all and he tells me that he had the wrong number for Ken Borek Air. I suggest Fabian tries enquiries, 411, but he tells me to do it. I do so and find the correct number. He doesn't want to call, as he feels it will be of no use and we tussle for some time about whether we should. I try to persuade him to keep on trying and not to give up. Penny suggests that I call directly and I ask Fabian if he minds this. He doesn't say anything but waves me on. I then take it that I have his permission to take over and in the circumstances am not usurping his leadership role. I find out the cost of the call is two Canadian dollars in change but none of us have any coins. Cecil and Pam are nowhere to be seen, possibly staying out of the way on purpose. There is no one else in the hotel to ask and I don't want to lose any more time by trying to find change in the village.

I decide to call collect from the call box in the hall and luckily they accept at the other end. A woman called Joan answers (it seems that everyone operates on first names only, presumably due to the fact that very few people live around here, particularly out of season). I explain our predicament, tell her that we must fly out urgently if we are to make our rendezvous with Goldsworthy and ask for assistance in tracking down Harry Hansen whom she knows well. I also tell her that Sir (I emphasise the Sir) Ranulph Fiennes had stressed that he wanted every assistance given to our team and that I could use his name to obtain any help needed. I even drop the names of other supporters, Lord Tonypandy, Nicholas Serota, the Tate Gallery and even members of the Royal Family. I'm so totally desperate to persuade Joan to do her utmost to assist us I would have mentioned the Pope if I had thought it would help.

Joan finally seems to understand the urgency of my request and tells me she will do everything she can. In fact she says the airport was closed for a while but is expected to open shortly. I am not totally certain if this is so or whether she is covering for the pilot. It doesn't really matter as long as it will open now and the aircraft can fly out. Joan says it might take up to an hour to resolve and she will phone back as soon as she can (perhaps she really knows where Harry is holed up).

I tell everyone the news and they all, including Fabian, cheer up immediately. I tell them not to get their hopes up too much as things can still go wrong but it looks very hopeful. In the meantime whilst we are waiting, I invite everyone to come with me to the home of the carver to see if they are interested in the other two carvings he has. Outside I think the cold air has some immediate effect after the alcohol that has been consumed, as they all start singing and making an enormous racket. It certainly disturbs the peace and tranquillity of this exceptionally quiet place. Fabian is especially noisy and keeps wanting to sit down in the snow. He reminds me of the Russians I saw in Moscow enjoying themselves rather too much on vodka and also sitting in the snow in the kerb. Some were still sitting there the next morning completely frozen to the ground and no longer of this world. What many fail to realise is that alcohol dilates the blood vessels and enables the body to cool even faster than normal. Too much alcohol or too little food can quickly reduce resistance to the extreme cold. The St. Bernard dog with a flask of brandy around his neck makes a charming picture but it is not accurate. The time to have a drink in the cold is when you are safe and warming in front of a fire or heater.

When we arrive at the carver's home I try to get everyone to quieten down but am not very successful. He is somewhat alarmed at seeing us all together and becomes reluctant to show the two sculptures. I finally manage to persuade him to bring them out. They are truly magnificent and I am again very tempted to offer to buy them. But I have already purchased mine so it is only fair that I let the others have their chance too. There is so much noise and confusion in looking at the pieces that I think the carver becomes nervous. For whatever reason he tells me that they are not in fact any longer for sale and are committed elsewhere. I don't really blame him as I would only want such fine pieces to go to a home where they would really be appreciated and where they could harmonise within tranquil surroundings. They have a Zen-like quality and need to be treated with gentleness. The others don't understand but I do. It means of course that I also can't purchase them but in a way that is all for the best as I am carrying too much weight already.

Back at the hotel, Pam has a message for me from Ken Borek Air. I phone back, collect again, and Harry Hansen is there waiting for my call. He is now very friendly, we mention Ran Fiennes several times in our conversation, and it seems the airport is now open. A miracle indeed! Harry says that Camp Hazen is closed however because of heavy mists so we couldn't fly on tonight anyhow. That means that he will have to stay overnight at the lodge and wants to know if I will pay for the costs. I willingly agreed and he says he will be with us in two and a half hours. We can then fly on to Hazen in the morning as soon as the airport there is open. I tell Harry I am looking forward to seeing him.

Of course everyone is absolutely delighted with the news. To celebrate I volunteer to organise a superb dinner at another hotel and go off to telephone again. I come back and describe the succulent Chinese meal with all the trimmings I've ordered and once their mouths are dripping with saliva in anticipation, I reveal that the other hotel is shut as it's the end of the season. They are all now in such good moods that I am forgiven for my jest and we are all happy enough to eat here. Anyhow Fabian still has a large stock of champagne. As we may be leaving, Cecil agrees to open his shop for us, he didn't take much persuading and we all buy woolly hats which we immediately put on.

Harry arrives at 10 p.m., still in time to share dinner. He is now really friendly, completely responsive and it seems he has definitely erased the episode of my waking him during the night. He explains the changeable weather patterns around this area and perhaps I have misjudged him. It certainly sounds very unsettled. Resolute was impossible to fly out from due to very high winds until 4 p.m.; Hazen has been closed all day and will definitely be shut until 7 a.m. tomorrow; Eureka, the other Inuit village with an airstrip is also doubtful. The North Pole is good for landing and take-off at the moment but that could change very quickly. The other pilot who may be used for the final flight into the North Pole is already based at Hazen, so even if we couldn't get in there, in an emergency he could fly solo and go in to pick up Andy and the others from the North Pole. Of course we are determined we should take the chance of flying into Hazen but Harry just shrugs his shoulders – the weather will decide. It's the definitive saying throughout the Arctic and Antarctic regions; the weather always finally decides.

We must wait – I've always been good at waiting. It's part of my philosophy. Wait and think and then decide and act. Don't rush it. Often you only get the one chance and you must make it count. There's no coffee for the morning so I volunteer to try and get some from the co-op shop. It's another chance to walk outside and experience the wonderful atmosphere of this Arctic place. The shop is also the home of Cecil and Pam; I never did discover if they were married or not but they were certainly together as a couple. Luckily I meet them coming back from somewhere and explain why I've come. Pam states the coffee is actually back at the lodge but in the locked storeroom and will return herself on her ski-doo to get it and put it out for the morning. I ask Cecil if he will open the shop again just for me as I'd like to see what it stocks in case I want to buy some other things, but he says he must repair a refrigerator at the hotel and doesn't have the time. They both set off and I find it rather odd that neither offers me a lift. They are a very independent lot, here in the territories, and keep themselves rather reserved. It's possibly something to do with the fact that people come through here once only and usually don't return; it's also possible that the intensely cold weather makes people less open and more insular.

I don't actually mind in the slightest and I'm very content within myself as well. It's again part of my personal philosophy. Anyhow it is only a few hundred metres back and I enjoy the brisk walk. I find Cecil, not working on the refrigerator, which now doesn't seem so urgent to repair and show him the muskox skull I found earlier. He tells me that someone has buried several skulls in the snow in various places and will return in May when it's much warmer and the snow's melted enough to reveal them. Therefore I shouldn't take it. I accept what he has said and place the skull outside in the snow. Somehow I feel that someone else will now have a fine muskox skull to display. We all agree to get up at 6 a.m. as there will be a weather report phone call at 7 a.m. to tell us if we are able to take-off and fly on to Hazen.

Suddenly I am awake and wonder if it is six yet. But my watch shows 1.30 a.m. There are all kinds of sounds and noises coming from outside my window and these must have woken me. I quickly look out and see two sledges pulled by ski-doos, crammed full of baggage of one kind or another. I am now fully awake so decide to go down to investigate. I meet Harry Hansen coming back up. He's not happy. It seems that Big Luis is back from hunting and has taken back his room which they had given Harry in his absence. Presumably Luis had also paid for the room or pays a higher rate. They had been letting the same room twice! Still it was their business but obviously Luis had not been too happy to find someone in his room and in his bed when he returned in the middle of the night, even though it still looked like the middle of the day. Luis is definitely a bear of a man but Harry is certainly no Goldilocks. Harry doesn't know whether Luis shot a bear or not but I don't see anything that could resemble a body on the sledges so guess and hope not. There are no other spare rooms so I offer Harry one of the bunks in my room. He's used to these noisy conditions so is asleep the moment his head hits the pillow. I can still hear the dogs howling and yelling for some time before I manage to drift off for a few more hours. In my dreams I see a three-headed dog beckoning me forward. It's presumably Cerberus, the guard dog of Hades, but fortunately I wake before accepting his invitation.

Chapter Thirteen

To The Pole

I actually wake up at 5.30 a.m. but knowing it's going to be a long day, I rest until 6 a.m. I then shave and shower, dress quietly and finally wake Harry at 6.30 a.m. It's misty outside and snowing slightly but Harry says it's going to lift. That's good enough for me. We can shortly take off from here and then the big question is whether it's going to be clear enough to land at the Hazen airstrip. But I'm very optimistic. I try to wake Fabian and Erik but they don't want to get up and prefer to wait for the 7 a.m. call with the weather conditions, to definitely know if we will be able to take-off. I go down on my own to have breakfast; plenty of toast, scrambled eggs and coffee. I'm then told Luis has shot his bear. It is disappointing news but part of the Inuit/Arctic life I suppose. The others also appear finally but no telephone call comes through with the weather conditions. It's a nail-biting time.

Then at 7.20 a.m. the telephone rings. We all look across at each other but at first no one moves. Slowly, nonchalantly, Harry gets up from the table still clutching a piece of toast. 'Hurry up, quickly, before they ring off,' I want to scream, but keep my words contained. I don't want to risk antagonising Harry again. It's all up to him. Although the weather will decide, in this instance I know it's Harry who will decide. The telephone is upstairs on the landing, and it seems like ages before he returns. His face seems to show disappointment. I hold my breath. Then he announces, without the glimmer of a smile, that it's clear enough to take off and to land at Hazen. An involuntary cheer goes up from the four of us. It's very exciting news!

Almost in a flash of inspiration I suddenly realise Harry's real situation, what's going on inside his mind. He's been flying these Pole trips regularly since the 1970s. There's no excitement for him anymore and every new flight is one he would rather not do. He'd jump at any chance not to have to undertake yet another one. I guess any expectation of mists, fog or high winds would be seized upon as a reason not to go this time around. Whether Resolute Bay had been closed in or not yesterday and then re-opened or not, I am now convinced that if I hadn't persisted with Fabian in taking over the arrangements and contacting Ken Borek Air and being insistent with them, Harry wouldn't have flown back in the evening. We certainly wouldn't have him here with us now getting ready to depart. His personal flight times would involve him flying around one and a half hours from Resolute, two and a half hours from Grise Fiord, then possibly four hours from Camp Hazen to the North Pole, plus fuelling and preparation time, then all the flights back. Certainly a tremendous pressure on him not to fit in yet another series of similar journeys, probably the last ones of the season. I wonder how many people may have been disappointed in the past, when he had decided it was impossible to fly on. Much later Penny confirms my thoughts by telling me she was also convinced that only my intervention made the final flight legs happen.

We quickly rush upstairs to our rooms to put on all our layers of undergarments and our thickest clothes and bring down our bags. I put the secret I've carried with me all through the Arctic under my top T-shirt, held in place by my heavy coat. A few quick goodbyes all round but we are very keyed up and our thoughts are already far ahead. Fortunately Luis is still sleeping so we don't have to say goodbye to him. Assuming he has bagged a polar bear I certainly wouldn't have been able to congratulate him on his kill. I decide it's as well to go to the toilet before we set off. I am, of course, well layered up and in my haste had put on one of the pairs of underpants back to front. Therefore I have to take off about eight layers first. Better before we start out on the plane, even if there are facilities on board, which is doubtful, or even more so when we land. Everyone has started walking to the tiny airstrip and I am left far behind. Fortunately Cecil is still to start out and has the luggage buggy attached to his ski-doo. I have learned my lesson with him, if you don't ask you don't get – he never volunteers anything – I quickly ask if I can ride pillion on his ski-doo. He reluctantly agrees. We sail smoothly past the others, they wave but I don't suggest we carry their hand baggage. Of course it means we are the first to arrive at the plane and I help in loading up.

We take-off at 8.15 a.m. We are really on our way! It is immensely exciting even though in flying time alone we are still seven hours away from the Pole. Our take-off is over a range of mountains; the scene is rugged, powerful, extraordinarily beautiful, to me it is an exquisite sight but the mountains have seen it all before, so many times. I need to sleep and doze for over an hour. Then I wake and decide to write down some notes. There are so many thoughts and incidents and I must put them down before I forget or they will become jumbled. I take the top off my pen and ink explodes everywhere. Probably a combination of the constant shaking of the tiny plane and the air pressure. I mop it up and continue with a pencil. We are now flying high above the clouds and there is just a pale sun reflected across them. Through occasional breaks I sometimes see the endless, white, flattened plains and plateaux beneath us. Finally we arrive at the Camp Hazen airstrip at 10.45 a.m. We are not visiting the base itself, there isn't any time. We must keep tightly to the schedule, otherwise we won't make it. We refuel and additionally heave on board two huge drums of spare fuel. That's mostly the key to surviving out here, being able to fly on in time and comparative safety, particularly if the weather changes, as so often happens.

The plane takes off again about twenty minutes later and flies on 89 degrees until 1.45 p.m., two hours on, when it lands at an isolated landing strip where we learn for the first time it is necessary to make a quick change of planes and of pilots. It seems Harry Hansen has done his stint and it is essential we have a fresh pilot to take us on the final leg. The waiting pilot has his own plane already fuelled for us. I wasn't really sorry to leave Harry behind as he had always been too contrary for my liking and I felt we had to watch what we said and did too carefully in case we upset him and he decided against flying us on.

The new pilot is called Henry Perke and he is perky by nature. He is enthusiastic and exuberant and seems as keen as we are, if that is possible, to get us to the Pole. This time we take on board three extra fuel drums. I just have time to walk once around the plane and take a look at the vast vistas of ice and snow stretching away into the distance in every direction that seem to go on forever. It is intensely cold and there is a fierce wind. I clamber on to the tops of some giant ice blocks to give me a greater view but it is still the same. Now I am the king of the ice castle. Henry had flown in Andy Goldsworthy and his team to the Pole only yesterday and had left them overnight to tent in the area. He tells us they have been hoping for and expecting us to arrive to meet up with them. Of course he couldn't leave the aircraft there as it was much too cold and the engine would likely freeze and prevent any subsequent take-off. Henry is flying a larger aircraft, an Otter which seats 16–18 persons; this is needed because of the greater number of people he has to bring back with us as well as their tents and equipment. The Otter has a low ceiling and we already feel cramped without the inclusion of the others and everything we also have to bring out. No matter, we are about to head for the North Pole!

Henry revs the engine twice; obediently and urgently it fires into life. It's a short runway and the plane quickly climbs upwards and we are on our way. We are initially flying low and fast and Henry handles the flying machine with utter confidence. He obviously knows the route like the back of his hand but nevertheless I still see him regularly checking his GPS instruments. The Arctic is not a place where you can afford to take chances. There are invisible signs everywhere 'Gamblers not welcome'. However, the flight still feels as exciting as winning a jackpot!

After a while there is tremendous excitement as we see far below us a tiny expedition team slowly edging their painful way across the ice, attempting to walk to the North Pole unaided. It can only be Robert Swan and his team. We circle once and they wave momentarily but they must need every bit of energy and concentration to continue and we are a distraction so we fly on. I am feeling tired and want to be totally alert for the Pole, so again try to doze and rest for at least an hour but it just isn't easy to relax.

Then suddenly, without any warning, we are there and the pilot starts circling as we see the Goldsworthy tent below us and he looks for a safe place to touch down. He explains he needs a firm and flat run in, without broken ice that could damage the undercarriage or might cause difficulty when he attempts the take-off. It is absolutely vital not to land on ice which is too soft and might not support the weight of the plane. Henry knows how much it means to the four of us to be here and he wants to land us exactly at 90 °N.

Henry makes his decision, the plane starts its final approach and we descend rapidly. Is he coming in too fast? No it is perfect! A few bumps, no skids, the plane holds fast and we taxi smoothly and come to a complete halt. We are in Pole position.

Chapter Fourteen

On Top of the World

At 3.20 p.m. the Tate four, Neville, Penny, Fabian and Erik have arrived at the Geographic North Pole. We are all wearing our T-shirts: 'Monday at the North Pole 24 April'. It is an absolutely glorious moment to savour and I think we all shed a tear or two, even someone as hard-bitten as Carlsson. There is often an imbalance between the expectation and the reality but in this case the reality is absolutely overwhelming. My skin is on fire.

We are so excited that we practically jump out of the aircraft and start running, slipping and sliding in our haste to reach Andy and the others. This is what we have come all this way for, to be part of this great adventure, to be part of Andy Goldsworthy's art project – Touching North. We are touching north and each other and everything; all roads lead southwards. Now it is time to reveal my great secret, a secret I have carried with me all the way from England. It is lodged under my coat, after all this time almost a part of me.

A strange, heavily muffled, bearded creature of the Arctic bounds towards me, looming out of the immediate distance, becoming defined and accentuated as the mists clear around it. I hurry towards it, my arm outstretched in anticipation. 'Mr Goldsworthy I presume?' Shades of Dr Livingstone, somewhat melodramatic, but I can't resist. The occasion calls for it, even demands it. He nods his response. We embrace, there are really no need for other words. The emotion felt by each one of us speaks volumes. Now for the special moment. I have to remove one of my mittens, the intensity of the cold bites deeply into my fingers but no matter. I undo my coat, retrieve and reveal my secret. It is an early Andy Goldsworthy catalogue, aptly named 'Rain sun snow hail mist calm', containing photographs of some of his other ice and snow sculptures. 'Will you sign it?' Andy responds generously as I had hoped he would. He enters into the spirit of this wonderful occasion. I produce a biro, praying it will work in the sub-zero temperature. Andy grasps it, he also has to take off his mittens to use it. He is truly touched that I have thought of this and have brought the catalogue all this way. He pauses and thinks for a brief moment. Then he draws a circle of giant ice blocks, like one of those I realise he has sculpted here, also drawing a long North Pole to the left of it, and writes – 'Signed and given to Neville Shulman at the North Pole 24 April, Andy Goldsworthy. Between the voids.' Andy then takes a fragment of snow and rubs it into the bottom part of the page to etch for all time the memory of this exquisite moment. It is utterly poignant. Words are not needed. What a treasure to gain and enjoy! One of the greatest Zen masters, Shunryu Suzuki has the words which say it all, 'The world is its own magic.'

There are three others with Andy – Julian Calder the photographer, Gordon Wiltsie the guide and photographer and Mike McDowell the team leader. I learned later that all three had pitched in to help Andy complete his North Pole sculptures. It is so amazing to be here and on top of the world! The temperature is only about -15 °C, which for this place and time is surprisingly mild. I unbutton my coat again and loosen a few layers. The sun is bright and the glare makes everything seem surreal and magical. The team have been sleeping in one red and yellow bivouac tent and they cooked, ate and washed inside. It is impossible in this cold intensity to do any of those duties outside. I suspect that very little washing actually took place. The brightness of the tent stands out vividly within the clear whiteness of the surroundings. But we haven't come to see the tent. Where are the sculptures?

Andy had only arrived just over two days ago, so he'd had a very short time to create anything. Still we are in for quite a surprise. With his companions trying to help, Andy has laboured extensively to sculpt four huge circular voids. Each void consisting of over forty blocks of ice welded together to form a large circle with a base for support. They create monuments of stillness and simplicity. Defining emotion down to its bare essence. As Tao Te Ching puts it with his direct clarity, 'We shape clay into a pot but it is the emptiness within that holds whatever you want.' He has also stated, 'The more you know the less you understand.'

The voids are grouped in a wide square, in some way forming an open room, through which the winds and the elements can pass at will. It is something of nature, for nature, yet not intruding against but blending with nature. Portals through which giants of another time could have passed. The strength needed to cut and form the blocks and make certain they wouldn't collapse in on themselves seems almost to have been superhuman. Andy had toiled from the moment he had arrived and with the perpetual daylight had gone with very little sleep to finish the voids in time for our arrival. We look, we touch, we embrace them. Strength, simplicity, flowing and free. I can walk through, climb through each circle and stand in the centre of this Arctic square, this cosmopolitan piazza, this international plaza. Simple but so effective and majestic, quiet almost beyond understanding. In Zen, 'Knock on the sky and listen to the sound.'

Although the whole project is called Touching North, these four glorious objects, forming one whole, are the cornerstones and therefore this ultimate sculpture is also named Touching North. They will last such a short time, perhaps days but probably much less. The sun will melt them, the wind will tear into them and they will implode as the structures weaken. That is part of their great beauty and uniqueness; the fact that they are so impermanent. They were built as a symbol of art, an emotional statement, a grand gesture and the intense memory is just ours alone, the eight of us standing here. We take our photographs of the sculptures, of each other, of this vast, incredible landscape, but nothing can compete with the actuality. There are no flags, no markers, and no poles at the North Pole. Nothing to indicate that man has been here before. There are no signs to say that daring, brave, extraordinary men and women of the twentieth century have somehow, often by the proverbial skin of their teeth, managed to get here. In every direction stretches absolute solitude.

Just for a few moments in time there are sculptures at the North Pole and we have witnessed them and feel part of them. Briefly the North Pole ceases to look like every other point in the Arctic and is marked by the magnificent ice edifice created by Andy Goldsworthy. But not for long. Within hours possibly, certainly less than even a nano-second in Arctic history, the sculptures will be reclaimed back into the ice. No one will see that they and we were here. But we know and are aware; imprinted images that can be instantly recalled exist within our memories. White blueprints.

The pilot, Henry Perke, is anxious we should all depart. We have been here just a few hours and we are greedy for more. But he is careful to explain how dangerous it is to stay any longer. It is the end of the season, this is the last flight in, after this it would probably be too unstable to fly here and to land. The ice would be softer and more unstable and anything could occur. The ice is actually imperceptibly softening as we speak. He has actually left the engine running the whole time, as he couldn't know if it would restart if he switched it off. The temperature can drop dramatically in a very short space of time and it is too big a risk to take. He tells us that on one previous occasion the pilot had left his aircraft along with his passengers and as they started to walk away they suddenly heard a rumbling sound. They all turned around to see the whole plane, as if in slow motion, sinking gradually under the ice. It had proved too heavy for that particular section and its sinking momentum had then quickly gathered pace so the plane had very shortly vanished into the Arctic depths forever. They had managed to radio for help and it took several, nail-biting hours before another plane had been able to come and rescue them. Of course they hadn't then waited for more than a few moments before scrambling on board and for the rescue plane to take-off and fly them back to safety. Possibly it is an apocryphal story, told to convince everyone to leave when the pilot decides it is necessary. But out here, in these frozen wastes, far removed from direct contact with the outside world, it is all too easy to imagine it happening.

Sadly, it is time to go. We load all the equipment and spare supplies on to the plane. The sculptures will be the only signs that man was here. They will disappear and then there will be nothing here to show we have visited. But we will always know. We carry with us the poetry and thoughts of this extraordinary setting, in which a determined Englishman lived his dreams for a moment in time and sculpted four voids in this vast ice landscape; Touching North.

The plane has only just enough fuel on board to get us back to Camp Hazen. But first we must take one final set of photographs, some by camera and others by imprinting the images deep within our minds. The plane makes one slow, lingering, almost loving sweep of the area. We look down at those four mystical, circular, ice shapes, truly squaring the circle. As the plane pulls away they stand out starkly, remotely, full of beauty. A sight to remember for all our days.

Chapter Fifteen

Flowers at Camp Hazen

Andy asks us to sign eight, small, white cards as mementoes of the occasion and for his use. We are happy and honoured to do so. I have my own Goldsworthy drawing and message. As if reading my thoughts, perhaps realising it for the first time, Andy says to me, 'Neville, do you realise you have the only art work that has been created at the North Pole?' Until then I hadn't realised the implication myself of what had occurred. It was, and probably is always likely to be, the only work of art actually created at the North Pole by an artist of international standing. What a gift to receive! I feel humbled by what I hold in my hands. It is something that will certainly stand the test of time and will be a constant reminder of this incredible event. For evermore I will only have to take the catalogue down from my bookshelf, hold it and glance at the drawing and inscribed message to be instantly transported back to the North Pole.

We all fall silent as each of us remember those precious moments and draw them down into a private and personal sanctum. There they will always remain, ready to be unlocked at a moment's recall. We are in a strange way, although perhaps it is not so strange, emotionally as well as physically drained and exhausted.

I look out of the aircraft's windows to try and catch a glimpse of Robert Swan and his valiant team, but no such luck. It's like looking for the proverbial needle in the haystack. How lucky to see them on the way in. I'm convinced they are still battling on. That's their special spirit.

Some days later, after I've returned to London, I obtain the newspapers for 24 April and read Robert Swan's reported journal at that time, 'I had lost my spoon. Misha his balaclava. Minor incidents in the explorer's almanac of calamities, but inconvenient nevertheless. Misha eventually found the balaclava on his head and, at the end of a day's uncomfortable travel, I found the spoon in my boot. I knew then, we were exhausted.' If only I had known and could have given Swan my spoon! They were only halfway to the Pole and must have been feeling desperate. Swan goes on to record, 'We heard tonight that Pam Flowers with her dog team (attempting to be the first woman to claim the Pole alone) has now pulled back.' Perhaps this very sad news helped to inspire him onwards to eventual success.

I can't help thinking about the brave men and women of so many different nationalities who have attempted to struggle, against overwhelming odds, across this harshest of all terrains. I doze for a while then wake suddenly to stare intently out of the tiny windows. There's just whiteness in every direction. We all sleep off and on, as we fly back for several more hours across the plains of snow and ice to reach again the mountain ridges, themselves full of wild, wonderful and colourful shapes and designs. We reach Lake Hazen, one of the largest fresh water lakes north of the Arctic Circle, and start our approach to Camp Hazen. I understand 'hazen' translates as 'fear' and can well understand within this totally isolated and desolate landscape why it is so named. There are scores of seals along the edges of the lake. They pay us no attention whatsoever as we fly slowly but triumphantly to land.

The luggage is loaded on to a trailer attached to a snow tractor and it trundles off at a leisurely pace to the actual camp. We set off in pursuit. It's about 10 p.m. The only way to ever know the time is to look at a watch as the day never changes. That's why it's always so important to change your watch as you hit another time zone, otherwise you'd become totally confused. Camp Hazen isn't a luxury hotel or even a simple hostel. It's a small, corrugated iron hut with just two dormitories, one communal eating area and a bedroom for employees of Ken Borek Air. That's their given luxury I guess. Still, in the middle of this immense desolation what else could be expected and to me now it seems such a very inviting sanctuary against the elements. Here have stayed many of the polar explorers on their way out or back with their expeditions.

Harry Hansen is one of the first to congratulate us and he will be flying us out and back to Grise Fiord the next day, weather permitting of course. Henry Perke has done us proud and I tell Harry briefly what has occurred. He is genuinely pleased at the outcome. Perhaps I have misjudged him. I should just put it down to the Arctic. It's a place that can play havoc with a person's mind. The act of imagining things to be different in the Arctic to how they really are is called looming. It's possible for distances to be considerably foreshortened and even huskies to be mistaken for huge monsters. Being out here for too long can certainly play tricks on the explorer's mind.

I guess I should mention, as I know it's one of the first things people ask, who have never been cut off from so-called civilised society, something about the lavatory arrangements, female and male. Well there's no difference in treatment between the sexes, either in the Arctic or indeed in the Antarctic. There are no plumbing facilities at Camp Hazen and the ablutions inside the lavatory cabins are performed with pans and buckets. You have to choose your moment and dash in and hope that the person before you was reasonably tidy and actually cleaned up to some degree. However, we are all so high from our successful adventure that I don't think it would have mattered if there had not been any privacy and we'd had to use open facilities. I choose a bunk, one of the top ones and it's so warm that I take off most of my clothes, down to my long johns. Everyone more or less does the same, but Penny is more modest. I rest on my bunk whilst the dinner is prepared. It's pleasant and relaxing to listen to the kitchen sounds and to smell the food cooking.

Wait a moment, I'm not here to be waited on and I quickly get up to offer my assistance. Mostly I seem to get in the way but my offer is appreciated and I lay out the plates and cutlery, such as they are. The cook tonight at the Camp is Pam Flowers, the explorer referred to in Robert Swan's diaries, she is a very interesting person. Pam is now working and cooking at the camp to earn some money to pay for her fare home. She's Canadian and had tried to walk to the North Pole, using only four huskies to pull her sledge loaded with her initial supplies. The plan was that she would receive further supplies by some five to seven air drops, depending on her progress. Pam actually walked alone for 130 miles but the trek was taking longer than she had anticipated and eventually she ran out of money and couldn't afford to pay for any more air drops so unfortunately had to give up. This time!

Her dream is of course to try again as soon as she has raised more funds. Pam looks like an ordinary woman but inside obviously beats the heart of an extraordinary adventurer. She is under five foot, weighing less than 50 kg, bespectacled and her normal job is working as a therapist in an Alaskan hospital. She will try again as soon as she can raise 50,000 dollars she estimates is needed to sponsor her for a total of 60 days. The huskies have to be fed three or four times a day; she can cut back on food but they can't.

Pam prepares a delicious meal for us, steaks, sweetcorn, mushrooms, potatoes, followed by several kinds of cookies, Canadian style. This is washed down by punch, orange juice and coffee. I help collect the dishes and whilst stacking tell Pam what I hope is an appropriate story. A husky rushes into a Western Union office and asks to send a telegram to his girlfriend. The message reads, 'Bow wow wow, Bow wow wow.' The clerk looks at the form and says, 'For the same money you could add another Bow wow.' The husky barks back, 'That would just make it sound silly.' Pam laughs and likes it but makes me help with the washing up. I just know she won't stop trying until she makes it finally to the Pole.

Afterwards I walk outside to spend some time on my own. I listen to the silence. The sun refuses as always to set and is a glorious symbol of the power of nature and how insignificant we all are individually. There's no room for the ego in these places, particularly as we are so dependent on each other. Some people have gone off to fish, there are plenty of fish holes, but I need to be completely on my own. A perfect place to contemplate. I guess I won't be back here for a very long time, if ever. It's a sobering and somewhat saddening thought. Therefore the important thing is to take as much inside as possible, so I can draw on this memory whenever I need to. Time moves on slowly but at 1 a.m. I still don't want to lose a moment of my experience here and go to sleep. Everyone else feels the same and also stays awake.

The four of us are still wearing our special T-shirts and they prove a great success and are of interest to everyone. They all find it hard to believe that in advance I had printed the expected date of our arrival at the Pole and that we actually made it. No one arrives there at the intended date! As always only the weather can decide and it doesn't follow rules. This time, lucky for us, it did. All the others in our team want one, I promise to arrange to have more printed and will send them out on my return. On the camp notice board I pin up a Rotary Club Of London flag and write on it the date. Hopefully some Rotarians will see it one day. (At the time I had no idea that I would subsequently have the honour of becoming the President of the Rotary Club of London, the premier club outside North America.) Suddenly I feel really exhausted and climb on to my bunk and sleep for a few hours.

I can hear signs of life from the communal eating room, so someone is preparing breakfast. It's 5.30 a.m. and I get up at 6. I'm the first from our group which means I can use the facilities to wash and shave before the others. I pull on a second layer of clothes and join the pilots who are already up and preparing for departure. They are listening on the wireless to the weather reports from Grise and Resolute. They aren't too wonderful and the pilots express their concern. Finally they are given the OK to depart and we load our luggage back on to the trailer to be ferried out to the aircraft. We say goodbye to everyone remaining behind but particularly to Pam Flowers. She is so slight it is still difficult to imagine she has the strength and determination to try to walk to the Pole. However, we all know she has and I hope she is able to set up another attempt soon. It seems to be her most important objective and everything else in her life is just biding time until the next attempt. She's a woman full of guts and I greatly admire her spirit. She is just so matter of fact about what she has achieved and her intended goal.

We walk out on the ice and make our way to the aircraft. This time Harry is already waiting, impatient to get underway. There is an ABC crew that has been filming in the Arctic and before they board their aircraft they film our plane revving up, our climbing on board and waving energetically from the small windows as we taxi ready for our take-off. We then have to taxi all the way back when it's discovered that one of the crew has forgotten his case. We go through the same procedure all over again and are just about to take-off when the urgent message comes through to abort. The weather has dramatically worsened and we couldn't land at either Grise or Resolute. Again the weather decides. Neither plane can take-off so we must all return.

We re-enter the camp and are quietly welcomed back, it happens often, we sit drinking coffee and listening to the continual weather reports. Finally Harry says we can try again and we all race down to the two planes in an effort to go whilst there is still permission. This time the ABC cameramen have their cameras and equipment still on board so fortunately can't hold us up by filming any more. Anyhow it would probably be the same shots. Though I know most directors like to shoot the same scene many times over, just in case they can capture something different or better; they actually rarely do. It's all part of their fear about taking a wrong shot, or a bad one, and missing the one they really wanted. It's a long and costly exercise to have to re-shoot. But of course it could be just the excuse to return we are all looking for!

Chapter Sixteen

Resolutions

We fly across some of the wildest country in the world with superb views of rugged ice ranges, ravines of blue-white snows and so many secret and hidden places. Ludwig Wittenstein expounded it as, 'The mystical is not how the world is, but that it is.'

The flight takes about two and a half hours and Harry makes an easy, smooth touchdown on the Grise Fiord runway. Cecil and Pam meet us together with the refuelling truck. They have heard about the poor weather conditions and know we don't have any time to waste. However, the ABC crew have immediately disappeared from their plane to film around the village. Harry, despite the deteriorating conditions, is willing to try for Resolute, he's obviously anxious to get back and doesn't want to have to spend another night in Grise Fiord if he can help it. The ABC crew has first to be rounded up, as it's preferable if both aircraft take-off at the same time as a protection in case of any emergency. Looty and his wife also turn up to see us off. He tells me the bear Luis shot was a small one, much less than two metres. It doesn't make me feel any better. We finally take-off at 12.50 a.m.

The mists soon close in around us and the clarity of the sky and the scenery has completely vanished. It's impossible to see anything in any direction. Harry and the pilot of the other plane are flying on GPS. I only hope they aren't flying too closely to each other. We are all concerned that we may not be able to land at Resolute and have to turn around.

The only problem with that scenario is that by now Grise is probably also weather-bound and then where would we land? We continue on and now the mists have become a soup fog and it's looking pretty serious. As we slow even more and descend I count down the last ten miles (16 km) from the pilot's instruments. Ten, nine . . . six, five, still totally fogged all around, four, three. It looks like we might have to abandon the flight and return. We are just two miles out when we drop beneath the thick, cloud level. It's actually clear enough to land. Harry's skills as a pilot really show themselves and he now proves his worth. It's 2.30 p.m. local time.

As soon as the plane comes to a halt we unload everything and quickly enter the airport itself. Surprisingly it's much colder here than at Grise Fiord, mostly because of the intensity of the wind. We will need to wait for Bezal and his wife Terry to drive in and take us to a hotel. There's a little time to spare and I quickly visit the airport co-op shop as always to look at the Inuit carvings. There are a number of really special ones but the piece that particularly catches my eye is a multi-coloured, stone carving of a seal lying on its back, legs raised and exquisitely and delicately carved. It's very heavy and I already have too many items to carry back with me but it's too beautiful to resist. Although I am running low on funds I buy it and immediately feel that it was the right decision. I find out there is no bank in Resolute, which possibly makes its own statement. There is however a police station but with only two officers. There is also only one school.

Terry arrives on her own and drives us to the Narwhal Inn near the airport to rest for a few hours and also gives us back the liner bags containing the clothes we left with her. The rooms at the hotel are small and windowless but after Camp Hazen they seem like pure luxury. There's a communal washroom where I can shave and shower and change into some reasonable, ordinary clothes. For the fun of it I decide to put on a tie. It feels rather strange after doing without one for so long but no one comments. There's a spacious dining room where most travellers have congregated but I've had enough to eat. I want some time alone before setting out on the journey back to our so-called civilisation. Fabian is still fretting as no alcohol can be purchased in Resolute and his own stock is rapidly diminishing. I walk outside and it's bitterly cold. It feels far colder than at the North Pole, of course I am wearing thinner clothes and less layers. There is a research centre which I try to enter but find it completely locked up, after all it is very early in the morning. I come across the Hudson Bay Services shop which, not surprisingly, is open and sells everything. The Inuit carvings there are more expensive and I prefer my previous choices.

An Inuk is leaving at the same time and seeing my keen interest in the carvings asks if I've come across or seen any *Inuksuit*. When I express my ignorance of this he volunteers to take me on his ski-doo to show me. My curiosity gets the better of me and we drive a short way beyond the town where we dismount and I see two stone columns built on top of a small hillock. They are the *Inuksuit*. *Inukshuk* in the singular, it means, 'Something representing a man.' It is meant to resemble the human figure and is composed of a series of stones, one on top of each other, the smallest, the head, at the top. They have many purposes and were created as mystic figures, as guides for travellers, to act as markers, to ward off evil spirits, also to frighten animals (especially the caribou) into various channels where waiting hunters could spear them or shoot them with their arrows. One Inukshuk is about 3m tall, tapering upwards and the other is shorter but has protruding side stones to represent arms. Anil my Inuk friend tells me there are Inuksuit all over the island and throughout the region and they are very much part of the Inuit heritage.

The Inuksuit remind me of the sets of stones I've seen in many parts of the world, particularly in the mountains, again used to show the way to follow or to climb. Anil offers to show me more but I know my time here is fast running out so reluctantly I ask him to take me back. Also it's become much colder and despite my numerous layers I feel it biting through. Anil says that when it gets really cold, usually between 30 °C to 50 °C below, they call it a three-dog night, arising from the fact that hunters would cuddle up with three huskies for warmth during the night. There have been times, in their houses when the temperature has dropped so low, that even with heaters they would still bring their dogs to bed with them.

After Anil drops me off near the store, the wind reduces considerably and as I don't feel that cold I decide to walk to the airport to explore around there. But it's difficult to find my way easily. Finally I decide to cross the airfield and I walk past a few standing aircraft. Some crew and maintenance men suspiciously stare at me, presumably wondering who I am but no one challenges me. The airport is now very crowded as a number of other flights have obviously come in as well as many other travellers who are waiting for their connections out. The ABC crew seems to have only just arrived and are bustling around trying to find some rooms to rent. It seems practically everyone else here is also meant to take off with us early in the morning at 2.55 a.m. As always it's unlikely the flight will leave on time. I've accepted the Arctic has a time schedule all of its own.

I walk back to the Narwhal where everyone is eating a meal, although I have no idea whether it's lunch or dinner or even a late or early breakfast. The Arctic does that to you; your internal time clock freezes and you are ready to believe it's any time someone tells you it is. Throughout, the continual daylight is whispering into your ear that you've just got up and it's time to get going. It doesn't really matter and after my forays outside in the intense cold I'm ready to eat anything. It's self-service and I take lamb, carrots, salad, olives, followed by apple pie, ice cream, various cakes and delicious apples. I hadn't realised how hungry I was.

Andy Goldsworthy has started an etching, initially made with snow on vellum and tells me he will finish it and give it to me in London. He asks to see the catalogue again with the drawing he drew for me at the North Pole and I can see how really special he thinks it is. He's very pleased that I had the idea to bring it with me from London, although possibly wishes that he had done one for himself. It's a totally unique piece. I return to my room and pack ready for our flight out. My bag is bulging from the many Inuit objects I've purchased. I lay fully clothed on the bed and in an instant am flat out.

I wouldn't have got up in time but fortunately for me Julian Calder checks and wakes me at 1 a.m. I am still very tired and slowly wash and go for breakfast. Julian's next photographic assignment is in Japan, then to China with Prince Charles. We have a light breakfast and then board the van the hotel has provided to take our luggage and us to the airport. We check in to find the incoming plane is again delayed and it's expected we will eventually take-off at 3.30 a.m. Somehow Fabian still has a half-filled whisky bottle left and it seems appropriate, even at that time of the morning, to finish it off by all of us once again toasting the Arctic, our journey, our memories. Bezal has come across to say a final goodbye and I hand him a copy of one of my books, *Exit Of A Dragonfly*. He is genuinely touched and will presumably have plenty of time to read it in this slow-moving, leisurely, frozen territory that only comes to some kind of bustling activity for a very few months of the year. There's a solitude and a special peacefulness here that is waiting for those that have the mind and inclination to search for those priceless treasures.

Chapter Seventeen

Homeward Bound

After flying for 700 km the first stopover is Cambridge Bay at 5.15 a.m. and I get off for 15 minutes to stretch my legs. I look up and see three white tundra swans flying majestically across the sky. They are a poignant reminder of all I've experienced and I watch them slowly vanish into the distance. We take-off again at 5.40. Then it's on to Yellowknife at 7.10, leaving there at 7.25.

Some new passengers have joined the flight and one sits next to me, on my right. Ralph Berg, a taxidermist, the first I've ever met. He works mostly on Arctic animals particularly bear, muskox and fox. He also makes miniature copies of them. Ralph is very talkative and interesting; his family was originally from Germany but he has never been there himself. He gives me his card, 'Berg's Taxidermy' and invites me to make contact the next time I'm this way. I suggest a business card strap line of 'Getting Stuffed' and he thinks that's quite a hoot. Sitting on my other side is Wendy Reece, a dance and acrobatics teacher, who has been funded by the Ottawa government to teach dance for a few weeks to the Inuit communities. Once Wendy finds out I'm on the dance committee of the International Theatre Institute we are able to exchange dance stories and compare the movements of animals to the best choreographic work. This was of course many years before the *Lion King* burst upon Broadway and the West End to exhilarate and delight their captivated audiences.

We arrive five hours later at Edmonton and check in for the final leg to Toronto. It's several hours before we will depart and we look for something to eat to pass the time. Then it's a flight of three and a half hours before we touchdown at Toronto airport. Only one more flight to go now before we arrive back in London. So many adventures, so much has happened, there's so much to think about. I continually look at my watch as the time seems to drift slowly. It must be the way I'm feeling. I'm both mentally and physically tired, although still so stimulated by all the extraordinary experiences. I determine to find out much more about the Inuit and their way of life within this vast frozen territory.

We still have an hour before boarding. Penny Govett and I are now sitting on our own as Fabian and Erik have already left for Norway and Julian was booked on a different flight. Andy Goldsworthy has gone on ahead to the gate as he wants to work on his etchings. At first I think I am dreaming as I hear our names called out. The gate is about to close. I hadn't adjusted my watch on this last leg and it is wrong by one hour. We start to run and just make it by seconds as they close the gate immediately behind us. It reminds me of the race to the Athenaeum in *Around The World In 80 Days*, when Phineas Fogg realises he hadn't adjusted his watch after crossing the International Date Line. Like Phineas, Penny and I breathe sighs of relief as we sink into our adjoining seats.

On board there is a Canadian tag team, enormous wrestlers who seem to fill the plane, so everyone is, or appears to be, very cramped. I would perhaps like to tell them about my sumo studies and ask if they know about the practice of shin, the use of mental force to overcome a stronger opponent, but I have too many Arctic memories to revisit and the hours pass too quickly. At the airport in London James Bustard is waiting eagerly for our return and we all emotionally embrace. Andy gives Penny and myself the etchings he has been completing on the way back, ice he had dripped earlier on to vellum paper and subsequently carved into unique designs. It's not easy to say goodbye but we must part; each of us has an individual story to tell. All the way home I stare at my North Pole Goldsworthy drawing and it's forever imprinted on my inner mind. Over the years in pensive or reflective mood I often turn to it.

Chapter Eighteen

Our Land: Nunavut

1 April 1999 is possibly the most historic date in the history of the Inuit. On that date an area of land, bigger than Western Europe, changed hands. The first new Canadian territory since the Yukon was formed in 1896. Canada has willingly given back to the Inuit nation, after 15 years of reasonably amicable talks, the 350,000 square kilometres of territory now called Nunavut (meaning Our Land). It stretches from the Hudson Bay almost to the North Pole and is eight times the size of Britain. It includes the Kitikmeot, Keewatin and Baffin regions and most of the Arctic islands including those in James Bay, Hudson Bay, Hudson Strait and Ungava Bay. Nunavut comprises 60 per cent of the original North-West Territories. This immense territory was taken some 300 years ago by British and French explorers, before then becoming part of Canada. Also, an amount equivalent to 400 million pounds (650 million US dollars) is being passed over to help with the new administration and arrangements. The total territory governed will amount to 2 million square kilometres of pristine wilderness – almost totally unspoilt environment with an abundance of wildlife.

Initially there will be approximately only 23,000 Inuit in Nunavut and then a further 4,000 people of mixed nationalities including the Canadians. There needs to be a rapid expansion of Inuit to people greater tracts of this immense region. They will be scattered over 28 communities throughout this huge land mass. This wise and open action on the part of the Canadian Government and all its peoples has given a sense of real worth and understanding to the entire Inuit nation but particularly to the Inuit children. They really have something to believe in and strive for. 'Nunavut gives us responsibility and a sense of pride in our history and our people. It is truly our land.'

The real beauty of Nunavut lies in its almost totally pristine open spaces and wilderness. It also has an abundance of wildlife and reveals a raw and natural environment that is a real joy to behold. The land is generally flat although there are large mountains, cliffs, fiords and vast valleys. In the words of the Japanese philosopher, Prince Shotoko (574-622), 'Harmony is the most precious thing'. Nunavut is an unspoilt territory that must be protected and the harmony that exists between the land, the wildlife and the Inuit should always be nurtured.

There is a particularly urgent need to obtain from Inuit elders as much information as possible about past Inuit culture. In Africa there is the saying, 'When an old man dies, a library burns down', the same could be expressed here as the older Inuit pass away. A century ago the Inuit were virtually living in stone-age conditions, in hunting camps, semi-nomadic, using weapons just of rock or perhaps the bones of the animals they killed. Fifty years ago they moved, or were moved, to settlements funded by the administration and conditions deteriorated as this hunting nation tried to fit into surroundings which didn't take account of their nomadic backgrounds and traditions. Now everything has the capability to change as they will self-govern one-fifth of overall Canadian land. The Inuit writer, Mary Carpenter Lyons, emotionally expressed the feelings this wonderful action has created within the nation, 'Nunavut speaks to the soul of the Inuit.'

The weather of Nunavut is predictable in that it is unpredictable. That's a Zen koan if ever I've heard one. Nunavut has the coldest weather in Canada; winter lasts about nine months and there are absolutely chilling winds even in June, July and August. Not the usual place to go for your summer holidays! Residents are often weathered out and it's not difficult to understand what that means. The extraordinary fact to realise is that much of this area has minimal precipitation, most places receive less than 300 millimetres each year – the north-western part of the Arctic Archipelago is a polar desert and receives less moisture than parts of the Sahara.

The earliest Paleo-Eskimo cultures date back in these arctic regions some 4,000 years and were formed by hunting tribes moving across the Bering Straits, the present Inuit descended from the most recent of these tribes, the Thule. Iqaluit, my original point of entry to this vast territory, is the capital of Nunavut. The population is about 4,000 and it's nearer to London than Hollywood but still manages to obtain the latest films before London does. There's only one cinema theatre to show them though. Iqaluit is more heavily populated than other Inuit towns or settlements. There's Pangnirtung with a community of 1,200, its single hotel the Auyuittuq Lodge and Arctic Bay with only 650 inhabitants, where the Enokseot Hotel is the only place to stay. Most communities are what they would have called in the Wild West days, 'one horse towns'. The Arctic and the Inuit communities are the new 'Wild North' towns where a few people live and die and the rules are often still being worked out. Everyone knows everyone else and their business, and isolation is the name of the game.

From Pangnirtung it's possible to take a perilous boat ride to Cumberland Sound and up the fiord to the Auyuittuq National Park, providing spectacular views of ice-capped, granite walls, capable of tempting the hardiest of rock climbers who are prepared to risk all. The Inuit names are very descriptive and full of strangeness and humour. One of the peaks has a name which translates as 'Cold peak doubled up like woman with period pain holding belly'. Try telling that to a stranger from out of town without starting a fight. Here every place and often the people have strange and ancient names. One of the tracks out of Iqaluit is called the Road To Nowhere as it is just that. Once an American army base was at the end of it, long ago it was abandoned and closed down but they still keep the road. That's part of the enigma of this region.

THE ANTARCTIC

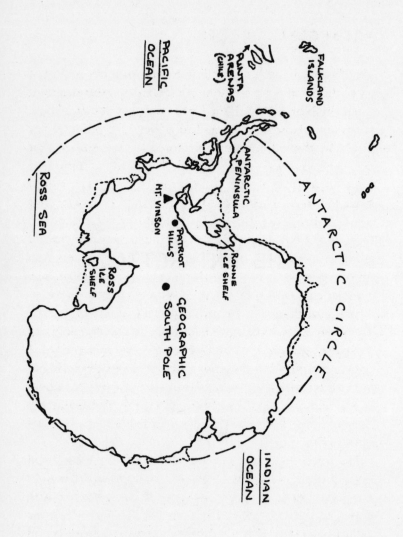

Chapter One

Antarctic Dreams

My primary dream of travelling to the Antarctic and then on to the South Pole had long pre-dated my great desire to reach the North Pole. Now I had achieved one and some years have elapsed, how was I to achieve the other? What would be the initial motivating force to start me on that very long journey? In order to deal with the complicated logistics, the costs and the time involved there would probably have to be something particularly special that would point me southwards, to the bottom of the world. Otherwise I'd just keep my dream ticking over and carry it forward to another year. That is also part of my Zen philosophy: waiting, thinking, acting and reacting, experiencing still moments, until something propels you in a particular direction, towards a certain course of action. Then you sense your movement towards the decision and invariably you know and feel when the moment is right. I hold numerous files of cuttings, reports and papers relating to the travels of many other fortunate explorers, incidents and adventures occurring throughout the globe, but my Antarctic files have gradually become the biggest. Perhaps now was the time!

My travel maps are an integral part of my library and many times I like to take them out and spread them over the floor, just to contemplate some of the magical places there are, some of which I've seen and many of which are still to be explored by me. I love to browse the wonderful place names to be found throughout this extraordinary world and to feel the magic calling out to the adventurous.

Today I am fortunately alone. No one else is at home. I can examine my maps at my leisure and without interruption. Books of poetry are kept purposely in the shelves above travel and as so often happens, the inspiring words of some of the emotive poets are soon tumbling out. Wordsworth and his 'Daffodils' are a special favourite, the sense of the ordinary having the power of the extraordinary is very much part of the Zen philosophy, 'I gazed and gazed but little thought what wealth to me the sight had brought.' Then I switch to the inspiring Coleridge and his sumptuous richness, 'In Xanadu did Kubla Khan a stately pleasure-dome decree – a sunny pleasure-dome with caves of ice.'

Across my maps I trace affectionately the contours of remote, high mountains, red-burnt deserts and white-iced terrain, gorging, winding, flowing rivers. I start to run my finger over exotic lands with unpronounceable names, faraway, valley-cradled countries; distant, remote nations trying to exist within adversity from man and nature. Africa remains at the heart of the Old World, always the cradle of mankind, yet where so much misery has been caused and still is extensively occurring. My friends at the Red Cross continue to work heroically in so many countries there. I so very much want to help their valiant efforts. The name of the continent of Africa in the atlas is writ large and as always so many of its volatile countries seem to be calling out to me. Some of the hottest places on Earth, regions continually suffering from famines, tribal wars and horrendous genocides between peoples. I decide I should again try to fund-raise for them, to make another personal gesture, hoping to encourage others to help, to show that they also care. But I had travelled to Africa before in order to raise funds, most recently to Tanzania and to Kenya, to climb the two highest mountains in Africa. Now I need to travel within another of the world's zones.

So to search out Coleridge's mythical 'caves of ice'; this will be my goal. Some like it hot but also some like it cold. One koan states, 'Hot, cold, it is you who feel them.' Many love the coldest places on Earth. The Antarctic at last! I will try and travel to the South Pole, to achieve at last my childhood dream.

Some of my earliest memories are of the tales of Captain Robert Scott, following the story of his driven but ultimately tragic journey to try and be the first to reach the South Pole. Even though his expedition had arrived second to Amundsen's, he ultimately became known as 'Scott of the Antarctic'. The terrible disappointment had served to break him. His team of five had subsequently all perished, not knowing how close they were to reaching a supply hut which would have saved them. But Scott and his men had lost the will to continue, to survive. The three attributes of Zen you always need to carry with you, never more so than on an arduous expedition are: a great root of faith, a great ball of doubt and a fierce tenacity of purpose. It seems they had abandoned them all after receiving the heart-breaking news that Amundsen was first. However, the Zen philosophy always explains that it's not necessarily important to achieve your planned goal, it's making the effort which is more important, retaining the will not to give in and often the strength to turn back.

Shackleton, by some acknowledged to be the greatest of all the polar explorers, never achieved his ultimate goal of reaching the South Pole, but throughout his heart-breaking journeys he never gave in. He knew his responsibility to his men was paramount and he brought them all back out of the frozen wastes of the Antarctic to safety. He never lost a man. He was truly a brilliant leader as well as a great explorer. But I, like many others, have always loved Scott; we can understand his pain, his tremendous sense of loss, his feeling of utter dejection. We can imagine what was going through his mind. If only he had realised, had understood what an inspiration he would be to us and would always be, that might have helped him to keep going and return. Then his infant son, Peter, would have really known his exceptional father.

Peter Scott was only two and a half when his father died. However he had been left a legacy which was to inspire him throughout his life. Robert Scott's farewell letter to his wife included the following words: 'Make the boy interested in natural history if you can, it is better than games; they encourage it at some schools. I know you will keep him in the open air. Above all he must guard and you must guard him against indolence. Make him a strenuous man. I had to force myself into being strenuous as you know - had always the inclination to be idle.' I think the words used on Robert Scott's memorial in Antarctica, taken from Tennyson's *Ulysses* describe his character better - 'To strive, to seek, to find and not to yield'. Sir Peter Scott had been left a historic legacy and certainly took his father's words to heart. He became a distinguished naturalist as well as a fine fauna painter and his contributions in his field were very important. He was co-founder of the World Wildlife Fund International and the first person to be knighted for services to conservation.

OK, so that's where I am going. To Antarctica. To stand where Amundsen and Scott had stood, all those years ago.

Just the thought of it is absolutely thrilling. I am finally going to travel to the coldest region on Earth, hopefully to feel what so few polar explorers had experienced, when trekking and fighting across those vast ice lands.

I announce my plans. I will travel to the Antarctic to raise funds for the work of the Red Cross. Everyone at first thinks I am joking. They find it hard to believe. My family look at me askance. Some of my friends decide to humour me, thinking I will change my mind but my friends and colleagues at the Red Cross are delighted. They realise it is a totally unique challenge and hope it will also act as an encouragement to their many supporters to take on other challenges, to set up other events where they too could raise funds for the vital work of the Red Cross. I state that all the monies I raise I want to go to their work within Africa, particularly in Rwanda and Burundi and they readily agree. In my mind's eye I am already on my way to the South Pole.

When to go? How to travel? I start making enquiries. There are a few organisations that can help and provide information. However, I have known for several years of a travel and exploration company arranging specialised trips to the Antarctic – Adventure Network International. On several previous occasions I have discussed the possibility of my travelling out with them but for one reason or another I hadn't been able to commit. This time I will, no matter what, and I again contact the owner, the indomitable Annie Kershaw. Any remaining doubts quickly vanish as Annie immediately and mouth-wateringly conjures up the delights and thrills that will be waiting for me in the Antarctic. There are several possible dates available, all within the months of December and January. It is necessary that travel to the region takes place in the period of Antarctica's summer when there are greater chances of actually getting to the South Pole. Going in the subsequent months would make it extremely difficult and dangerous to travel through the huge tracts of ice wastelands, particularly those that separate their base camp from the South Pole Station. After considering the various options I decide to plan my journey in order to have the opportunity of perhaps spending New Year's Eve or New Year's Day at the South Pole. What a memory that would be! My family finally understands and agrees to waive their objections. They accept it will be the chance of a lifetime and they then actively encourage me to go ahead. We have often travelled together abroad at that time in previous years and have celebrated the New Year in such diverse places as Ecuador in the tropical rainforest, Cairo and Luxor in the Valley of the Kings and in the eternal Jerusalem. They know there will be other family opportunities like that in the future. This is one journey I will have to take alone.

My preparations are soon underway and as usual I train to get myself fit. I am not certain what difficult situations I might have to face but I know that being stronger and fitter will stand me in good stead and I must be prepared for anything. Now I want to learn as much as possible about Antarctica, its human and animal inhabitants, Antarctic weather conditions and habitats and of course the history of those who have gone before me. Indeed, first of all I need to read up on some of the incredible explorers who have carried out, in this most remote of all the continents, so many inspiring exploits of daring, adventure and bravery. Their stories are astounding. They make me more determined than ever to follow their way.

Chapter Two

Ice Warriors

Although even the ancient Greeks were convinced there was a southern land territory, it still remained unknown or at least undiscovered for most of the first two millennia. The Maoris and Polynesians in their ancient cultures also tell of legends of a huge white land far to the south. *Terra Australis Incognita*, meaning 'Unknown Southern Land' is first titled on a map dated 1513, discovered in the Topkapi Palace, Istanbul only as recently as 1929. (The title clearly illustrates the origin of the name Australia). Sara Wheeler's wonderful story of her time spent at several South Pole bases is also entitled *Terra Incognita*. There are some who argue that the legendary lost world of Atlantis was actually based where Antarctica now lies and that a tremendous disaster, natural or otherwise, destroyed that civilisation and caused it to become the ice wilderness it now is. Of course it is only a theory, like those that claim Atlantis was originally in South America or in the Sahara. Until real evidence can be provided we must accept only the knowledge we presently have and honour the great adventurers who tried desperately for so many centuries to find this most remote of all the lands.

Captain James Cook was the first seafarer to circumnavigate the continent of Antarctica on his voyages in 1772-1775 in the ships, *Resolution* and *Adventure*. Cook was the first to cross the Antarctic Circle and he reached 71 °S. His initial, harsh opinion was, 'That the world would not be benefited by a country doomed by nature to be forever buried under everlasting snow and ice.' However, once some new territory has been discovered, a new land sighted, the curiosity of the human spirit will never be satisfied until that place has been revisited and explored. There were also intriguing stories coming back of the massive seal stocks to be found in the sub-Antarctic islands. Commercial considerations of the likely wealth implications were to prove another tremendous spur in encouraging the exploration of the region. Soon the planning of the early Antarctic explorations would commence and from then it would become only a matter of time and national pride before one explorer would be able to claim the ultimate prize. But who would it be and for the honour of which country?

Shortly after the beginning of the nineteenth century the Antarctic explorations really started in earnest. In 1819 William Smith set sail in his ship, appropriately named the *Williams*. The Russian explorer, Thaddeus von Bellingshausen, was also making voyages at this time. It is claimed he was actually the first to see the Antarctic continent, sailing there in his ships, *Vostok* and *Mirnyi* in 1819-21. In 1820, Edward Bransfield, claimed to be the first person to see the Antarctic Peninsula; although it might have been Nathaniel Palmer, aged only 19, a sailor on the *Hero* also in 1820. Due to the length of the voyages and the fact it might be a year or more before ships could return with information, imprecise data on initial sightings would easily occur.

In February 1821, a sealer, John Davis, became probably the first person to actually land on the continent. Later James Weddell sailed to 74 °S, the farthest south yet reached and the sea he initially named after King George IV, now bears his name. The Frenchman, Dumont d'Urville, who earlier had persuaded the French Government to purchase the Venus de Milo, discovered Louis Philippe Land and explored down the Antarctic coastline which he proceeded to name Adelie after his wife. Her name was also given to a breed of penguin, presumably intended as a compliment, but whether to them or her is uncertain! In 1838-42 Charles Wilkes organised the largest expedition to date, its aim being to map the eastward coast, consequently it was named Wilkes Land.

Now the voyages were following thick and fast upon each other. The British expedition under Sir James Clark Ross was especially prepared to work in polar waters and its voyages took place between 1839 and 1843. His two ships, *Erebus* and *Terror* were strengthened for work in the ice, adding double hulls and reinforcing all their beams. His reputation was well established as he had located the Magnetic North Pole in 1831, when he sailed under the command of his uncle John Ross. It was a great time for discovering previously unknown places and naming them. He reached, and named, the Ross Sea and then Ross Island and also the Ross Ice Shelf (equal in size to France). Prophetically Ross's opinion was that this enormous ice sheet, stretching as far as the eye and telescope could see and obviously far beyond, rested on a polar archipelago.

The enormity of the task that faced those endeavouring to sail southwards and the overwhelming odds against success mostly turned thoughts of further exploration to other areas, particularly again to the Arctic which was considered to be more easily accessible. Therefore for some 50 years little further was achieved in the Antarctic region.

There were a few attempts to travel deeper in but they didn't accomplish very much. There was some continuing scientific interest but the research stations were all set up outside Antarctica and therefore were not really effective. The mysterious white region still attracted periodic attention but the extreme conditions usually repelled ships which had little chance against the overwhelming strength of the crushing ice.

Antarctica was still virgin territory with little known of what would be encountered and the unknown perils awaiting those who ventured there. There is a classic Russian fairy tale which sums up the difficulties faced: 'Go – not knowing where. Bring – not knowing what. The path is long, the way unknown.' Several expeditions were organised over the following five decades by many countries including Norway, Sweden, Germany, France, Australia, Japan and of course by Britain. But the impenetrable Antarctic easily thwarted most efforts.

Now we arrive at the golden age of Antarctic exploration and the three greatest names associated with it, Robert Falcon Scott, Roald Amundsen and Ernest Shackleton. Scott was the first expedition leader of the three to explore the region, in leading the British Antarctic Expeditions of 1901–04. His famous ship *Discovery*, built in Dundee, Scotland, was frozen in at McMurdo Sound (which Scott changed from McMurdo Bay as originally named by Ross) for two successive winters. Although exceptionally strong the wooden ship had developed a persistent leak, which led to the crew's standing joke, 'What's the worst vegetable we have taken with us? Well, of course, the Dundee leek.' The *Discovery* had also taken on board 800 gallons (over

3,600 litres) of rum, 42,000 lbs (over 19,000 kg) of flour, 10,000 lbs (over 4,500 kg) of sugar, and 3,000 lbs (over 1,350 kg) of roast beef, as well as 23 sledge dogs and 45 sheep. On this occasion, despite the numerous setbacks, Scott eventually managed, on dog sledges, to reach 82 °S before being forced to return.

Shackleton had been on Scott's expedition in 1902 but had been invalided home with scurvy. At the end of 1907 he determined to try on his own account and set off with his team on his first expedition in *Nimrod*. They reached to within 175 km of the Pole before a shortage of supplies forced them to abandon this attempt and return home in 1909. However, they had located the Magnetic South Pole and team members had climbed to the summit of Mount Erebus (3,794 metres).

Ever since his own return to England, Scott had been planning his next expedition to Antarctica. Shackleton's close encounter immediately acted as a spur to move his plans forward quickly. Although he had married in 1908 and his son, Peter Scott, had been born in 1909, nothing would deter him. By early 1910 he had secured sufficient funding and after a rousing send-off party by the Lord Mayor, his final expedition ship set sail from the port of Cardiff, Wales, for Australia.

Learning that Robert Peary had reached the North Pole in April 1909, Amundsen, the totally dedicated Norwegian explorer, without even telling his crew, secretly changed his original plans to try for the North Pole. He determined to make the South Pole his and they set off in August 1910 in his polar ship, the *Fram*. Only when they reached the island of Madeira in the Atlantic Ocean did he inform his confused crew of his new decision. 'We are going to try for the South Pole, not the North Pole. Anyone who doesn't want to come with me, leave now.' None of his crew left the ship and they all became completely committed to his challenge to be the first.

Scott was in Melbourne, preparing his own South Pole expedition when he received the telegram that must have literally sent shivers up his spine, 'Beg to inform *Fram* proceeding south. Amundsen.' The race was on. But this was like no other race. There was no official starting date. Each of the bitter rivals had to decide his own course of action. First the two teams made their way down to the Ross Sea where patiently or impatiently they both would have to wait out the next winter and then decide when and how to head off across the frozen ice. Scott arrived in the Bay of Whales on 4 January 1911 and Amundsen ten days later.

In fact neither was aware of each other's arrival until February when in an outward expression of comradeship, their inner feelings presumably quite the opposite, Amundsen had lunch on board Scott's ship, *Terra Nova*. This was a great ship also built in Dundee in 1884, which had been used on several earlier expeditions. It was subsequently continued in service until it sank in 1943 off Greenland, fortunately without the loss of any lives.

Amundsen's expedition was meticulously planned and he decided to rely solely on dogs, not concerning himself overly with any suffering they might endure. He also chose to ignore all scientific aspects of the expedition and reduced his party to a minimum to save on the supplies needed. The race was all. His team were expert skiers and this in particular was to prove a tremendous advantage. Scott had been considerably disturbed by the sufferings of his dogs on the earlier *Discovery* expedition and therefore only wanted to use them as a back-up resource. His initial intention was to rely mainly on his motor sledges and donkeys. It turned out to be a disastrous mix. In addition, his team were mostly inexpert at skiing and they took much too long to become reasonably proficient. Both teams had settled in for the long winter to make their final preparations but Amundsen's plans were to beat Scott no matter what, and he was determined to embark first.

After an even earlier false start, Amundsen finally set off across the ice shelf on 19 October 1911, with 48 dogs, 5 men, and 4 sledges. Scott was unable to follow him out as his much larger team had immediate problems with the donkeys which were having difficulties in dealing with the intense cold. He finally set out on 2 November 1911 and the pressure this delay caused never allowed him and his team to find a way to catch up.

Of course Amundsen never knew when Scott had set off and throughout the push for the Pole, Amundsen remained unaware of where Scott's team were. He was terrified that they might somehow have got ahead of him. In that vast landscape, mists, fogs and blizzards blanketing everything all around them, each team could have passed within a hundred metres of the other and still not have been seen. Amundsen, in order to move faster, even decided to shoot the weaker of his dog teams and feed them to the others. Eventually he and his four colleagues, 16 dogs and two sledges reached the South Pole on 14 December 1911. Their return to the *Fram* was relatively uneventful and was achieved in record time, so fast in fact that those waiting for them thought they hadn't made it and at first were frightened to ask the question, 'Have you been there?' It was only 25 January 1912.

The struggle against the elements had proved a nightmare scenario for Scott and he and four others had eventually reached the South Pole only on 17 January 1912. He had fought so hard to reach there first and was shattered to find the black tent with the Norwegian flag flying. Inside was a note from Amundsen confirming his success and sending his 'good wishes' to take back to the King of England. On the return journey, Scott and his team, demoralised and physically exhausted, encountered even more severe and extreme weather conditions; they all perished.

In the tent with Scott, at the bitter end, were the last two surviving members, both barely hanging on, Edward Wilson and Henry Bowers. Edgar Evans had earlier fallen to his death and Lawrence Oates had a few days earlier walked out into the blizzard to die. Oates was suffering from severe frostbite and gangrene and he knew he was delaying the others and limiting their already slim chances of surviving. He decided to sacrifice himself and left the tent declaring, 'I am just going outside, and I may be some time.' Meticulously, even when he knew he would not survive, Scott kept a detailed diary and the words he left behind have since inspired many, 'Had we lived, I should have had a tale to tell of hardihood, endurance and courage of my companions, which would have stirred the heart of every Englishman. These rough notes and our dead bodies must tell the tale.' Scott's last diary entry was 29 March. Those poignant and emotive words of Scott are, as Humphrey Bogart would express so many years later in one of his classic films, *The Black Falcon*, 'The stuff which dreams are made of.' They certainly helped to fuel my childhood dreams, decades later.

1912 was a year of great triumph and incredible disaster. Scott and his men would never know of the catastrophic encounter between the *Titanic* and the giant iceberg on 14 April 1912 which was to cost so many hundreds of lives. Yet Scott's death and those of his four very brave companions, in a uniquely and perhaps peculiarly British tradition, created a special kind of personal victory and he has for evermore been acknowledged as one of Britain's greatest heroes.

Shackleton found it very difficult to accord the primary role in Antarctic exploration to Scott and was still as determined to enter the history books. His stark, brutal advertisement for possible crew members couldn't have put it more plainly: 'MEN WANTED FOR HAZARDOUS JOURNEY. Small Wages, Bitter Cold, Long Months of Complete Darkness, Constant Danger, Safe Return Doubtful. Honour and Recognition in Case of Success.' In August 1914 he set off from Plymouth to attempt an Antarctic crossing from the Weddell Sea to McMurdo Sound in the Ross Sea, via the South Pole. In January 1915 his ship, rather poignantly called the *Endurance*, became trapped in the pack ice for ten months. It drifted slowly with the ice and finally broke up in November. The whole crew then had to live on the floating ice floes for five months before Shackleton eventually got his men to the deserted Elephant Island. He left most of them there and set off with three of his strongest members in one of the lifeboats, the *James Caird*, to cross 1,300 km of extremely perilous ocean in order to reach the whaling station of

Stromness Bay. Three months later, arriving by 30 August, Shackleton returned to Elephant Island to rescue his entire crew, not losing one; a survival record totalling 590 days on the ice and in open lifeboats. It's not difficult to imagine how ecstatic they were to see him. This is certainly considered to be one of the foremost feats of seamanship ever accomplished. His recorded stark statement afterwards surely says it all, 'We reached the naked soul of man.'

This legendary adventure story and rescue was to prove an enduring legacy which has rightfully established Shackleton's Antarctic role. Another epic sea journey of that magnitude which also springs to mind is that of Captain Bligh (captain of the HMS *Bounty*) in April 1789. Bligh survived after being set adrift with a small loyal crew in an open boat, by his first mate, Fletcher Christian. He then navigated and sailed for more than 5,800 km to Timor. Captain Bligh's probably well-deserved, harsh reputation (although they were very harsh naval times) has generally eliminated this remarkable feat as being eligible for similar heroic consideration. Shackleton was to make one more unsuccessful attempt to reach the South Pole, but is mostly acclaimed because of his incredible perseverance and the fact that he never personally lost any of his men.

One of Scott's own scientists, Sir Raymond Priestley, actually remarked, 'As a scientific leader give me Scott; for swift and efficient polar travel, Amundsen; but when things are hopeless and there seems no way out, get down on your knees and pray for Shackleton.' Of all three, Shackleton above all exemplifies the tenets of Zen in his character. He carried with him at all times the three great attributes of Zen, particularly the fierce tenacity of purpose, which Scott probably abandoned after his crushing defeat at the Pole.

Scott's flag, handmade in silk by his wife Kathleen, bearing the sewn words, 'Stretched wings towards the south,' was auctioned in 1999 at Christie's and fetched £36,000. Shackleton's Royal Standard fetched £65,000. They will always be remembered and honoured. All three explorers died young. Scott was only 44 when he perished in Antarctica, Shackleton just 48 when he collapsed and died in South Georgia. Amundsen was 56 when he died in a plane attempt to rescue the Arctic adventurer Umberto Nobile, despite the enmity that had eventually developed between the two men who had earlier been flying colleagues.

Strangely, after Scott, the South Pole wasn't visited again until 31 October 1956. On that date, Admiral George Dufek and several US Navy crew landed in a ski-equipped R-4D aircraft in order to survey the area in the anticipation of a research station being established. Construction of the original South Pole Station began in November and was completed by February 1957. A new station was subsequently conceived and it replaced the first one in February 1975.

Vivian Fuchs made the first surface crossing of the Antarctic in 1957–58 leading the Commonwealth Trans-Antarctic Expedition. Fuchs set out on 24 November 1957 from Shackleton Base on the Weddell Sea, planning to reach the South Pole and then afterwards meet up with a team led by Sir Edmund Hillary (the first Everest summiteer), who had set out from the Ross Sea to provide supply dumps and guide Fuchs back to Scott Base. Hillary's team, however, made such good time that they decided to push on rather than wait and themselves reached the Pole on 4 January 1958, the first overland crossing after Scott's. Fuchs was still some 650 km away and there was an argument as to whether Hillary should wait or return, to avoid the dangers of the imminent onset of winter and whether Fuchs should try again next season. Fuchs' answer was short and very much to the point, 'We will find our own way out.' This forthright statement was enough to persuade Hillary to stick to the original plan. Fuchs then reached the Pole and left on 24 January, fortunately the second leg proved much easier. Fuchs and his team finally completed their epic 3,472 km journey after 99 days.

As an indication of the tremendous difficulties faced by anyone contemplating an Antarctic crossing, it is worth noting that the second land traverse only took place in 1980–81 when Sir Ranulph Fiennes, Charles Burton and Oliver Shepard crossed in sixty-seven days as part of their Transglobe Expedition. The third crossing was then in 1989–90, in part a celebration of Amundsen's journey, this time using forty dogs, travelling the longest route from the tip of the Antarctic Peninsula to the Russian base Mirnyi via the Pole. It took seven months and all the dogs survived.

One of Antarctica's most famous explorers is undoubtedly Richard Byrd. He was the person most responsible for introducing the use of light aircraft into the Antarctic region. Byrd led five successive expeditions to Antarctica, beginning with the historic one of 1928–30. He also discovered the Rockefeller Mountains and the Edsel Ford Mountains (now called the Ford Ranges). Initially thwarted by blizzards, on 28 November 1929, Richard Byrd as navigator and three companions became the first to fly over the South Pole, after a 10-hour flight from their base at the Bay of Whales. I decide to take it as a good omen that his radio operator was called Harry Neville Shrimpton. Subsequently, on another solo expedition, Byrd decided to test and measure the winter weather far inland. He then became trapped in his tiny hut, the first built in the interior, and suffered from carbon monoxide poisoning from a faulty engine used to power the radio as well as from the oil-burning stove. Byrd hid his plight from the outside world for many weeks in order to prevent a rescue operation, as he knew, in those present weather conditions, this would end in tragedy. As his radio reports and messages became stranger and stranger it was eventually realised that Byrd was unwell and a successful rescue was finally staged. Byrd was the first real user of the radio in the Antarctic. His own words are a statement of pure Zen, 'A man doesn't begin to attain wisdom until he recognises that he is no longer indispensable.'

The first full length flight over Antarctica was commenced in November 1935 by an American, Lincoln Ellsworth, who discovered and named the Ellsworth Mountains, situated close to where the Adventure Network Camp was to be sited at Patriot Hills over 50 years later. Together with his British pilot, Herbert Hollick-Kenyon, they flew a metal monoplane, appropriately named the *Polar Star*, from Dundee Island next to the Antarctic Peninsula, to Ross Sea (totalling close to 3,700 km). They had to land four times during the flights and they set up Camps I, II, III and IV directly on the snow. Not unexpectedly after the final take-off they ran out of fuel and from then on had to man-haul a sledge carrying their survival rations. Against all the odds they made it through and were eventually rescued on 14 January 1936.

This successful flying adventure of course changed things forever. Now airdrops of vital supplies, medicines, replacement equipment can be flown in to assist explorers and supplement their expedition needs. If someone is in grave difficulties it now means that there are more chances of being rescued and saved. Those who have gone before, with no chance of help, have really risked all and the heights of their heroism can never really be achieved again. There are, as always, those who have tried to use the power of polar flight for less scrupulous ends. During the Second World War, Hitler and Goering even arranged to send Dornier flying boats to Antarctica to try and claim it for Germany. Marker poles with swastikas were thrown on to the ice in the name of the Third Reich. If only Hitler and Goering had been thrown out instead! Perhaps Goebbels had once been to the Antarctic, which might account for the popular army song which rhymed his name with the supposedly lack of certain manly parts.

The first woman to visit Antarctica was Caroline Mikkelsson, the wife of a Norwegian whaling captain, when she stepped ashore at Vestford Hills. Edith Ronnie and Jennifer Darlington were the first women to winter in Antarctica in 1947–48 on Stonington Island on the Antarctic Peninsula. There continue to be many who attempt to cross the Antarctic or reach the South Pole in a new or special way in order to be 'the first' in their particular goal. The Norwegian Erling Kagge was the first to ski alone to the South Pole in 1993 (having with Borge Ousland in 1990 become the first team to ski to the North Pole; although, as with Peary, there are disputes to that latter claim). In 1994, Liv Arnesen, also of Norway, became the first woman to ski alone and without re-supplies to the

South Pole from Hercules Inlet, hauling her sledge containing the food and equipment for 1,120 km for 49 days. Ms Arnesen is currently planning, together with Anne Bancroft of the US, to become the first woman to cross the Antarctic. Robert Swan, and two companions, completed the longest unassisted trek to the South Pole in 1986 and was awarded the Polar Medal. Swan was totally inspired by Scott's heroism and dedicated his expedition to him. As a further act of self-reliance, his team, like Scott's, took no radios or dog teams with them. He then went on to become the first man to trek to both Poles when he reached the North Pole in May 1989. With a name like Swan I guess the white ice was always likely to be his natural habitat.

In what has been termed a classic re-run of the fierce contest and rivalry between Amundsen and Scott of 1911, a similar contest was played out over 85 years later. The Norwegian, Borge Ousland, and the Brit, Sir Ranulph Fiennes, separately tried to be the first person to walk alone across Antarctica, both starting out on 15 November 1996. There were two other main contenders fighting their way across the ice at the same time, a Pole, Marek Kaminski, and a South Korean, Ho Young Heo. (I suppose if they had jointly made it they would have been referred to as the South Korean Pole.) Kaminski is the first person to ski to both Poles in the same year and Ho has also skied to both Poles. Unfortunately throughout his attempt Fiennes suffered badly from kidney stones and finally had to drop out on 27 December. Ousland battled on to win through and completed his journey in freezing temperatures of less than -40 °C on 17 January 1997. Ousland's route started from Berkner Island in the Ronne Ice Shelf, across the

South Pole, then down the Beardmore Glacier. He crossed the Ross Ice Shelf, finally and triumphantly reaching Scott Base, on skis, 64 days later instead of the originally predicted 90 days. Awaiting him was a telegram from Fiennes, 'Enormous Congratulations.' It was a terrific achievement. In September 1999 Fiennes purchased a biscuit found next to the body of Scott for nearly £4,000. He then generously donated it to the UK Antarctic Heritage Trust so it could be put on display. I suppose you could really call that taking – or rather giving – the biscuit!

There will always be someone who wants to find a new 'first' in attempting to reach the South Pole. Recently there has been the story of a married couple, Mike and Fiona Thornewill, who became the first husband and wife team to trek to the Pole. In recording their success their motto undoubtedly should be, 'where there's a Thornewill, there's a way.' Unfortunately there was also a price, as with most polar expeditions; Fiona suffered some frostbite facial injuries which are likely to remain. The Thornewills are currently planning to trek to the North Pole together. In January 2000, a British team became the first women to trek to both Poles, a terrific way to salute the millennium. The permutations are obviously endless. But the hazards also remain and no one should venture into the Antarctic without being fully aware of the dangers that will always be faced. In 1997 a six-strong band of sky divers attempted to join the handful of those who have sky-dived over both the North and South Pole. All had jumped successfully at the North Pole but sadly, in the south, three parachutes failed to open and the three men died. No one is exactly certain why this tragedy occurred. Perhaps it was the fact that the air is much thinner and colder so the dives become faster. They might also have experienced a white-out and misjudged how close they were to the flat ice terrain. Perhaps I will be the first man to reach there with his fingers crossed all the way!

Chapter Three

The Loneliest and Remotest Continent

Antarctica is the coldest of the seven continents and the most isolated. It is an extreme and extraordinary wilderness, frozen in time. The Antarctic can be a very dangerous place to visit, as so many explorers have found to their great cost. 'In the wilderness, expect nothing – simply do the best you can.' If you dig down just a little way you touch snow that fell before you were born and before your grandparents were born. Only one hundred metres below the South Pole itself is snow that fell over a thousand years before.

There are no human inhabitants living in the Antarctic, although up to 10,000 scientists and support staff work in the region during the summer months. This immediately falls to 1,000 with the onset of winter. It then truly becomes the land of the Big Freezer. On average up to 10,000 explorers, travellers and tourists also visit every year. It is by far the windiest of all the continents (sometimes gusting up to 320 km/h) easily the most inhospitable. It is 58 times the size of the United Kingdom, twice the size of Australia and one and half times the size of the United States. It is an area of 14 million square kilometres, 10 per cent of the Earth's land mass.

The epicentre is the South Pole which is 1,235 km from the closest coastline and is on a high polar plateau (rising up to 3,850m). At the South Pole it can be as cold as -75 °C although the world record for the lowest temperature occurred at the Russian Antarctic station Vostok, where -89 °C was logged in July 1983.

In recent years, a vast freshwater lake has been charted in the Vostok region, appropriately named Lake Vostok, some 200 km long. Its deepest waters are estimated to be a million years old and there is a surface area of some 14,000 square kilometres. It is believed that the lake, some 4 km under the ice, is kept from being frozen by the heat radiating from the Earth's core as well as the insulation provided by the ice. At a depth of 3,000 metres the pressure would be so great that water would only boil at 400 °C. No one yet knows what could be lurking in these waters but certainly ancient bacterial life forms and microbes. It is essential that the continuing exploratory drillings through the ice cover do not allow any contamination to penetrate through. All drillings take place in several slow stages, allowing the ice to refreeze above until the titanium probe finally bites through, first releasing a sterilant before the breakthrough. At some stage the probe will send out a swimming robot the size of a small thermos flask containing a video camera, a computer, a spectrometer, lights and sensors for measuring heat, light and pressure and whatever else they can cram in. The Natural Environment Research Council has also created a submersible robot, Autosub, which will have the ability to explore places no manned research vessel or human divers could ever reach. It will have a range of 1,000 km and a diving depth of 1,500m.

In this unexplored lake, as in other parts of Antarctica, undoubtedly there will be found resilient extremophiles. These are minute organisms that have adapted to live in extreme conditions: thousands of metres under the sea, hidden within the coldest Antarctic conditions, surviving in boiling water or even living inside rocks and stones. Whichever kind they are, they are undoubtedly some of the hardiest of life forms and a great deal will be learned from studying them. Everything in a wilderness has a use or possibly even multiple uses, the secret is to learn what they are.

Antarctica is also the iciest place on Earth and is capped by an ice sheet up to 4,800 metres at its thickest part but on average it is 2,160 metres. It is so heavy that in places it has pushed the land below sea level. It was formed from the compacted accumulation over some 100,000 years of snow over 25 million years ago. The weight of the snow above has turned the snow below to crystal-clear, blue-green, glacier ice. The total volume of ice is over an incredible 30 million cubic kilometres. Due to the ice thickness Antarctica has the highest average altitude of all the continents. It's hard to believe but here there is approximately 90 per cent of the world's ice and over 70 per cent of its fresh water in frozen form. If the ice sheet ever melted it would raise the overall sea level by at least 65 metres. The wealthier countries could probably cope but the effect on the poor countries would be absolutely devastating.

There is a constant process of ice movements and recessions and consequently the land rises and changes the coastlines; to geologists this process is termed as isostasy. In winter the surrounding sea totally freezes and, in ice terms, the continent doubles, extending in size to 78 million square kilometres. There is approximately eight times more ice in the Antarctic than the Arctic. Under the ice sheets are the valleys, hills and mountains, the tops of which sometimes stick up above the surface to create rock peaks which are a challenge to any mountaineer.

The ice sheets end at the coastlines in huge ice cliffs and their slow moving glaciers can create massive ice shelves the size of some countries, which in turn create icebergs as large pieces break off and fall into the ocean. The world's largest glacier, the Lambert Glacier, is in the Antarctic and is over 500 km long, where it reaches the ocean it is 200 km wide. Most of the world's icebergs are in the Antarctic Ocean and can be enormous lengths with ice 45 metres or more above the water. Some are the size of cathedrals and are wind and water sculpted into inviting caverns and caves of extraordinary design and beauty, but beware ever trying to explore inside for they can be sudden death-traps. More Coleridge *Xanadu* imagery springs to mind, 'Caverns measureless to man.' A 15 metre (50 foot) schooner will appear to be a child's toy boat in comparison. A very large iceberg might weigh 400 million tonnes and could contain enough fresh water to supply a city of 3 million inhabitants for a year.

Every year the unstoppable iceberg impact totally removes many large animals and microscopic organisms from the marine shallows. This devastation can actually prove to be very beneficial as it enables new life forms to develop and flourish. As the icebergs collide or break up, air, which may have been trapped inside the ice for thousands of years, is suddenly released and can create a sound like a thousand champagne corks popping all at once. These constant ice changes and forces also drive the Southern hemisphere weather patterns, which then modulate the world's climates and have a major effect on ocean and atmospheric circulations. It is convincingly argued that the world's climate and weather patterns are materially affected by changes in the Antarctic region over very short periods of possibly between 10 to 100 years.

This enormous area is a treasure trove of information which scientists are only very slowly starting to uncover. Palaeontologists are hoping that perhaps here at last will be found the Holy Grail of evolution – the missing fossil halfway between tetrapods, the land-based animals with four limbs and backbones, and their original derivation from fish. When fins became fingers, the pelvis was also rebuilt and became attached to the backbone and the skull completely transformed. It's even possible that the secret of longevity will one day be unlocked from studies in the Antarctic; if you remove a piece of lichen from a rock in the Antarctic Peninsula you could be destroying a thousand years or more of slow organic growth; the skua gull flying overhead might be 30 years old; the fish you catch could be 12 years old and even the krill living on the bottom of the ocean floors can live to 7 years.

Many creatures and plant life have longer lives compared to those in warmer climates and grow at a slower rate. This is connected with the way in which creatures hibernate during the intensely cold winters and how some life forms, including humans, can put themselves into a state of suspended animation. Some Tibetan monks, themselves Zen masters, have perfected this technique, so perhaps the stories of Shangri-La and the Himalayan peoples who could live for centuries are not so completely far-fetched. Our own lifespan expectancy is even now starting to reach 120 years. The Tibetan monks can also raise their body temperatures by meditation and breath control, the art of Tun-Mo. They've even used it for drying out wet sheets by wrapping them around their bodies. Of course, these are all more reasons why it is so important to protect and preserve this region and all its inhabitants and organisms, particularly as it takes much longer for everything to regenerate.

Antarctica is an arid place and officially classified as a cold desert, where, on average, there are snowfalls of only 150 mm of water each year, although at the South Pole it can actually be less than 25 mm. It certainly seems a strange contradiction in a region which houses the vast majority of the world's fresh water supplies. The powerful and awesome blizzards that occur are mainly loose snow being blown by the fierce winds that constantly arise but there is only minute precipitation.

Surprisingly, there are some plant species which continue to exist and survive but naturally they are very low life forms. There are hundreds of algae species, lichens and mosses clinging to life in these very harsh conditions. Some even grow inside the rocks (endolithic plants). Refugia are the minute areas where organisms escape to in order to avoid harsh climatic conditions. The further north you travel, the warmer it gradually becomes and more types of life can be found, including minuscule midges and flies. The Southern Ocean completely surrounding the Antarctic continent is extremely cold and around latitude 50 °S its waters meet and mix with the warmer, saltier waters of the Atlantic, Indian and Pacific Oceans; this invisible area is called the Antarctic Convergence or sometimes the Polar Front.

Several bird species breed south of the Antarctic Convergence and the most famous, the penguin, accounts for 85 per cent of the bird population. They build their colonies at the ocean's edges so they can hunt for the plentiful supplies of fish to be found there, of course, penguins are one of the few breeds of bird which do not fly. The immutable rule is that there are penguins only in Antarctica and polar bears only in the Arctic. It has always seemed somewhat strange that in each of these intensely cold regions only one of these two species exists. It's another of nature's great mysteries. It would be extremely interesting to discover whether it would be possible to transfer and breed polar bears in parts of the Antarctic and breed penguins in the Arctic.

Interestingly, some ancient Greeks, against most of the prevailing concepts of the time, believed the world to be round. They therefore reasoned that to balance the land at the top of the world, the north, there must be a similar area at the bottom of the world, the south. As they had called the north region *Arctos*, meaning 'the Bear', based on the northern stars in the shape of a bear, they called this land region to the south *Antarktikos*, meaning 'opposite the bear'. Presciently this was before anyone knew there weren't bears in the region and that polar bears only lived in the Arctic. The largest carnivore living permanently in the Antarctic is a wingless midge, measuring just 12 mm long. Not much of a contest for the North's fearsome carnivore polar bear.

About 0.4 per cent of Antarctica's surface is actually free of snow and ice. Various mountain chains push up through the ice, with the highest being Mount Vinson at 4,897 metres above sea level. Antarctica is a land continent, covered by ice and surrounded by ocean whereas the Arctic is an ocean covered by sea ice and surrounded by the northern continents. That is why a marker at the North

Pole cannot be fixed as the ice is continuously moving, whereas a marker at the South Pole can be fixed and moves only fractionally. Therefore it is possible to stand at the actual current position of the Pole and see, just a few metres away, the marker where Scott and Amundsen themselves stood over eighty-five years ago.

The Southern Ocean is a continuous sea surrounding Antarctica. In winter more than half freezes over to about a depth of one metre, creating a further ice area larger again than Antarctica itself. This invariably melts during the summer period. The waters of the Southern Ocean have an effect on all oceans of the world and they also support an abundance of fish creatures including fin fish, crab, squid and krill. Continuing scientific studies are taking place of the food resources that are found there. The krill, which are shrimp-like crustaceans, are at the bottom of the animal food chain but are possibly of prime importance – the killer whale attacks and feeds on the leopard seal, which in turn attacks the Ross and Weddell seals and the penguins, which then feed on squid and small fish, and these feed on krill which survives in huge quantities and itself feeds from the plankton.

The polar vortex of Antarctica is between 10 to 20 km above the Earth's surface and needs constant monitoring in order to report on the current position. It is capable of causing immense damage to the ozone levels in the stratosphere. This ozone hole is over 26 million square kilometres and tragically it is increasing. It is presently more than three times the size of continental US.

Antarctica also provides a unique place and opportunity on many fronts to study terrestrial and extra-terrestrial phenomena. The ionosphere above Antarctica provides an exceptional viewing window through which it is easier to research nearly all regions of geospace by remote sensing processes. Geospace, possibly a million kilometres long, is where the atmospheres of the Sun and the Earth meet. On a continuing basis, thousands of tonnes of ionised material are thrown out of the Sun into space. This outflow is called the solar wind and rushes towards the earth's magnetosphere at hundreds of kilometres per second. The results could be devastating but fortunately the earth's magnetic defence systems deflect and divert the incoming attacks. The greatest dangers from the solar wind occur during the most violent phase of the Sun's 11 year cycle, a period known as solar max.

One continuing special effect, when the ionised particles collide with other neutral particles, is the creation of a gossamer curtain, aurora, the multi-coloured, dazzling, shooting lights which astound at both polar regions where the magnetic fields are at their strongest. The aurora australis, the 'Southern Lights', can reach up to one thousand kilometres into the sky. During solar max the aurora can also be seen from time to time in the lower latitudes.

Possibly some of the Antarctic rocks can provide the answers to evolutionary questions concerning the southern continents, as well as other parts of the world and even the universe itself. In Antarctica, in 1984, a meteorite was found but only more recently have tests been able to establish it as having come from Mars. The rock plummeted to rest in the Allan Hills ice field of Antarctica and was named after its discovery place and date as ALH 84001. The mineral content of the rock and the composition of its gas bubbles sealed within it, match those of the surface rocks of Mars and relate to the Martian atmosphere which was measured by the Viking probe that reached the red planet in 1976. The rock was formed about 4.5 billion years ago. The conjecture is that an asteroid or a comet struck the surface of the Mars planet some 15 million years ago and the impact sent a mass of material on a long journey into orbit. This finally culminated, about 13,000 years later, when some material entered the earth's atmosphere.

The meteorite is riven with tiny fractures caused whilst still on Mars which contain carbonate and iron sulphide particles. These may contain some of the original building blocks of life. Several more Martian meteorites have since been found and are being analysed. Their journey across space was truly an odyssey of epic proportions and there are likely to be many more meteorites waiting to be discovered which will contain more vital and revealing information.

There is a 17 square kilometre area near Patriot Hills that is considered very rich in meteorites and an expedition by the Planetary Studies Foundation is being mounted there in the next year or two. The fact that many meteorites (or parts of one larger one) have been found there, does lend some credence to those who try to argue that thousands of years ago a gigantic meteorite crashed into this territory we now call Antarctica, and caused this white wasteland to be created.

NASA has a continuing programme of sending a series of spacecraft to Mars, in order to find out primarily if there has been, or even still is, water there. This would prima facie indicate that conditions could have supported life at some time in the past and therefore perhaps could again. One day in the future, even in as short a time as only 500 years or so, it may be necessary to think of colonising another planet and Mars is of prime consideration for that.

Fortunately it has now been accepted, although there were some considerable tussles before this occurred, that the continent of Antarctica must be only used for the benefit of all countries and for science in particular. In essence it has become one gigantic science laboratory. Those nations interested in Antarctica, and there are many, have developed a framework, known as the Antarctic Treaty, by which the Antarctic is managed and which provides an acceptable means of co-operation. The original twelve countries who were active in the region, especially during the historic International Geophysical Year of 1957 (IGY), first entered into this treaty in 1961. Many other countries have since also signed up. The National Science Foundation (NSF) was given responsibility for the US research efforts and in 1959 also established the US Antarctic Research Program (USARP). Mapping, biology, meteorology and ocean sciences were added to the other active disciplines, geology, geophysics and glaciology.

The much maligned US President Nixon who, despite his tremendous failings on other fronts, was a far-sighted man in foreign policy and overseas activities, was enthusiastic about safeguarding the interests of Antarctica. He stated three US essential principles relating to this vast and mostly unexplored continent and they are important enough to restate here.

1. To maintain the Antarctic Treaty and to ensure that this continent will continue to be used only for peaceful means and shall not become an area or object of international discord.

2. To foster co-operative scientific research for the solution of worldwide and regional problems, including environmental monitoring and prediction and assessment of resources.

3. To protect the Antarctic environment and develop appropriate measures to ensure the equitable and wise use of living and non-living resources.

Chapter Four

Punta. The Windiest City

My initial flight is to Santiago, the capital of Chile, but after 11 hours flying across the Atlantic there is first an hour stopover in Sao Paulo, Brazil. I wander through the airport but it is 8 a.m. local time and all the shops are closed. In one of the windows of a pottery and gift shop I see some strange, painted clay figures which are of doctors carrying out operations on half-naked bloodied patients. There is even one of a dentist vigorously and enthusiastically pulling out a man's tooth. There is painted blood on this figure as well. They are typically Brazilian, primitive art forms depicting scenes of pain inflicted by medics and I wish I could purchase them for some doctor friends. It reminds me of the Zen saying: 'If you show me a stone and I say stone, they say stone; if you show me a tree and I say tree, they say tree; if you show me blood and I say blood, they say paint.'

The flight to Santiago takes another four hours. It is starting to be a long day (or is it really night?) although now we are on South American time, three hours earlier. I am relieved to find both of my bags have arrived safely and am met by my arranged driver, Juan. He drives me to Hotel Plaza San Francisco where I am checked into a pleasant, wooded room decorated in an old Spanish style. Although tired, I don't want to waste any part of this Chilean opportunity, so after a quick shower, Juan drives me up into the Andes.

Juan waits at an inn which is more or less closed but is still serving coffee, while I set out on foot to explore the nearby mountains. Almost immediately I see my first condor of this trip and then am lucky enough to see several more in quick succession. I climb for an hour or two feeling beneath my feet the strength of this enormous mountain chain that stretches throughout most of South America and crosses borders with impunity. If only people were as fortunate. The mountains were there before me and will still be there after. Some hours later, I reluctantly return. Juan drives much faster on the way down and takes the mountain bends with reckless disregard for anything coming the other way. Probably he calculates that it is unlikely we will another vehicle. We make it back alive and I have another shower. Later that night I meet some Chilean friends for dinner, Fernando and Monica Friedmann. They take me to a fish restaurant, Loco Loco. The owner is definitely mad as well and insists I have the fish speciality of the house. After several pisco sours it is difficult to tell the taste of the fish but I am assured it is excellent.

Next morning my flight is at 8 a.m. Juan is already waiting as I check out and we leave for the airport at 6 a.m. The town is still mostly asleep. If I miss my returning connections I promise to contact Juan on my way back to let him know if I reached the South Pole.

The first flight is out over the mountains and then along the coast. We stop once before arriving in Punta Arenas, some three and a half hours later, having flown a distance of 2,200 km. The population of Santiago is 4 million but here in Punta it is only 125,000. I am met by Steve Pinfield, one of the guides from the base camp who has been assigned to assist us and had flown in from Patriot Hills the previous night. I am weighed down by my packed coat, heavy clothes and hand luggage whereas Steve is in shorts and looks as if he has just come off safari. He has already been stationed at the camp for seven months and this is his second tour of duty there. Fortunately again, my two bags arrive safely and I know from now on there will be no chance of anything going astray. Only me.

After quickly checking into Hotel Jose Nogueira and being allocated a small but comfortable room with a double bed, Steve takes me to meet the others who will be travelling out with us. There are only three; Ian Ford a military doctor from New Zealand and two Swiss climbers, who go by the delightful first names of Hans and Christian. I never can get it right and always call Hans Rauner, Christian and Christian Steiner, Hans. They don't mind and are good sports and happily put up with my ribbing, even when I continue asking if Anderson will be joining us.

They have all been waiting here for several days, so Steve takes me, on my own, over to the offices of Adventure Network International, to meet at last the company owner, Annie Kershaw. I learn subsequently that her husband, Giles Kershaw and two friends had set up the business in 1987, but Giles had been killed in March 1990 flying a gyrocopter type of aircraft. The plane had crashed on the Jones ice shelf, east of Adelaide Island. Kershaw had been quite an adventurer and was the first man to fly around the world over both the North and South Poles as part of the Transglobe Expedition of 1980–81. He had also carried out a number of daring rescues in the region, including the recovery of three Argentine officers, from the battleship cruiser *Belgrano* (later sunk in the Falklands war), who were marooned on an ice-floe whilst on an Antarctic expedition.

Following in his heroic footsteps or perhaps more accurately 'flightsteps', Annie has bravely decided to continue the company and the polar expedition programme. It has been a tough struggle but she is managing well and has built up a reputation for fairness and straightforwardness. People trust her and like to do business with her. This trip is a case in point. Originally she had been expecting that at least twelve others would be coming and possibly even up to twenty and had budgeted costs on that basis. Now there were only four of us, the expedition would no longer be economic but Annie wouldn't cancel out or increase the costs as that wouldn't be fair to us.

I have also brought her greetings from my friend Rebecca Stephens, the first British woman to climb Everest. Annie had met her previously when she had helped to organise the climbing team in which Rebecca had summited Mount Vinson. Annie can hardly believe I am here at last. We have been corresponding for several years, as I have tried to come out several times previously. She said she always knew I would make it some day and had understood my dream that I wouldn't rest until I had come to the Antarctic. Of course a main part of the reason for this expedition is raising monies for the Red Cross and Annie is also a firm supporter of their invaluable work. The Punta office is run by her two assistants, Lesley McGhee and Fay Somerville, who are just as welcoming and they immediately volunteer to assist me in any way they can. We have all corresponded so many times about the arrangements and possibilities that I feel I know them well.

As usual, I decide that I must learn a little about this strange and totally remote city and the area surrounding it. Punta Arenas means Sandy Point and is the capital of the

Magallanes Region, named after Ferdinand Magellan the famed Portuguese explorer. Magellan had reached the sea passage, also named after him, the Straits of Magellan, in 1520. The area had previously been the haunt of pirates, explorers, seal and whale hunters for centuries. Only the hardiest individuals came to this place and were able to survive the very harsh climate as well as attacks from the indigenous Mapuche Indians from the north. The Spaniards were the first to settle permanently and founded Punta Arenas in 1848. They commandeered the land which was then inhabited by the more peaceful Tehuelche Indian tribe, who sadly died off soon afterwards from measles brought in by the Spaniards. There's a salutary lesson to be learned there somewhere; as Fred Astaire might easily have said, 'You say Tehuelche, I say Mapuche, let's call the whole thing off.' Nowadays there is a very mixed population of Spanish, German, Italian, British and Yugoslav ancestry, but all speaking Spanish.

The extremely ferocious winds can easily average 30 to 40 km/h throughout spring and summer. It is known as the windiest city in the world and after being tossed across its streets and squares I certainly wouldn't disagree. At least the winds keep the town very clean and tidy, apart from the odd body or two still trying to argue the toss. Here you cannot survive if you refuse to adapt, 'The tree that does not bend with the wind will in time break.' It's known as a mean city and not surprisingly the annual mean temperature is low at 6 to 7 °C, the average yearly rainfall is only 425 mm.

There is still some time to spare as it is planned we will all eat together in the evening. There are no possible flights out to Patriot Hills until tomorrow morning when we are booked to leave. However, no one seems in a rush to do anything and I presume they have already looked around the city and beyond. However, I certainly don't want to rest. Although I have been travelling for such a long time I want to see whatever I can in the time available. I have heard about the Torres del Paine National Park where there are all kinds of interesting wildlife as well as the towers (*torres*) of metamorphic granite rising to 3,000m which I had hoped I might have an opportunity to climb. However, Fay suggests that in the time available the best place to visit is the penguin colony (*pinguineras*) based out at Seno Otway, Ruta 5. This seems the best option so I hire a car and although the drive out takes nearly two hours it proves to be well worth it. On the way we pass several flocks of sheep as well as rheas and ibises flying low overhead. A lone condor flying purposely towards the west is a special thrill to observe, perhaps it's on its way to the Chilean Andes. We park at the outside entrance to Fundacion Otway. I purchase a ticket and start the long, meandering walk through to the nesting grasslands.

Chapter Five

In Life, Some Things Are Black And White

All penguins are wonderful creatures but out here the penguins of the wild are not like the rather sweet, domesticated zoo penguins we are all mostly familiar with. On this bleak and barren coastline penguins have to fight to survive, to combat gale force winds and to live in extreme conditions without any shelter except that which they can organise themselves. Their legs are short and set far back on their bodies which causes the waddling effect which is so appealing. They have about 12 feathers to every square centimetre of body surface. Their feathers are short and form a very dense, waterproof coat which, together with the thick layer of blubber, protects against excessive heat loss. Penguins build their homes in the sandy ground, in tiny stone castles, set within the grasses where there are any, and every one seems to inhabit a separate burrow. They all have imaginary penguin 'Keep Out' notices which someone ignores at his or her peril. Penguins have a built-in confidence and are not intimidated by anyone else's size. Some breeds of penguins use the beach stones to build their nests and will often steal stones from other penguins. The best fighters and stealers naturally have the highest nests. Penguins like to have fun and will use small icebergs as excursion boats; using their own built-in paddles.

Primarily of course they have to eat. Here they are not fed fish from a zoo keeper's bucket. They have to dive into the freezing Atlantic waters and catch their own meals.

Otherwise they go hungry. To see the penguins battling high, turbulent waves and diving again and again into the water really is a sight to behold. Raising and feeding their chicks is particularly arduous. The parents have to fight their way again and again into the ocean to find food and bring it back. Initially they take it in turns, presumably to rest up, as the chicks are never satisfied and drive the obliging parent quickly back to the sea.

Within the few months of summer the chicks need to grow quickly from tiny balls of grey to full-size penguins with waterproof feathers if they are to survive through the long, harsh winter. If the winter comes early as sometimes happens, then many chicks will not get sufficient to eat and will die. If all goes well however, the baby chicks start to resemble little bulging sacks of food. Soon both parents need to work at food gathering in order to satisfy the growing appetite of their young. They may all look alike to us but to the parents there is obviously a world of difference and they unerringly find their own offspring each trip they make. By the time the feeding process has ended and the chicks are grown enough to move off, the tired parents have lost half their own weight. They have also lost their old, worn feathers and must wait for new ones to grow before they can themselves swim off.

On the coast there are no Emperor or King penguins but several kinds of Magellanic penguins which are much smaller and without the distinctive yellow plumage the more majestic ones have. Early Antarctic explorers thought penguins were fish and initially classified them as such. They are of course birds, but superbly designed for 'flying' underwater as they cannot fly in the air – although every so often a penguin attempts to launch itself forward as if to question this fact. Perhaps there is a Jonathan Livingstone Seagull kind of story waiting to be written about William Shackleton Penguin. Unlike other birds their flippers cannot fold and are used to propel them forward at speed when under water. Their compact bodies, packed in blubber, have breastbones that work as keels and they also have massive paddle muscles. Their heads can actually retract so as to form a perfect hydrodynamic shape. The prime food here is krill, which is in plentiful supply in the Antarctic waters, and they can dive if necessary up to 500 feet for prey, although mostly they remain in the shallows. Fish are more a delicacy than a regular diet. It all depends whether a school of fish unwittingly visits the coast waters. Then watch the penguin feast.

In addition to the very impressive Emperors and Kings there are many species including the chinstrap, gentoo and Adelie, which are the kind mostly found in these parts. The latter, like the Adelie coastline, were named after the wife of the French explorer Dumont d'Urville. Either he missed her very much or she walked in a rather funny way; perhaps it was because of the stays and corsets most women wore in those more courtly days. Luckily he didn't consider renaming the great auk (*pinguinus impennis*) after her, a bird often considered or mistaken to be part of the penguin family. Also flightless, plumper than the penguin and much sought after as a great delicacy, the great auk was eventually hunted into extinction. First by the indigenous peoples and then by the European sailors who found them easy and defenceless pickings. It is generally believed that collectors clubbed the last two great auk to death on Eldey Island in June 1844. What a tragic way to collect and what a loss to the world of nature. The Iceland Natural History Museum in 1971 paid $18,000 for a stuffed great auk, the highest price paid for a dead bird. A live great auk would be priceless. Ralph Waldo Emerson stated the principle with sad resignation, 'Nature has decided; that which cannot defend itself shall not be defended.'

Fortunately the penguins are survivors, they seem completely fearless and are absolutely fascinating to observe. Oceanites is an international organisation set up to study living marine resources and specialises in penguins. The founder, Ron Naveen, is very concerned about the gradual warming continuing to take place, as penguins often suffer from overheating. Heat can only escape from the bare areas on their feet, at the base of their bills and from underneath their fins. Also, the reductions in the winter ice surrounding the continent diminishes the larval krill, their main food source. Naveen believes that studying penguins is a great way to understand the Antarctic ecosystem.

I collect some strangely-sculpted stones and a few pieces of oddly-shaped driftwood, all of which will help remind me of my time with the penguins. I wander constantly up and down the beaches, always keeping my distance and spend at least a further two hours watching their highly amusing antics. They ignore me but are still so aware of my presence. The youngest member of Scott's earlier Antarctic expedition, Apsley Cherry-Garrard, stated in his fascinating but terrifying expedition book, *The Worst Journey In The World*, published in 1922, 'They are extraordinarily like children, these little people of the Antarctic world, either like children, or like old men, full of their own importance and late for dinner, in their black tail-coats and white shirt fronts and rather portly withal.'

Chapter Six

Herculean Efforts

Dinner has been arranged for 10 o'clock. Just before it is served we all gather in a private dining room arranged by the hotel manager. Annie, Lesley and Fay join the five of us travelling out. They prove to be great fun and do everything to make sure our last night in Punta is enjoyable and memorable. The wine flows like wine and I order the most enormous Chilean steak that comes covered in cheese. It's absolutely delicious. I stand up and propose a toast, 'To tomorrow and our long journey into the depths and wilderness of the Antarctic.'

To my utter amazement this is met by downcast looks and much shaking of heads, almost as if I've put a bad spell on our chances of leaving. They all explain, almost tripping over each other's words, that it is unlikely we will be able to take-off tomorrow. Once again I hear those ominous words, 'only the weather will decide'. I had actually thought the others had been waiting for me, so we could fly off together, but it turns out this is not the case. They have in fact been trapped in Punta for the last two days, waiting for the weather to break. The high winds to the south have totally prevented any flights taking off across the Magellan Straits. I had been lucky to arrive. The flights in were also subject to constant delay and cancellation arising out of the current uncertain and highly changeable conditions.

They all tell me that I must be prepared for the worst and could even be stuck here for up to a week before we can take off. I have to fight hard not to laugh out loud at their solemn faces but they don't laugh back in response. They can't understand my own rather laid-back reaction. Perhaps I haven't understood. They repeat the decisive statement – the weather will decide. Yes, I respond, but the weather shouldn't decide our attitude. We must think and act positively and must always assume that everything will go according to our plans, yet be prepared in case it doesn't, then we can change if necessary.

I try to explain some Zen philosophy which has got me through and out of some difficult situations but I can see they are unconvinced. I expound further about the basis of karma, the necessity of creating positive thoughts, fighting negativity and sometimes just going for it. The more I argue my case, the more they try to counter and I quickly realise that I will need a small mountain of positive karma to overcome the negativity they are setting up. I quickly change the subject and offer to tell them a joke in an effort to lighten everything up. Hopefully it will put everyone into the right frame of mind. We are going on a great adventure; it is important to enjoy each moment as it unfolds, no matter what it may bring. The wine waiter fills our glasses again and they all quieten down to await my story. I only hope it won't strike the wrong chord.

I stand up, the joke comes over better that way: 'As you will all know, in any position of command it's absolutely vital and important to lead with responsibility and decisiveness. But also at the same time to show some delicacy and respect for those in your command. Well, to illustrate, the Captain of a platoon calls in his Sergeant. "Sergeant Brown, I have just learned some bad news."

"Sir?" Sergeant Brown responds.

The Captain continues, "I have heard that Private Jones' mother has just died. I want you to tell him the news but break it to him gently."

"Sir," Sergeant Brown responds again, smartly saluting. "No problem, leave it to me." He goes into the mess hall and shouts for attention. "Men, all those with mothers put your hands up. Not you Jones, keep yours down.'"

It might have been the wine but the joke goes down well and naturally after that the evening deteriorates as the wine flows even more freely. When we have finished yet another bottle or two it is definitely time to call it a day. But what an incredibly full day it has been. I feel as if I am thousands of miles away from my usual life and of course I am. We are all on the brink of setting off into deepest Antarctica and who could know what tomorrow will bring. We all agree to be up early, ready to fly out, just in case the weather decides to allow.

I am in fact up at 3.30 a.m. and phone through to make certain Ian is also ready on time. I have some tea in the lobby and am checked out by 6 a.m. Amazingly Lesley and Fay are already waiting outside in the van to take me to the plane. Now that's what I call service! We pick up Steve, Ian, Hans and Christian on the way. Now to find out whether we can fly out or if we will have to abort our plans and return to the hotel. Ian tells me, as the weather has been so volatile for the last two days, he is not expecting anything different today. I discover he is always generally pessimistic about things throughout our time together and I am continually pushing him to expect the best, not believe the worst. Luckily the omens are looking good and weather reports so far are excellent.

We are driven out to the Presidente Carlos Ibanez del Campo airfield and meet our flight crew. They are all South African and we will be flying with the airline SAFAIR, whose headquarters are actually based at Johannesburg International Airport. The crew had moved out from South Africa to take up overseas positions after the wonderful, to me at least, collapse of apartheid. Because of apartheid, I hadn't been able to visit South Africa up till now, but it is certainly on my future travel itinerary. No nation owns Antarctica and therefore there are no customs facilities to go through in or out. There is no need to show a passport to anyone. This is definitely a first!

We board an old Hercules C-130, which obviously has done Trojan service in its past flying life. It certainly carries many battle scars and resembles a huge ship with wings. It has an enormous, cavernous interior and gives me some hope that if it comes down in the sea it might float, for a while at least. It is the kind of plane that was used in Vietnam and other war areas to ferry huge numbers of men, quantities of equipment, supplies and sometimes even tanks. Now it resembles an empty circus tent after the circus and the crowds have left. There are wires and ropes hanging down, untied straps and loose items everywhere. The toilet is at the front of the aircraft, just outside and to the right of the cockpit, half-hidden behind a torn curtain which will hardly cover anyone's modesty. The curtain has to be hand-held when used, which makes it a rather precarious activity.

We have been joined just before take-off by Lorna, the girlfriend of the Patriot Hills camp manager. She is feeling very anxious on how she will be received and I try to cheer her up, telling her not to be so forlorn. I nickname her

Lorna Doone. Travelling south to the land of frozen water it seems appropriate for her to be considered a Sir Walter Scott heroine. It's time for all of us to go with the floe!

On board there are only the six of us and the crew of four. There are no announced regulations or instructions to follow and we settle in for the six-hour flight, of 1,000 kilometres. The only thing the Captain tells us is that we can expect some turbulence as we hit differing air currents over the mountain ranges, sea and ice fields, and to be prepared for a few sudden jolts. His voice is nonchalant but creates an expectancy of unusual surprises. In my inner ear I hear the legendary star Bette Davis, in her 1950 film classic *All About Eve*, drawling to her friends in that incredible husky, sexy voice, 'Hang on to your seat belts, darlings, you're all in for a bumpy ride.'

Initially we fly over Tierra del Fuego, the southernmost land in Chile. To the left is Estrech de Magallanes, the Straits of Magellan. We rattle around inside this vast aircraft enclosure and are allowed to wander whenever and wherever we wish. The pilot is pleased to see us come to the cockpit at any time and is happy to chat about his own travel and flying experiences. We cross the stormy and unpredictable Drake Passage (Sir Francis Drake rounded Cape Horn in 1578) and at 60 °S we reach the winter limits of the frozen ocean. This is the Antarctic Convergence and is an area rich in plankton and other minuscule creatures that are part of the food chain that all life in this region depends on. At 66 °S we reach the Antarctic Circle and initially pass over a series of icebergs and then the gigantic ice shelves from which they were created.

At the back of the plane just before a slew of motorised sledges, oil drums and boxes of food provisions there is a large wooden table which serves as in-flight service. On it are a variety of breads, slabs of different cheeses, heaps of blood-red tomatoes, a variety of soft drinks only out-numbered by the bottles of beer. Nothing is served directly but whenever you feel like something to eat or drink then passengers or crew can help themselves.

Our first sight of the continent of Antarctica appears as we reach Charcot Island close to Alexander Island (named after Tzar Alexander I by Bellingshausen in 1821). We are now at 71 °S. The plane is incredibly noisy and we have been advised to wear earplugs but they don't really help much. The plane has tiny porthole windows so there's not really much opportunity to see out and anyhow the views all seem the same. Endless miles of snow and ice as we head deeper and deeper into the remotest regions of the Antarctic. Mike the pilot tells me that the plane is carrying 57,000 lbs (26,000 kg) of fuel and will use up 19,000 lbs (8,600 kg) on the outward journey. It's clear that Adventure Network will not cover the necessary payment for that kind of extensive cost with only four paying passengers. I bless Annie Kershaw again for being so honourable and sticking to her commitment to take us, even though all the others she had expected had dropped out.

It's a long journey of six hours, covering 3,200 km. It makes me appreciate even more all those mad, crazy, wonderful, beautiful people who have walked these remote, icy wastes for weeks and months in an endeavour to reach the South Pole. I'm reminded of the song about two friends 'walking the barren wastes without a drop of water' but that actually took place in a sand desert. However, although it is not so often realised, Antarctica is also a desert. The definition of a desert being a place where there is very little or no rainfall over a set period of time. The Antarctic has virtually no rainfall and therefore, strictly speaking, it is the biggest desert in the world.

We climb to 25,000 ft (7,620 metres) and it gets progressively colder. I put on my gloves, then my hat, then cover my knees with my parka coat. Steve comes over and tries to whisper into my ear what I learn is his most important instruction, 'KW'. I can't hear him and he has to shout it out several times to get through the heavy engine noise. 'What's that mean?'

'It's the one thing above all to remember,' he grins. 'Keep Warm.' I haven't anything more at hand to put on but nod and clap my gloves in response.

Steve is 43 today and later we break open a bar of chocolate to celebrate. Steve, guide extraordinaire, stunt arranger, location scout, lives in St Ives, Cornwall. He is still a bachelor although he says he has come close several times. The call of the wild and his guiding all over the world has always stopped him at the last moments. He's starting to regret his missed opportunities though and the fact that he hasn't put down roots and is wondering if it's now too late. Probably it's his birthday blues and a once-a-year time when he reflects on what might have been. Tomorrow he'll be as happy as he always seems.

The one thing that gets to him when he returns home, as it does to all of us that undertake expeditions of any length, is that perennial question, 'Where are you off to next?' We laugh it off but really want to respond, 'Wait a moment, we've just got back, let's relax a while before deciding on the next exploit.' I suppose it's something to do with the inability to understand why we go, why we risk injury or worse and why we don't just settle for the quieter life. As Louis Armstrong has said and I often quote it as my kind of answer, 'If you have to ask 'What is jazz?' then you'll never know'. It might be a non sequitur or might directly relate but a number of geologists and explorers over the years have remarked that the Antarctic light invokes 'the feeling of jazz.'

I look out the window to my left but the light is less vibrant as it's now becoming misty and there's little to see. It's still very noisy but I have more or less got used to it. There are only two more hours to go. We have been flying into the Antarctic interior for about four hours. Off and on I am reading Amy Tan's *The Hundred Secret Senses* and the subject fits in well with this mystical journey into the unknown. One passage particularly refers to colour, its meanings and effects and perhaps because of seeing so many 'whiter shades of pale' I start to wonder if maybe there are more colours than is generally accepted. Yellow is the most vivid colour to me and yet there are so many different variations that some seem more than just a shade. Is it possible some could be a separate colour in their own right?

Experiments have shown that in an overwhelming number of cases people's heart rates increased when placed in red surroundings. This has proved invaluable in the treatment of cardiovascular ailments. Shades of green can reduce fatigue and yellow is said to counteract monotony. After factory workers complained about the weight of crates painted black they were repainted green and everyone reported they were now much lighter. A sailor is shipwrecked on a tiny island. As he recovers he notices the beach is purple, as are the trees and the grass. Even the birds flying overhead are purple. Suddenly he notices his skin is changing to a similar colour. 'Oh no,' he cries out, 'I've been marooned!'

Humans, of course, do not have the monopoly on colour. Many of nature's creatures have colour vision and use it in defence and protection as well as in attracting the opposite sex. No one knows if all the colours they see are the same colours we know. Just because something seems similar it doesn't mean that's how it really is. As in Gershwin's *Summertime* and Porgy's poignant comment to Bess, 'It ain't necessarily so.' On a journey such as this, to the bottom of the world, it feels quite acceptable to pose questions that ordinarily one would not try to answer. We are heading into an unreal world, or at least a world that has different rules to the ones we have accepted without question before. Biologists actually claim that before the earth was green it may have been purple. This hypothesis is based on studies of genetic sequences which reveal that purple bacteria have the most ancient photosynthesis genes.

We have reached Ellsworth Land and are approaching the Ellsworth Mountains. These are named after Lincoln Ellsworth who made the first flight across Antarctica in 1935. Only one hour to go and the excitement for all of us is mounting. I am hungry and make myself a cheese sandwich. I am also feeling tired but don't want to miss any part of this thrilling journey and unique experience by sleeping through it. After drinking too much water I need to use the toilet and try to hold the curtain across but no one cares anyhow.

It is now 45 minutes to landing and we are warned to tread carefully when disembarking as it's extremely icy out there at the landing strip. We are now flying along the east face of the Sentinel Range, which has the highest Antarctic mountain, Mount Vinson, and then across the Nimitz Glacier. We will shortly be landing on a natural blue-ice runway at 1,000 metres above sea level, immediately after passing over the Ellsworth Mountain Range. We are told we must leave through the rear of the plane.

Only a final 15 minutes until touchdown. I decide to strap in. I have a window seat and can snap away with my camera at the swirling, energising whiteness stretching in every direction. I can see there are lumps and bumps everywhere. The engine noise is totally deafening, the coldness is absolute. Presumably the runway has been cleared for touchdown. The Hercules has no skis and lowers its wheels. We continue to descend rapidly; the hard ice is approaching fast. Here we come!

Chapter Seven

The Max Factor

The plane's landing is perfect. Mine isn't. As soon as the Hercules rolls to a halt the rear hatches are opened and the first boxes and equipment are immediately unloaded. I am champing at the bit and once there is room to get by, I am straight out of the plane and take my first joyful steps on to this frozen continent. Wham! I slide and slip immediately and can't prevent myself from doing an impression of the Pope kissing the ground as he arrives in each new country. I quickly pick myself up but fortunately no one seems to have noticed. Either they are all too busy making certain they don't slip or are helping unload the equipment from the aircraft. I offer my services but they are not needed. I can do whatever I like; stay around to watch the further unloading, hitch a ride on a ski-doo going to base camp, take photographs or just hang out. Do they mean chill out? I can hardly make up my mind; it's all too wonderful. But I am not going to rush it. One slip is already one too many.

It's a moment to take stock. The stunning ice views cry out for superlatives. I can only stare in wonderment. We are close to the Ellsworth mountain range, with snow-capped ridges, interspersed with rugged rock formations surprisingly clear and stark, edging upwards to the skyline. We are at 80 °S and are over 1,100 km from the nearest inhabited place; the South Pole Amundsen-Scott Base Station. This is a place you can only access by aircraft, or possibly by an exceedingly long foot slog. Approximately the same distance as from New York to Chicago or Paris to Madrid. There are no cities or towns for nearly 3,000 km in every direction. The nearest place in case of emergency is the South Pole itself.

Finally I decide to start my walk in, I'm told it will take about 30 minutes. First I quickly take some photographs of the plane as it is being reloaded with equipment and other boxes that need to go back. The backdrop of the mountain is entrancing and the huge Hercules is dwarfed into toy mode. Idly I wonder why equipment has to go back rather than be kept at the camp and I reflect on what's in the boxes. They could of course be empty although they seem too heavy for that. At first I assume everyone around the plane is helping unload it but I soon realise that a number of the people are waiting to return to Punta and are to board as soon as the loading is completed. There are another six hours of flying before they and the crew will arrive back. A fast turnaround is always called for, as it's vital to head out whilst the weather holds. The pilots won't even stop for tea. They've learned from experience that delaying even for an hour can move you into another weather frame and they've obviously been framed once too often.

As positively as I dare I step out towards the camp, my companions have already gone on ahead and I follow along their fairly obvious pathway. The light seems to bend, perhaps an interaction between ice and wind. There's a Union Jack flag raised on a small hillock and someone offers to take my photograph next to it. It's an offer I can't refuse. The wind lifts it at just the right moment. I still don't feel inclined to hurry and I continue on at an uneven pace. I stop often to drink in the heady atmosphere of this icy land and it is an unreal feeling. I am actually here! I am so happy I could almost burst. In fact, I do burst into song. Fortunately there's no one near enough to hear. Richard Eyre, the National Theatre director has just done a production of *Guys and Dolls* so those are the songs that most easily come to mind. 'Luck be a lady tonight!' Later on someone reminds me that sound travels much further in these intensely cold conditions and my singing carried across the ice and was a source of considerable amusement to those waiting to greet the new arrivals! Perhaps it was the real reason why they gave me a tent to myself.

I am still sliding all over the place and try to find the crunchy sections to try and prevent falling over. The sun is beating steadily down all the time and I am soon overheating. I need to stop and loosen the two heavy over-jackets I'm wearing and apply some sunblock. When I finally arrive at the camp I am amazed by the size of it. I hadn't really appreciated up to now how permanent a base it would be and it looks pretty substantial. There are in fact several large, fixed Weatherhaven tents that are left standing to be used each year. When the season is over they have their innards removed and stored and then kept more or less as shells until the next season begins, when they are refitted as necessary. Adventure Network chose to base itself here in order to improve and maintain the first bare ice runway to be used anywhere in the Antarctic. It is the most southerly runway in the world and is actually a natural phenomenon. This is a place where wheeled landings can take place. All other runways in this area, as I was to discover to my discomfort later, are used by aircraft with ski landing gear.

On arrival I am initially ushered into the long dining and cook tent (3.5 x 14.5 metres, and nearly 2 metres high). It's the hub of the camp and everyone congregates there whenever possible. It's always warm and there's plenty of room to sit around and do whatever is the order of the day. Repairing kit, discussing that important subject, the weather, and of course the most important of all camp activities, eating. There are two cooks, Ros Cooper and Fran Orio and I soon learn that their standard of cooking is excellent. 'Eat, eat,' it's as if my mother has sent feeding instructions ahead. I am happy to oblige and down whatever is put in front of me. It's absolutely scrumptious.

I discover the extent of the other base facilities and they are equally impressive. Probably the most important is the wireless tent, essential for obtaining up-to-date weather information and relaying news of whatever emergencies are occurring, either here or at another station. There are several stores, a reading and library tent, and a medical and treatment tent which possibly doubles as the doctor's sleeping quarters. Also electrical and service tents which house the aircraft spare parts. The larger tents have full-sized entrance doors, windows and the dining tent has insulated floors. It's essential out here as you can easily experience a complete weather white-out and will have to wait until the storm lessens or passes which can be anything from two to twenty hours. A white-out can be completely disorientating and if caught outside in one you can be totally lost even if only a few metres from a tent. It's impossible to see or hear anything and you will quickly lose all sense of direction. You should only step outside if it's really essential and then you must make certain you have a rope or cord attached to guide you back.

Fortunately now the weather seems perfect, very little wind, clear in all directions, sunny and even warm. I'd like to take off for the Pole immediately but that's not possible. Normally the camp houses about 20 visitors, which means sharing tents, but as there are so few of us I am allocated one to myself. Is it something I've sung? Each tent is named after a polar explorer; I have the large Byrd tent. Is it another sing-song joke? I don't mind and I have the luxury of two mattresses which means I can put my sleeping bag on one and spread out my equipment and spare clothes on the other.

After sorting my bags and laying everything across the mattresses I make my way back to the cook tent. Everyone calls it that, rather than dining or eating tent, as out here you don't use two syllables if one will do. It saves on breath and also means your mouth is open less to let the cold in. Ros immediately presses me to eat something; all I want is tea and I'm given a huge mug with several biscuits. Two large, standing containers of heated water are situated in the centre of the tent to spread the heat in all directions. They are used for all purposes, including cooking, cleaning and washing, although the latter I soon learn is far down the list of priorities. There is no running water in the Antarctic and the only way to get water is to melt ice. This is more laborious than it sounds. You need to go outside to find a section of clean ice, cut a large number of chunks from it, carry them inside and drop them carefully into the containers to melt. It is a ratio of four chunks to one of water so it can take a long time. Therefore water is considered very precious and must never be wasted. That's why, I guess, some consider shaving and washing extravagant.

In the cook tent I meet the most important person in the camp, to me at any rate. The man who will have the

<u>Antarctic:</u>
Penguins as far as the eye can see

Tenting in the wilderness of Patriot Hills

Inspecting the crashed DC6

Snowed in at Patriot Hills

New Year feasting at Patriot Hills

Trekking to the mountains through the icy mists

Loading a Twin Otter in preparation for a flight to the mountains

Huge snow and rock climbs in the Ellsworth Mountains

Hastily refuelling the Cessna at White Fields

Flying over mountain ranges towards the South Pole

Mystical Antarctic cloud formation creating Pegasus, the flying horse

The current South Pole marker

Standing exactly where Amundsen and Scott stood in 1911/1912
after their heroic journeys to the South Pole

Entrance to the underground Amundsen-Scott base at the South Pole

Ferdinand Magellan's statue in
Punta Arenas, Chile

Fighting the immense winds to kiss Magellan's lucky big toe

most impact on the success or otherwise of my journey through to the Antarctic – Max Wenden the pilot of the Cessna 185. I learn almost straightaway that Max will be the one to decide when and if I can go to the South Pole. The weather will initially decide but it is Max who will have the ultimate say so. I learn now to my horror, although I do my best to disguise it, that there is as much chance of my not getting to the Pole as there is of making it. The weather patterns mostly originate from the South and there can be katabic winds which gust up to 100 knots, although the usual strength is around 15. But when the powerful katabic winds strike, everything and everyone are immediately paralysed into staying put.

The air in this region is actually dry, more like that you'd find in the states of Wyoming or Colorado. Therefore even when it gets to -10 °C it is not uncomfortable. I lead the conversation gently back to our chances of getting to the Pole. Max gently, but also rather too nonchalantly, tells me that several times those who have come out to Patriot Hills to travel on to the South Pole have had to abandon their plans. Either the weather and flying conditions were too dangerous or sometimes the plane wasn't serviceable. Flying to the Pole is no joy-ride and if there is the slightest problem or concern then the flight mustn't take place. There have been too many mishaps in the past, with other companies or organisations; Adventure Network are justifiably too proud of their safety record to take any chances.

Apart from expressing that scary scenario Max says, all things being equal, his plan would be to fly in and perhaps even tent overnight at the Pole. He would try this if he could rig up a heating system for the Cessna. I wanted immediately to shout out, 'What are you waiting for? Why waste time talking to me? Get on with it!' But I didn't. Max is not the kind of man to be hurried. Here he is king and he will take his own time. He tells me the Cessna only seats three or four persons, including the pilot, so I realise how lucky I am that there are only four of us. Hopefully that means that I have a good chance of being one of the three who could fly out on the first flight that is permitted. Max's Cessna is nicknamed the 'Polar Pumpkin', because of its orange colour, but I hope the name also means I will also go to the Ball, I mean the Pole!

There are two other pilots, Steve King and Greg Stein, who fly the camp's two Twin Otters and they come over to chat. At this time their planes are being used for flights to the mountains, particularly for those wanting to climb Mount Vinson and are therefore not presently available for Pole flights. In fact one of the Twin Otters needs repairs and servicing so is not in the equation anyhow. Throughout my stay in camp I may joke and talk with Steve and Greg but Max is my main man. He has my polar destiny totally in his hands, he is the only one to decide whether I will achieve the ultimate goal and make it to the South Pole. He is a straight guy and understands my strong desire but he has been, and wants to stay, around for a long time. The thing he has learned well is that you don't take chances, especially out here where the back-up is so limited.

We had arrived at 1.15 p.m. and the reloading of the Hercules had been completed in just 45 minutes. But it's now 4.30 p.m. and the Hercules is still on the ground. It looks ominous. The problem is that one of the propellers is not turning fully and they must get it right before risking the long flight back. Repairs continue the whole time, there are a lot of huddled consultations and visits to the electrical tent but no one appears flustered. This can happen any time in Antarctic conditions. It's a problem that will be solved, only the time it will take is uncertain. Additionally the temperature has risen to only -1 °C and that's too warm for the take-off and initial flight; they mostly prefer about -8/10 °C. It's also starting to blow quite hard and that is another concern. If they take off the outgoing passengers and they stay over it means there will have to be a reallocation of the tent places, meaning I'll have to share with someone and move everything to one mattress. I hope she plays chess at least. Another half-hour or so and there is good news. The propeller is fixed and with a whoosh the Hercules lifts into the sky and is on its way back. It's a great sight.

Duncan Haigh, the camp manager, comes back from the Hercules to welcome us. He is feeling pretty chuffed and it's not to do with the take-off. Not only has his girlfriend Lorna come out to join him for a while but he has just received important news. A letter came in on our plane informing him that he has been awarded the Polar Medal from the Queen and this is being Gazetted. It is signed by Rear Admiral Myres and is from the Ministry of Defence. It relates to Duncan's work in the Antarctic region and his masterminding the handing over of one of the polar stations to the Canadians.

Duncan tells us about the camp and its working arrangements and gives me the most important information of all. Details about the latrine facilities. There are two and they are situated several metres away, divided inside an igloo, specially constructed to house them. Outside are two small red flags. When either latrine is occupied the flagpole is kept the right way up with the flag at the top. As you leave it is important to invert the pole so it's at the bottom, as a signal that particular latrine is empty and available. Although there are only two the system works reasonably well. Latrine duty is allocated once a day and the person on duty is called the mouse. I suppose anyone who declines is called a rat!

I decide to inspect and fortunately both flags are upside down. There is a slight slope down and inside the hollowed-out cavern I am surprised to see an actual toilet with a seat. There are toilet rolls on a stick stuck into the ice wall. Very civilised. It's bitterly cold inside so it's not a place to linger on several accounts. I remember to invert the flag as I leave. There's nowhere to wash hands and I now know why people just waved their greetings at us and didn't shake hands when we arrived.

Nearby there is a small hut in which there is a narrow shower and an adjoining washroom set with a small basin and mirror. You can use the hut for washing, shaving and showering but you have to bring in your own water obtained from the cook tent. As water is so precious and it's so laborious to melt the ice into the containers in the cook tent, it is necessary to use it very sparingly. For that reason as well as the inconvenience of transporting the water across the ice to the hut, most people shower rarely, if at all. During my stay I had an occasional overall body wash but it seemed many people who were there even for months didn't shower. All the men, except Steve, didn't shave and had long, unkempt beards as well as bushy, overgrown hair. That was certainly the norm and out here the wild look is certainly in. I guess Steve keeps clean-shaven because one of his duties is to fly back regularly to Punta to pick up new travellers; they probably don't want them to be too alarmed, not to begin with at least. Some of the hairstyles, women as well as men, are strange to the extreme and everyone wears a mix of clothing that has no rhyme or reason and are primarily put on for warmth. Max Wenden is always wearing a very torn, long-sleeved jersey that I am told he never changes during the whole of his season at the camp, which is at least four months. Max waits until a jersey has literally disintegrated and then throws it away before putting on another one. Lorna Doone professes herself to be very tired, throwing a meaningful look across at Duncan and he eagerly takes her away to show her where their tent is. We won't see them again until very late tomorrow. Ian, Hans and Christian also soon disappear off and the cook tent is rapidly emptying as most people drift away. I am also feeling tired, so quickly have something to eat and then make my way across to my Byrd tent. It is of course still completely light outside as it will remain throughout my time in the Antarctic. After snuggling inside my sleeping bag, I put on some eye shades in order to blot out the brightness and it helps me get to sleep. In a moment I am flat out. One of my dreams is of a mouse in the shower hut eating a bar of soap which gradually turns into cheese and perversely becomes impossible to eat. There is water cascading down but in the dream the mouse never gets wet.

Chapter Eight

Getting My Rocks Off

Finally I sleep well and then wake early. I quickly dress and use the latrine and wash hut using some of my precious container water. The atmosphere in the camp is surreal and gives an impression that it's floating in a slow-moving, luminous-white sea. There is a slight mist which is slowly lifting. I walk around the tents which seem abandoned and are spaced one from another before going over to the cook tent for breakfast.

I am the first apart from the two cooks who are already busy preparing everything. They are happy to chat at the same time and I learn that they are using this work opportunity as a way of travelling out here and seeing something of the Antarctic. Although they have been here for several months neither have yet been to the South Pole. I express my surprise at this and they explain they would still have to pay for the fuel costs and this is very expensive. They are hoping there will be a possibility towards the end of the season.

Everyone else is now drifting in and I buttonhole Max to see if there is going to be any chance of going to the Pole today. He isn't enthusiastic and apart from some engine work he wants to carry out later, he tells me he's learned that there are a group of VIPs from New Zealand visiting the Amundsen-Scott Station. So even if we were able to go, there would be no chance of visiting the base itself, so it would be much better to wait. There is no hurry, from his point of view of course and he advises me to just relax and use the opportunity to tour around the camp area.

I am fast getting the impression that no one is likely to respond to my anxious urgency. The pace of life and activity at the camp is obviously on a much slower level than I had expected. Zen teaches you to be patient but also to use every opportunity. The Zen philosophy is always positive and would rarely suggest someone holds back and does not go for it. Of course it is important that all chores of the camp have to be carried out but it is still necessary to work out a balance and to prioritise. I am certainly getting the strong impression there is never any rush to do something here and it doesn't seem to matter whether things are done now or tomorrow – whenever that is. Perhaps all polar pilots are the same and Max Wenden is cast in the same mould as Harry Hansen, the pilot in the Arctic who had nearly stopped the Tate Gallery team from reaching the North Pole. I decide I will have to gauge my approach carefully if I want to encourage Max to take us to the South Pole. Ian is angrier and wants to demand Max makes the arrangements as a matter of necessity. Gradually I calm him down and explain that we have to accept their way of operating and must work within their system.

In the centre of the cook tent there is a blackboard where information and daily notices are pinned or written up. At a moment when everyone else seems occupied, I write in large lettering: 'Unless morale improves the whippings will continue' and sign it *The South Pole Gazette*. Also at the bottom I add *Carpe Diem* ('seize the day'), hoping Max might get the hint! There's considerable discussion on who might have written the messages but I don't volunteer and just hope both will have some impact. From then on a joke or similar wry comment appears from someone or other most days. There's one I suspect Fran wrote, 'Remember to empty the teapot and stand upside down on the draining board.' At least it helps to amuse us whilst we are waiting for the opportunity to take off for the Pole or the mountains. Hans and Christian have definitely decided to climb Mount Vinson, at close to 5,000 metres it is the highest mountain in Antarctica and therefore one of the seven summits (the highest mountain on each of the continents). They are as frustrated as everyone else however, as the winds are too strong for the Twin Otter to take-off yet and they must also wait in the camp.

Seeing our impatience Steve suggests a cross-country skiing excursion and Ian and I jump at the chance. Hans and Christian are not keen as they want to sunbathe outside their tent. They are sharing the one tent as they often climb together, it will get them used to the close quarters when they finally get their chance to attempt Vinson. Ann Ward, the camp's doctor hears about our planned trip and asks to come with us. She's good company so we are very happy to agree. The skis are kept in a storeroom and when we inspect them they turn out to be rather battered and worn. There are no special ski boots. Still beggars can't be choosers. The boots I have with me are really only for climbing and trekking and I have a difficult time fitting them to the skis. I manage it somehow but they feel pretty loose and I'll just have to take my chances.

Steve skis ahead with Ian and I follow with Ann. Soon we are all whizzing along and it's very exhilarating. The ice is bumpy and it sends us spraying ice in all directions. Ian is the first to come off and then Ann takes a tumble. Then it's my turn. Steve is as competent on skis as one would expect from his other skills and never falls over. We start to ski as a unit and fan out like easy riders moving more or less gracefully forward in formation across the great white Antarctic plains.

Steve leads us towards a small plane wreck, hardly visible in the snow unless you know what you are looking for. It's the body of a Cessna that crashed a few years back. Powerful winds had caught hold of it and toppled it on to its side. Although the pilot was relatively unhurt, the tangled body of the plane serves to emphasise the constant dangers there are of high winds and ever-changing weather that we all must be on our guard against. Max would be only too aware of these precarious situations and obviously wouldn't fly unless he felt confident enough he could cope with the conditions.

We take photographs of the crash and of each other on skis then it's time to turn around and race back to the camp. Ann is soon in front although I guess Steve is content to let her win, as he skis comfortably alongside me and has no difficulty matching my pace. Right on cue, as we ski into camp my bindings on both feet loosen and I nosedive into a perfectly placed snow ramp. Nothing but my dignity is hurt. I limp nonchalantly past the tent of Hans and Christian who, true to their word, are lolling in the sun outside. It looks so strange to see two men sunbathing wearing thick clothes and only allowing the sun to beam to their faces. It doesn't seem too wise, but then again, they are Swiss and they know more than most about mountains, snow and sun. We wave happily to each other and they seem more cheerful than I would be in their forced stationary circumstances. They seem quite content to sit it out till the weather decides. The four of us put the skis away and head to the hut for hot chocolate and biscuits. I am starting to get used to this life, insulated from contact with a faster moving pace. It's definitely a danger signal and I immediately get to my feet.

I decide I still want to explore some more today and would particularly like to climb on my own for a time. I ask permission and it is readily given. One of the managers just needs to know in which direction I am heading and my intentions in case they have to come looking for me. I point at the far ridge of the Ellsworth Mountains, just beyond the airstrip and say that's my goal. I load up my day pack with some food and water and a few other necessities which I feel I might need. I am asked if I want to wait for a lift on a ski-doo but on my first day I prefer to rely on my own resources. I put on loads of sunscreen, two pairs of gloves, my thick and heavy hat and thus suitably attired, set off.

Almost immediately it feels absolutely glorious and although it's as icy as on arrival I quickly put quite a distance between myself and the camp. I am now completely on my own. I cross over a high hump and the camp vanishes from sight. It's an eerie feeling. I am totally isolated and it would be so easy to head off in the wrong direction and become lost. The crystals in the ice sparkle like diamonds and lure me on like an illusion impossible to attain. The first mountain ridge is directly in front of me and I keep it firmly in view.

Occasionally I trek into a lengthy ice gully and then nothing can be seen in any direction and for several rather agonising minutes there is nothing to indicate the way ahead. But then there is always the sun to guide me and therefore I can't really go wrong. Or could I? But what if the sun were to exit? If heavy winds suddenly occur and whip up the loose snow it would certainly blot out any vision and it would be all too easy to lose one's bearings. Fortunately that does not occur. However, it is always a possibility in this totally isolated region and I wonder if it was a correct decision to allow me to go off on my own. Particularly on my first day, before I've got to know my way around or for them to know my capabilities. I guess they assume that anyone who chooses to come this incredibly long way is going to be responsible. Someone who is not going to behave in a manner which will not only endanger his or her life but cause others to be endangered in needing to send out a search party and attempt a rescue.

It's much further to the mountains than it initially appeared and even after I've passed the airstrip there is obviously a long way still to go. I remember that in these intense cold conditions it's possible to see much greater distances and this is why the mountains appear nearer than they are. Still, what else would I be doing? I need to understand something of this amazing wilderness of ice and snow desolation. This is one of the main reasons I came out here; to feel the emptiness of this extraordinary place, to experience the raw emotion of this vast landscape. I want to touch south, just as I had touched north all those years earlier with Andy Goldsworthy and my travelling colleagues from the Tate Gallery.

Every so often I stop and listen to the strange absence of sound. Can one really hear silence? Is it the sound of one hand clapping? This most famous of Zen koans leads me to consider again one of the most interesting and often debated philosophical questions; Does a tree falling in the middle of a deserted forest make a noise if there is no one to hear it? Or even just a leaf? In Antarctica is there a sound from the fall of one snowflake or several (although they rarely fall but are nearly always wind driven) or from the cracking of the ice, if there is no one there?

This extremely intriguing question actually stems from an Hindu view of mankind as the centre of existence and asks, 'What is the nature of reality?' The argument concerns the difference between subjective and physical reality. Objects are said to have primary and secondary qualities; primary are solidity, size, shape, etc., whereas secondary include colour, smell, taste. Secondary qualities are not intrinsic to an object but depend upon the reaction of the observer. I may consider ice to be white or blue or green or any combination of colour. It's up to me and therefore not intrinsic to the ice. Sound may not be heard for a variety of reasons. However, if you define sound as moving airwaves then a vibration of those airwaves will have taken place and an effect has occurred even if not actually perceived. Zen masters will ask students for their answers but will not say which is the right one. You either know or don't know.

It is as if I'm the last man on earth and there is no one to turn to for any assistance or any answer. It is an extraordinary feeling and I savour it to the full. Although it is mostly silent there are in fact occasionally things to listen to and observe. My boots make their own sounds and rhythms and every so often the wind starts up and whistles or breathes on me. Although mostly it is still. Very still. Very beautiful. The land forms over which I'm trekking are so very different to the ice forms of the Arctic.

I finally arrive at the base of the mountain ridge and start to climb. It's an ideal opportunity to use some Zen and concentrate on my breathing. A vital part of the practice of Zen is to be aware of the importance of breathing deeply in and exhaling fully. Breathing should occur from the lower abdomen – the hara – that part just below the navel. If someone is said to have hara then he or she is considered to be well-balanced, physically as well as psychologically. In breathing correctly it becomes possible to concentrate totally.

In order to focus the concentration more intensely it is very important to practice counting the breaths; this is called susoku. Every exhalation is the end of one breath. Susoku is counting each breath to ten and then repeating, again and again. The repetition acts as a mantra and helps to put you in direct contact with the land or ice beneath you. It's difficult at first until I get my rhythm going but soon it feels great and I start looking forward to reaching the top. On the way up I stop several times to look around. In the far distance I can see the camp now and it's comforting to know it is there. No one can hear me and probably can't see me as the tents appear tiny and I can't make out any figures. As I climb higher I am surprised, even shocked at the different kinds of stone and rock I come across. Before reaching the Antarctic one imagines the whole area as being one of endless kilometres of ice and snow. One doesn't associate it with rocks and mountains. Yet they are there. Although I knew about Mount Vinson being the highest mountain, it somehow seemed apart from the Antarctic itself and anyhow I thought of it as composed of stark rock faces, overall greyish in colour. The rocks and stones here are surprisingly full of colour and I spend a great deal of time handling and examining the smaller particles. The yellow ones, carrying the colour of enlightenment, are particularly wonderful to handle and there are all kinds of yellow and golden shades, as well as reds and silver and black. I gather together a selection of the smallest rocks and load up my pack with them. I am soon weighed down but I don't want to leave any behind, also I will probably climb down a different way and may not see the same examples again. I very much want to examine those I've collected when I return to camp. Rocks, stones and water are essential Zen elements and are used to design natural gardens to imitate and pay homage to nature's forces. Most stones speak but you have to listen with your eyes.

After climbing much higher, straining under the extra weight, I step on to an upper ice ridge. It's a moment to stop and listen. The ice glistens with a vast array of colours which refuse to submit to my intrusion. At last I reach the topmost ridge and I can see way into the distance in all directions. Zen Master Funei always declaimed, 'Zen study only aims at perception of essential nature.' I relish feeling the immense power of Antarctic nature. For a few moments I feel I am truly a part of it. I continue climbing along the main ridge for some distance. In parts it's knife-edged and I need to step warily to avoid slipping. I decide to trek off to the right and look for other rock and ice sections and different ways to proceed. It is still extremely icy and again I have to tread very carefully to avoid slipping. It would be all too easy to take off and zoom down. In view of the difficulties I am encountering it seems even stranger that I was allowed to go off on my own. Well I'm here now and it's too late to consider whether that was a wise decision of theirs, let alone my own. Still I climb and scramble ultra-carefully. I have certainly gained immeasurably by the fact they have let me go. Perhaps they understood this and that my gain would outweigh any dangers I might face.

I make my way along the ridges for several hours but always make certain I keep the direction of the camp in mind, to guide me when I need to make my way back. Although the camp is big the area around is so vast it would only take a small diversion in direction to miss it altogether. I could stay out much longer but as it is my first full day I finally decide it would be wiser to turn around before I become tired. Of course I take one or two more interesting small rocks with me from the top ridge. Rocks in this region range in age from as recent as 250,000 years old to more than 1 million. This is certainly the place to feel high!

I hadn't realised how far I had come and it takes a very long time before I eventually climb down the final section and reach the edge of the ice plain. The sight of the camp has now completely vanished and I am again all too aware how easy it would be to head off in the wrong direction. Still I set off very confidently and start on my way back across the ice. It's more slippery than ever and I am making slower progress than I expected. I soon start feeling more tired than I had anticipated, in my excitement I have definitely overdone it on the first day. However, there's no other choice but to keep going and I plod slowly on.

Suddenly I see a ski-doo making it's way across the ice and I wave enthusiastically to attract the driver's attention. At least this would be one way of confirming I am definitely heading in the right direction. At first whoever's driving it doesn't see me and it starts pulling away. I shout out but my voice doesn't seem to have enough strength to carry for any distance, I'm probably more weary than I realised. Just my luck, the wind has strengthened so that it is also preventing the sound of my voice carrying across. Then amazingly the ski-doo veers round and heads straight towards me. It is a wonderful moment. Although I am not really in any danger it is especially welcoming now to see another human being. My moments of solitude are coming to an end, for the time being.

As the ski-doo slows to a halt next to me I recognise the rumply, rotund figure of Art Mortvedt. Art, sweet man that he is, has come out specifically to look for me and bring me back. He thought that I had been out too long and he was worried. Art runs a wilderness camp in Alaska where he organises fishing, boating and a whole range of outdoor activities. His camp is called Peace Of Selby Wilderness and the name indicates the kind of place it is, as well as something of Art's own philosophy. His warmth and caring attitude show how much he must think about the welfare of his guests. He is obviously a treasure to enjoy at first hand if I ever have the chance to travel in Alaska. I clamber on board and Art drives off. I can feel my pack pressing down with the weight of the rocks and every now and then they clink rhythmically. I hope Art does not hear as my explanation might appear a little strange, although he is a man of the outdoors and would presumably understand.

On the way back we see the Twin Otter taking off and Art tells me that it is taking Hans and Christian to the mountains to enable them to attempt Vinson. That's really great news and it gives me hope that Ian and I might also have our chance at the Pole soon.

Chapter Nine

Telling Stories Out of School

Once back at the camp everyone welcomes me back enthusiastically and wants to hear about my adventures in the mountains. They are surprised that I had the energy to accomplish so much. After some much-needed tea I take out my stones and rocks and they seem interested in my theories. However, these are my memories and they have probably seen more than enough rocks for themselves. We look through just in case we can find a meteorite but it's not likely. I would have to break them open to really find out and I don't want to do that and anyway the odds are so much against.

After thoroughly cleaning and studying them, I put a few aside and carry the rest outside, where they will not be in anyone's way. Using their interesting and unusual colours and shapes I build a small, symbolic, Zen rock garden. Within the snow setting it creates a vibrancy and looks like a miniaturised Japanese rock and water garden. I am able to emphasise the effect by using some flat, circular shapes to imitate the flow of water around the rocks. Everyone comes out to see and they are finally impressed. Hopefully they at last understand what I have been trying to explain. By the next day the wind blows more loose snow around the camp and it quickly obliterates the sight of my Zen garden. Still I know it is there and in my imagination I see the rocks. With any luck they are still there, even now.

Max is still very non-committal about our chances of taking off tomorrow. I try not to show my disappointment or fears in case it sets him even more against making an attempt. Shortly afterwards, as if to prove his point and emphasise the dangers in the region, one of the other pilots returns with Hans and Christian. The winds had been so intense he hadn't dared fly close to the mountains, in case his aircraft was blown on to the rocks. Also there was a lot of mist, creating the very real danger of flying into them because of the poor visibility. He hadn't been able land anywhere near enough to set the two of them down, so they could tent for the night and try in the morning, even if the weather had improved. They were naturally disappointed but I had to admire their sangfroid as they merely shrugged, smiled and said they would try again when the weather improved.

We gather around one of the long central tables and start talking about previous expeditions in other parts of the world. At present there's little else to do and dinner is not for an hour. Everyone has stories to relate and no one more so than our guide, Steve Pinfield. He tells us about his difficulties on various films, acting as either stuntman or guide in some very inhospitable terrains. On location in Kenya one of the actors he had been hired to protect had been scared of practically everything, imagining snakes and spiders in his tent and inside his sleeping bag and luggage. Steve had to go everywhere with him and check it out before the actor would enter his tent, or even stand and deliver his lines to camera. The latrine tent always had to be meticulously examined first and afterwards Steve would stand on guard outside. Eventually the actor suffered a nervous breakdown and was flown home, which Steve said was just as well, he had been on the point of braining him!

Steve's story reminds me of the film actor, Victor Mature, who played Samson in the over-the-top Hollywood 1949 extravaganza, *Samson and Delilah* (the female lead was Hedy Lamarr, the incredible Hungarian beauty, who earlier in her career had swum naked in the subsequently banned film, *Ecstasy*). Victor Mature was also extremely frightened of animals and in one of the most important scenes where he had to wrestle with a lion he refused, claiming he was in mortal danger. The film producer, Cecil B. De Mille told him not to worry as the lion was completely docile and anyhow had no teeth. Mature wasn't convinced and still worried in case he was gummed to death! In the end they had to use a stand-in for the fighting shots and drug the lion for the close-ups. I told Steve if he'd been stunting on the set he would have had to allow the lion to chew him up a little. Most people, including Mature himself, thought his acting was rather wooden and that he couldn't act himself out of the proverbial paper bag. Mature, to his credit, tells the story against himself of the time he applied to join a snooty Hollywood club in the days when being an actor was mostly looked down upon. 'Sorry,' he was told, 'no actors admitted here.'

'I'm no actor,' Mature replied, 'and I've got a score of films and notices to prove it.' The ladies however loved him and every year he threw a birthday party inviting only former girlfriends and they all still came. The parties just got bigger and bigger. Only he stayed the same age.

Steve has also worked with an actor I've had some dealings with. He is such a heavy drinker that Steve spent his entire time on location in the rainforest hiding the alcohol from him or finding excuses why he couldn't fetch any. Somehow the actor still found his own supply, so there were many hairy jungle moments and the other actors had to shoot their scenes talking alone to the camera. The director was going completely crazy by the end and probably took to the bottle himself! The actor is extremely talented and skilful but I think now his drinking reputation precedes him and that's why he's not as successful as he might have been. Unfortunately, those who drink heavily usually become 'might-have-beens' or 'has-beens'.

Steve also tells about one film crew member who broke both legs and needed to be airlifted out. Steve eventually got a helicopter to fly into the jungle area but they needed to keep the man lying flat out and there was not enough room to do this inside the helicopter. So all they could do is strap him underneath with two huge pillows under him for support. The story then becomes very gruesome; one pillow flies up into the blades, the pilot loses control and the helicopter crashes, killing the man underneath. The pilot staggers out of the crashed helicopter but the engine is still running, the blades are still rotating and he is hit by one and loses an arm. It's a story to end all the stories and there is utter silence at this very sad tale. I imagine it will make Max even more likely to hold back from flying, if there is the slightest question of a problem. It's a story we could have done without.

I try to break the gloom by putting on the Ella Fitzgerald tape I've brought with me but it takes some time before everyone calms down and conversation picks up. I try to lighten the mood and throw in a kind of self-explanatory conundrum. 'A man suspects his wife is being unfaithful and she goes off with some friends, including the one he suspects, to an island. There are no bridges, no boats and no airstrip. She thinks she is perfectly safe. But no such luck, by helicopter!' (By-hell-he-copped-her.) Some faces are blank but Steve laughs immediately, he is such good fun to be with. He is very sympathetic about my concerns on making it to the Pole before I have to return and advises me to talk to Max's girlfriend, Ann. She is staying out here with him for a few weeks and Steve suggests she might persuade him to move the flying schedule ahead. Ann is actually British and has been with Max for some years. I ask her about his torn jersey and why he doesn't throw it away and wear another one and she laughs out loud. 'You should see the state of the other ones he has back home in New Zealand!'

Steve tries to buck Ian and me up and tells us that if we don't fly tomorrow he will arrange an excursion on ski-doos. We can travel to the nearby mountains where we can tent overnight and explore the ice and rock ranges. That sounds just great and my mood improves immediately. Ian Ford is keen and the doctor Ann Ward wants to join us. One of the cooks, Fran Orio, hears our plans and asks if she can come with us. As there are so few in the camp her colleague, Ros, readily agrees.

Also in the camp is a somewhat enigmatic Polish film director. His first name is Jerczy and his last name seems completely unpronounceable, as it has a whole string of consonants with possibly only two vowels to pull them together. He doesn't speak much English and only a little French. Previously I had made the big mistake of trying to converse with him in French. From then on as soon as Jerczy sees me he invariably makes a beeline in my direction and we have some very convoluted conversations. He's a nice guy but our talks aren't going too far.

Our rather hesitant contact immediately reminds me of my old Latin teacher who was rather ominously called Mr Judge. He had been blinded in the war and taught by relying purely on his amazing recall of the text books he'd used from before. Mr Judge was a stern, tough and exacting teacher, perhaps because of his blindness, and was always jury as well as judge. With him there was never any chance of an appeal. The reason Jerczy had made me think of him was that Mr Judge had the strangest explanation of why it was necessary to know Latin. He had been in a prisoner of war camp and his bunk companion was Polish. Neither could speak the other's language and they were only able to communicate by speaking in Latin. 'So you see,' he would exclaim triumphantly, 'Latin isn't a dead language, you never know when it might come in useful.' It seemed more than a little far-fetched, but I always took his explanation in good grace. He was such a brave man, I'd often walk with him to his bus stop and he would accept my companionship but never on the basis that I was in any way assisting him. Perhaps it was my first encounter with the Zen spirit which has come to mean so much to me.

Mr Judge was determined never to allow himself ever to be dependent on anyone or ask for any help. I very much admired his courage but he was, in reality, impossible to actually like. He was ramrod stiff, mostly harsh in manner and rarely smiled. He never gave any quarter, perhaps because he never asked for any. He was as tough on me in class as on everyone else, often tougher I thought. However, he is the teacher I remember the most. That's probably why I usually respond to Polish people more sympathetically, they invariably remind me of Mr Judge and his bizarre conversations in Latin in a POW camp.

When Jerczy hears I am going on this tenting expedition overnight he also wants to come along to take photographs in the mountains and Steve agrees he can. It is turning into a large party and I feel that soon we will be emptying the camp. But it also means that there will be fewer people in the camp for Ros to feed and that makes it easier for Fran to get away. I am really looking forward to the trip and to staying out in the mountains, but first there is the rest of the evening to enjoy. They have laid on a huge dinner, plenty to drink, music of a kind and I again try to manoeuvre my tapes into those being chosen. Most don't seem bothered either way whereas I like what I like, though my tastes are as broad as a broad can be (to quote from *Damn Yankees*, or is it *South Pacific*? Or perhaps both). I mix in Pavarotti and Duke Ellington and of course the Stones.

Then it's time to wander outside, buttoned up, hatted and double-coated into the utter brightness that is the Antarctic night in December. It feels like the end of the world, which in one sense it is and there's utter magic in the frosty, breath-swallowing air. I wander over to my Byrd tent, take out my toilet bag and make a quick dash over to the latrine igloo. Fortunately the red flags are pointing upwards and I can take my choice of either one. I check and decide the left one is the better for now. Tomorrow it could easily change. Then back to Byrd and bed.

Chapter Ten

Baby, It's Cold Out There

Next morning I wake up crouched way inside the sleeping bag, feeling very hot. I remember about the two pairs of socks and reach down to remove them. To my surprise my feet are bare. I must have taken them off in my sleep, unless I'd had a visitor! I re-dress hurriedly and make a quick dash over to the latrines. I hope to be the first into the cook tent but of course Fran is before me. She has already prepared our provisions for the journey to the mountains and staying out overnight in our tents.

Fran seems as excited as I do and I learn this is actually her first chance to leave the camp. I am surprised to hear that her cooking duties are so involving and they require her to be around most of each day and evening to prepare the meals. Although there are two cooks they are really always both needed, especially when there is a full contingent of explorers and travellers. It's as fortunate for her as for me that this time there are only the four of us making use of these excellent facilities. We are certainly getting the red carpet treatment. Her colleague is happy to double up in these circumstances and therefore Fran can take off most of the day and stay overnight with us. She seems to think that this opportunity has happened because of me and Ian and therefore she always tries to give me more. It's hard to resist and I need to exercise some double helpings away.

A 9.30 a.m. briefing on our proposed trip is organised in the Library tent, which also doubles up as a 'conference room' for any kind of special meeting or discussion. I am chuffed to find the US version of my book, *Zen In The Art Of Climbing Mountains* on one of the shelves. It's looking a bit worse for wear, as it's done the rounds and I promise to send out another one. Steve explains our planned route and what we will need to take with us. Principally our sleeping bags and two tents; the two women in one and three men in the other (Jerczy is taking his own). Also a stove, fuel, general and emergency rations and the essential shovel and flares – just in case. As on expeditions in the Arctic you always need things 'just in case'. The weather out here is like the most ferocious bear imaginable. Hopefully it will keep its distance but if it decides to roar and go for you, better be prepared for the long haul. Steve explains that a long haul here can mean several days or even weeks. Fortunately, Jerczy hasn't turned up for the briefing so I don't have to try and laboriously explain everything. He should be able to pick up what is necessary from watching the rest of us. Fran still needs to help prepare lunch so we agree to set off immediately afterwards.

We have a few hours to spare, so Art Mortvedt and Kris Hopping, the second camp organiser, arrange to take Ian and myself to visit a crashed DC6 that came down some years back. We travel out on two ski-doos and head out into what appears to be no man's land where everything looks the same to my untrained eyes. Fortunately Kris and Art have been this way several times so there is little chance of getting lost. Though if the winds come up suddenly, as they sometimes do, even they could quickly lose their bearings. However, they exude confidence so I place my trust in their judgement. We travel out for about 8 km and then we see it. It's eerie to see the way the aircraft has been slowly but steadily buried under the snow and little is now visible, just the nose and the tail where it snapped off on impact. But it is a clear statement of the power of the region and the need to take care at all times.

The aircraft came down in 1991. It was intended to be part of the commemorative expedition of Norman Vaughan, the famed polar explorer, who is the last surviving member of Admiral Byrd's 1928 expedition. The idea was to recreate one of his exploits in trekking through the ice fields with a team of huskies, as an homage to the fact that he was Admiral Byrd's dog sledge chief. Vaughan wasn't aboard this plane and fortunately no one was killed although the pilot and his one crew member were badly injured. The huskies mostly escaped and ran off into the wilderness and must have subsequently perished. This is an unsentimental place and it's a question of survival, not necessarily of the fittest but of those who understand the grave dangers which must be faced and overcome on so many occasions. It seems there were heavy mists at the time with strong winds gusting, the pilot was trying to avoid coming down at the Patriot Hills camp and was forced on to the rocks. Mt. Vaughan was named by Admiral Byrd after Norman Vaughn who heroically re-climbed the mountain in 1993 at the age of 89. He continues to live with his wife in a one-room log cabin, isolated in Alaska.

The last plane crash in these parts occurred in 1995 when a Canadian plane came down at Rothera, killing both of the crew. I am sobered at the sight and by the thought of the men and the dogs that perished and quietly take a few photographs. It is now bitterly cold and I worry that the camera batteries may not survive for long. I always put my camera away when it's not in use and keep it wrapped inside an old sock. All my socks are old socks!

On the way back I am very quiet, though on the back of a ski-doo it's hard to talk anyway. I feel the air currents moving aggressively around me and they dance without rhyme or reason as they try to force themselves belligerently into any uncovered space. Once back at camp there's a hot drink ready as well as lunch and soon it's time to take off again. We load up the two ski-doos, both with attached sledges full of tents, equipment and provisions and everyone in the cook tent comes out to wave us off. It's as if they won't be seeing us for some time. Do they know something I don't? Steve has me holding on at his back, with Ian lolling, king-like, on the trailer sledge. Fran has Ann behind her with Jerczy on their sledge. We can switch positions whenever we like, though I'm told only Steve, Fran and Ann are insured to drive. I wonder idly if my reputation for driving ski-doos and the story of my mishap in the Arctic has somehow arrived before me.

We set off at a leisurely pace towards the Ellesmere Mountains but I really want to experience speed and Steve is happy to oblige me. Soon we are racing along and Fran and Ann, alternating, are forced to keep up. I am guessing that they are finding it as exhilarating as I am. I glance back occasionally at Ian, though it's something of a risky manoeuvre, but he seems very content to be ferried at whatever speed we prefer. He has his own views and a different perspective. After an hour and a half we reach the destination Steve has chosen and smoothly slow to a halt.

We pitch tents in the plateau and I remember one of my first lessons in climbing and tenting. Always put up your tent in the open, away from the shelter of the mountain in case there is an avalanche, particularly during the night. Another way of expressing that concept; 'A good shelter in a bad location is a bad shelter.' Jerczy has of course brought his own single tent with him and pitches it some distance away from us. He decides he will do his own thing, concentrate on taking his photographs and make his own meals from the provisions he has with him. It seems more than a little strange, even odd thoughts of espionage flit through my mind but are quickly banished. If he wants to be on his own I can understand that and accept it is his way. Often it's my way.

Out here there is no such thing as a set time for doing anything; it's always the same light conditions. Unanimously we decide to eat first, then trek and climb afterwards. Steve is also an expert cook and as he has Fran with him the three others primarily leave the preparation to the two of them. We just set out the fold-up table and chairs, the plates and cutlery and await their culinary results. Ann, Ian and I can then wander around this beautiful landscape, there is much to marvel at. The snow and ice are rich in tonal colour with so many variations and I am gradually coming to appreciate the differences. At times it's difficult to believe I am actually here and trekking through the Antarctic. It's likely that all of us are making first time footprints, this is such a large territory and so few have passed this way. We don't have long to wait however and the food is soon ready. It's simple but plentiful and tastes absolutely delicious. Perhaps we should open a restaurant in Antarctica for travellers. We would corner the market, although there might be long gaps between customers. We finish everything to the last morsel and Ian and I volunteer to clean up. It's only fair. 'Be our guests.' At least that way we don't have to leave tips.

There's another important and necessary task, latrine duty, that's primarily why we needed the shovel. We all agree to share. Even out here in complete isolation, in an area that may never be visited again by another human being it is only right that we dig a hole and bury all human and food wastes. Anything that is not bio-degradable of course we will take back to camp with us when we leave. The latrine is dug just behind the parked ski-doos. We put in a black plastic bin liner to make it easier to transport it all away afterwards, when we decide whether the contents should be buried or taken back with us. It's very basic but we mustn't in any way despoil this ice paradise and in case of fierce winds we use two ski poles to hold the bag in place.

Now we are ready for our first sortie to the mountains themselves. We trek across the ice basin and up the snow lines and shortly reach the first rock formations. I am very keen to keep going but Steve advises that we keep it short. He suggests we have an early start tomorrow, so after just two hours we return to our camp. Now it's time for another meal, which probably is dinner. It doesn't matter here what you call a meal, all you have to do is eat it. Again I am a spectator at the feast, at least till it's prepared, but a full participant in the eating of it. Another delicious repast. There's just enough time for one more story: The famed detective Sherlock Holmes and his faithful companion Dr. Watson are tenting in the mountains. A few hours after they have turned in, Holmes nudges Watson and tells him to look up.

'What do you see?'

Watson replies, 'Millions of stars.'

Holmes continues, 'Well Watson what does that tell you?'

Watson thinks for a moment, knowing he is being tested once again, before gravely replying. 'Astronomically, it tells me there must be millions of galaxies. Horologically, I deduce the time to be about 4 a.m. Theologically, that God is all powerful. Meteorologically, I expect we will have a fine day tomorrow. What does it tell you Holmes?'

Holmes pauses, as always, for effect. 'Not bad Watson,' he begins, 'But what it tells me is that someone has stolen our tent!'

Now it really is time for us to bed down in our tents or 'Himalayan Hotels' as they are sometimes called and they are certainly roomy.

Ann and Fran are in first and we can see their flickering movements through the transparent tent material, illuminated by their torches. The images they conjure up are shadowy ghosts. They remind me of one of my journeys I made through China, at a time when there was very sparse use of electricity. In the evenings you would see, or in reality hardly see, hundreds of Chinese cycling through the gloom, without any bicycle lights, looking very much like ghostly figures, constantly appearing and disappearing. We decide theirs is the yin tent, the female one and ours the yang tent, the male. I stroll over to wish the girls a good night's sleep and interesting Chinese dreams, although they don't understand why. They actually look quite isolated and vulnerable but at least they don't have to worry about bears in the Antarctic. Besides we are only a shadow away and if there's a problem I tell them to whistle, a la Lauren Bacall. They both attempt to but without much success. Still they understand we can come running.

baby, it's cold out there

In our tent Ian has taken one side and Steve generously takes the middle position to leave me the other side. Ian is out like a light and his immediate and heavy snoring in such a confined space is deafening. Steve gives him a hefty nudge but it only works for a short time and he has to repeat the action throughout the night. I put in some earplugs and will myself to doze off during Ian's quieter moments and soon I am asleep in a tent on a plateau, in the middle of Antarctica. Apart from Ian's snores and Steve's nudges there is only the sound of silence.

We all seem to sleep late but I get up at around 6 a.m. to dress and stagger out to the luxury latrine we have created. Half-undressing in that sub-zero temperature is absolutely freezing. I recall the old saying about a brass monkey and can certainly appreciate here what it implies. Finally everyone else gets up and we prepare and enjoy a leisurely breakfast. It's fun eating al fresco in Antarctica and the food has a flavour all its own and even clearing up is an adventure of a kind. Still, plenty of hot drinks are called for until I remember how difficult and cold it can be to relieve oneself and decide to restrict the amount of my liquid intake.

Around 9 a.m. we start an extensive hike up through the ice fields to explore the higher mountainous regions. It's tiring but exhilarating at the same time and I can't stop myself marvelling at the vastly different landscapes that are always visible. I'm behaving like someone who's never seen snow before – but this is Antarctic snow! Before coming out I imagined that everything would look mostly the same yet I am finding that there are an endless variety of textures, colours, shapes, within the snow and ice fields, the rock and stone formations and the rolling hills and mountain ranges.

The sun is nowhere to be seen, mists cover the skyline, but it's still very bright, although bitterly cold and it's better to keep moving. We reach a section of enormous crevasses and skirt cautiously round them. Steve warns us, although I don't think we need to be told, that the edges are not safe and could crumble and take us down into the pit of the basin. It could be very soft snow there as well and falling might easily cause a person to be buried. Even if that didn't occur it would be extremely difficult to climb the crevasse sides and we don't have ropes with us that would be long enough to haul anyone out. The answer is not to fall in. We all keep a further distance back after hearing that.

There are all kinds of strangely-shaped peaks and the rocks look interesting for climbing. One in particular is known as the Minaret because of its high conical shape and I want to inspect it more closely. However, that wouldn't be fair to the others who would have to wait around in these freezing temperatures which is not advisable. It certainly seems climbable and when I learn it has never been scaled before it is a great temptation. Most people of course come here to climb Mount Vinson, the highest mountain in the whole of the continent of Antarctica, and therefore rarely have time to attempt anything else.

I wonder if Hans and Christian have yet had the opportunity to start off again for Vinson and I certainly hope so. I'll have to wait till I get back to camp before I can know. Steve has a walkie-talkie transmitter with him, but it is only to be used for emergencies and not for unimportant matters. Steve invites me to climb Vinson with him on another occasion and that seems too good an offer to pass up, but first I need to get to the South Pole. That is, if Max is happy with the state of his beloved Cessna and accepts the weather conditions as flyable. When we get back to camp I'll find that out as well.

We trek on for several hours and each new view is as spectacular as the previous one. I could go on and on. I guess we must have trekked a distance of well over 15 km but Steve reckons half that and explains that distances out here are often deceptive. However, because we are climbing diagonally I feel we may have done more. Whatever area we have covered it was a magnificently enjoyable journey through virgin territory. Due to the vastness and constantly changing landscape it is very likely that no one else has ever come this way before. I have to acknowledge more than ever the extraordinary feats of the really great polar explorers who trekked for thousands of kilometres, there and back through the Antarctic, in the quests to achieve their goals. There's a rock, silhouetted against the skyline, curved like a half moon. I refer to the immensely thought-provoking statement of a the Japanese actor/director Yoshi Oida. 'I can show you the gesture that indicates looking at the moon. I can teach you the movement up to the tip of the finger which points to the sky. From the tip of the finger to the moon is your own responsibility.' It's something to contemplate as we trudge onwards and upwards.

The weather starts to deteriorate fast, as it so often can in this region and we need to head back urgently. Being trapped in a snowstorm out here wouldn't be much fun, particularly as it could last for many hours, even days. We have trekked and climbed further than we should and perhaps my enthusiasm was partly to blame. I keep my head down and don't dally any longer and as a party, at the pace of the slowest, we head back to our tents. Steve has an excellent sense of direction, presumably a prerequisite for any guide, and in an unerring way leads us directly, and by the shortest route, back to our makeshift camp.

It is blowing hard and he thinks it wise to pack up and head back straightaway. We even consider hunkering down for another night but Steve doesn't like the look of the weather at all and decides we must get back. Also Fran of course has to return to help Ros in the kitchen with the preparation and serving of meals. It wouldn't go down at all well if she stays out another night. Besides, who knows, perhaps tomorrow may be the opportunity Ian and I have been waiting for to take off for the Pole. If that is missed there might not be another for some time. If anything is going to convince me, that last supposition is and I am the most active in taking down the tents and packing up the sledges. We have to find Jerczy who is peacefully resting inside his tent and oblivious to everything. He naturally agrees, although more reluctantly, to pack up and come back with us.

By the time we are ready to set off the increasing wind force has turned into a gale and the visibility is reducing rapidly. Steve appears unperturbed and I have every confidence in his ability to get us back safely. He drives one ski-doo and Fran the other. Steve takes Ann and Ian, Fran has me and Jerczy. She is strong and determined and seems to know exactly how to handle the vehicle. At times we are heading directly into the wind, visibility is greatly reduced and we have to slow speeds so as not to lose contact with each other. Both ski-doos are being battered by the ferocity of the winds and it would be very easy to turn over, particularly if we hit a hidden rock or a very hard piece of ice. If that happened it is essential that the others could rescue anyone hurt or help to right the ski-doo. If one is damaged I shudder to think how we would manage, I doubt that one ski-doo could pull two sledges and all of us.

Every so often Steve stops to make certain that Fran is alright and isn't too tired to continue. It is taking a tremendous effort to hold each ski-doo on course and keep it balanced. She has to fight hard not to allow the huge gusts of wind to rock it too much causing it to topple over. It is very slow and cold progress and all any of us who aren't driving can do is to keep still, hold on tightly and not get in the way. We try to give as much encouragement as possible, but in these worsening conditions it is almost impossible to hear what anyone is saying. It becomes absolutely freezing and even through our double gloves and mittens I can feel the intensity of the cold. I wish I was now wearing the two pairs of socks I left back in my Byrd tent. I know the two drivers holding tenaciously on to the steering wheels must be having a much worse time.

Time loses all meaning and we are in an imprisoned vacuum, filled with noise and turbulence which controls our destinies. Zen Master Bazo expressed the feelings that all of us must be experiencing, 'In the bitterness of the wind you feel the bottom of your mind.' I send every particle of my energy through to Fran and encourage her own will to continue. She seems to respond and continues to fight on with tremendous courage. I know she will make it through and so will we.

Chapter Eleven

Year In, Year Out

Hours later we see the lights of Patriot Hills and a more welcome sight it is hard to imagine. We are practically blown in. Steve and Fran drive in, very uneasy riders. We've made it, thanks to more than a little bit of luck and determination to get through the eye of the storm. The camp has endured the same horrendous weather conditions we have, but at least everyone there was inside. There are huge snow drifts covering everything and piled high around the tents and access areas. The pathways have been totally obliterated. We need to dismount to get through the last section. We quickly unload and dump our bags into our tents. It takes quite an effort just to push the snow from the flaps and scramble an entry.

Then it's a race into the cook tent where we hurriedly pour down several very welcome cups of steaming coffee which slowly work through to warm the extremities. Fran seems totally unfazed and is immediately in the kitchen section to help Ros continue preparing the evening meal. There are streamers around and everything seems unusually festive. Being so far removed from my normal daily life, here in a world where it is always daylight and dusk never occurs, I have lost track of time and date. It is actually New Year's Eve. We are going to have a special New Year meal and party. Wow! I will be celebrating the New Year in Antarctica. This will truly be a time to remember. I think back a few hours, how it could have ended so differently. I could have spent it huddled inside a frozen tent or even worse – crouching next to an upturned ski-doo. This is definitely going to be a night I won't forget.

There are still some hours before dinner is ready and the celebrations have been arranged later than usual to occur nearer the bewitching hour of midnight, Antarctic time. First I decide to trudge through the deep snow back to my tent to change. I think the occasion also calls for a shave and indeed an overall wash. Most of the others think I am going a little too far, as they don't think there's a need to change or clean up especially. One announces formally, 'There's no need to panic, the Queen's not coming after all.' What does he mean?

I return to find everyone else has already congregated inside the cook tent. There are coloured balloons, flags of all nations, streamers and anything else colourful draped across the sides of the tent. Immediately I walk in and have taken off my outer garments, I am grabbed and forced to join in the toasts to the numerous countries we represent. I don't need much forcing. When we finish those off we start on those not represented.

I am also delighted to learn that Robert Swan, the first person to walk to both Poles, is expected. Robert is heading up an expedition associated to UNICEF. They are taking a multi-national group of children to the Antarctic by ship. Robert had originally been trekking across the north-west peninsula to join the ship. After travelling for some days he changed his plans and had decided to travel across to us. He would then fly on to Punta Arenas and fly in to join up with his team. It seems an astonishing coincidence to me (although it is said there are no such thing as coincidences, only God's incidences), that on my original journey to reach the North Pole all those years previously, the expedition had flown in a Twin-Otter over Robert Swan's team as they had slowly and painfully trekked to the Pole and now we are to meet again on our way to the South. Over the years, Robert and I have met on several occasions. He has given me signed copies of his books and particularly *Icewalk*, the heroic story of his harrowing but triumphant North Pole saga. When Robert arrives, to everyone's astonishment and somewhat to my embarrassment, he gives me a huge bear hug. He is very pleased to see me and we swap stories of how we both came to be here in the Antarctic at the same time. Robert also feels it is quite something special that I also saw him in the Arctic, even from a plane. Robert looks wider than I remember but it's probably the numerous layers of clothing he is wearing, as he has been trekking through intensely cold winds. Gradually he unbuttons and removes layer upon layer as the hot wine he gulps down starts to do the trick. Like the other experienced polar guys he sees no need to change or wash up. He has several days growth of beard. I wonder if the facial hair grows slower in the polar regions. I hadn't noticed any difference myself.

Robert's arrival gives me the assurance and a lead-in to ask Max Wenden what the chances are of flying to the Pole tomorrow. He's as non-committal as ever and still gives me no encouragement. Max of course hasn't changed anything and is still wearing his torn jersey, although the tears seem to have widened. Dinner arrives and it's a feast! Huge portions of turkey (absentmindedly I wonder if they've got the holidays mixed up as it's not Thanksgiving or even Christmas), several kinds of stuffing, mashed potatoes, cauliflower, carrots; followed by mince pies, fruit and cheese. There is a non-stop flow of wine and champagne.

I am put in charge of the music, although most don't seem to notice as they just raise their voices louder to continue their noisy and excitable conversations. Robert is as loud as everyone else, he has tremendous energy and vitality. Every so often he hugs me and again we tell everyone *ad nauseum* how we have connected on the way to both Poles.

It's getting close to the midnight hour and we all don wigs and dress up in fanciful clothing Ann has gathered from somewhere. Soon we all start dancing, no one cares with whom or with what sex. It's almost midnight and the countdown is about to commence. As the seconds tick away everyone kisses everyone. We toast each other, our families and friends, those who are in our thoughts but so very far away. They toast the Ice but don't explain; I'll learn why much later. In return I offer a special toast to all the polar explorers of yesterday, now and tomorrow; the past is history, the future is a mystery, today is a gift, that's why it's called the present. Everyone thinks that deserves more than one drink and there are no further toasts needed to give us reasons.

It must have been pre-arranged as a quiz game is quickly organised. We are divided into three teams, oddly named Rednecks, Frocks and Famished. Max is on my team and I continue to try, but just as unsuccessfully, to steer our conversation to the weather being OK in the morning for a polar flight. The quiz questions are extremely wide ranging and often peculiar and we all get more wrong than right. Two of those I recall answering: Which English artist was in an asylum and killed his father? Richard Dadd (get it?) and who wrote the screenplay of *Dr Zhivago* after writing for miles? Robert Bolt who was married to Sarah Miles. We are all telling silly jokes and it's probably the buckets of wine we're knocking back, but that last answer leads me to ask what is the longest word in the English language. After several ludicrous guesses I reveal it's smiles, as there's a mile between the first and last letters.

The evening, although it's well into the morning, deteriorates even more rapidly and I cannot drink any more, although Robert and many others obviously can. I try one last attempt to influence Max to consider flying tomorrow. I have to give up as I can see he's also too far gone and I can't imagine him getting up early in the morning and wanting to fly all the way to the South Pole. I ask Ann his girlfriend to try and intercede on my behalf and then start to leave the tent to turn in. Duncan, his managerial responsibility still keeping him sufficiently sober, grabs hold of my arm. He shouts loudly into my ear, as if the drink has reduced all my senses, 'Go straight to your tent and don't wander around. When you've been drinking you chill much more rapidly and your body temperature will tumble fast; hypothermia could set in and you might not get up.' It's sound advice as I also know from my climbing expeditions and I step slowly but purposely to my Byrd tent. I only tumble when I reach the mattress, drag off my boots and coat and crawl inside my sleeping bag. Happy New Year! Instantly I fall asleep.

Chapter Twelve

Mountain Highs

I am up later than anticipated, too much wine the night before. I don't expect to see Max for some time but to my surprise he is already in the cook tent drinking his coffee. I give him an enquiring look but he doesn't respond, so I ask the usual, direct question. Max tells me he has already been at the Met tent checking out weather conditions. The forecast for White Fields, the intermittent stop on the way to the Pole, is not good and it would be taking too much of a chance to fly. It would be dishonest not to admit that the thought crosses my mind that perhaps Max just doesn't feel like going today, particularly as he must have drunk as much as anyone the night before.

I can't even begin to hide my disappointment and really feel the days are ticking ominously by. Perhaps there won't ever be a time when the weather conditions are perfect enough to make the whole journey. Max sees my impatience and concern but says he will only go when he feels all the elements are in our favour and there is a very good chance of making it all the way. He knows Ian and I are scheduled to fly to the South Pole as part of Adventure Network's commitment to us but that can only occur when it is likely to be a successful flight back as well as flying out. Otherwise the costs involved of starting the series of flights and not completing would be exorbitant. I wonder about hiring personally and ask the price if anyone was to hire the Cessna privately. Max tells me it's a staggering $2,500 per hour!

On an overall round trip taking well over 12 hours I can see immediately how costly this whole exercise of travelling to the South Pole would be. It again makes me realise how honourable Annie Kershaw has been and the special ethos of her company in agreeing to go ahead with the expedition, with only Ian and myself going to the Pole and Hans and Christian to Mount Vinson. Even though so many of those planning to come didn't follow through as she had expected, Annie still went ahead with her commitment to us. She must be making a considerable loss overall. There's no choice, I have to wait it out and hope the weather conditions will improve and more importantly that Max will consider they have improved sufficiently for him to take us.

Max reminds me that the Amundsen-Scott Station at the Pole is run on New Zealand time, being the closest country, which means it is 17 hours ahead. If we want to arrive with sufficient time to tour the base, assuming that we are allowed in, then we have to time our departure from Patriot Hills accordingly. The base is only officially open 8 a.m. till 5 p.m., again New Zealand time. Several of the staff have also arrived now and we start arguing about the possible times we could arrive at the Pole Base Camp. It's surprising, given that most have spent months out here, how widely different are their calculations and answers.

Eventually I am forced to write out a schedule of possible flight departures and flying times, showing expected arrival times, before everyone finally accepts one formula. We agree, assuming there are no unusual problems, that the flight time is 6 hours, not including the stopover at White Fields. That means that if we leave here at 9 a.m. we should arrive there on local time shortly after 8 a.m. the next day; if we left here at 4 p.m. we should arrive after 3 p.m. the next day. Ideally then we should always try to leave in the morning, to allow for problems and delays and provide us with sufficient time to tour around the base.

During the rest of the morning I spend most of my time walking between the Met hut, the cook tent, and Max, who is mostly tinkering with the Cessna, to ask him if it's time yet. I start to feel like Laurence Olivier, playing the fanatical Nazi ex-dentist in *Marathon Man*, interrogating Dustin Hoffman and continually asking him, 'Is it safe?' Hoffman has no idea what to reply or what Olivier really wants to hear, so first replies negatively, then positively, then changes constantly as Olivier keeps boring relentlessly into the root of one of his teeth. I am probably boring everyone with my enquiries although they all take it in good part. In the end we are down to my raised eyebrow and their head shakes and shoulder shrugs. Eventually I can anticipate their responses just by the slant of their heads or the position of their shoulders.

As the hours roll by I slow my pace as I don't expect any affirmative reply. Time relentlessly moves on until it is close to 1 p.m. I finally accept, as much to my own relief as everyone else's, that today we won't be going. Ian has left all the chasing and motivating over the last few days to me; he seems to have sunk into a kind of stupor in which he has no control over any events and must await the outcome of what ever will be. Another time I might have argued that he was being Zen-like and showing extreme patience but I know that this isn't the case. Zen, often misunderstood by those who haven't studied or learned any, is not about doing nothing and waiting for something to occur. It is about doing everything you can to make something happen, but then not being brought down if it doesn't. A form of

Zen I often use when climbing or trekking is known as kinhin. It is a very active Zen, full of strength and will keep you battling beyond your normal capabilities.

There are several *Antarctica Sun Times* to read but I've soon worked through the whole lot. In one there's a cartoon of two visitors being asked by the camp manager what they've been doing all day. Just behind the tent, dwarfing it, is a gigantic snowman; I can certainly understand the joke, although not necessarily appreciating it at this moment. I must accept that I have done all I can do for now and I will bow to the inevitable. Today we will not be attempting to reach the Pole. Tomorrow is another day.

Now I really have had enough of people. I want to be apart from everyone in the camp, kind souls though they are. I must be on my own. I decide I'll trek out again and the camp managers willingly agree. Perhaps they would also like some peace. They ask me to be cautious in my climbing and not to attempt too much. I promise to return for dinner. I'm so anxious to set off I don't want to wait for lunch and Fran makes me some cheese sandwiches. Additionally I take a full thermos of hot water, apples and bananas. Also, of course, plenty of extra clothing including my large parka and a ski stick. Rachel Shepherd, another camp assistant (camp is a noun not an adjective!), kindly lends me her portable walkie-talkie, to call back in case of any emergency and shows me how to operate it. It doesn't seem difficult and I think I understand. Let's hope I won't need it.

I set off at a fast pace, eager to put some distance between me and the camp. In a way I'm surprised how easily they let me go. But it's the way that climbers and explorers behave, one to another; a person is allowed to take any chance he or she decides is acceptable, provided it is not putting anyone else at risk. Art catches up with me on the ski-doo and offers me a lift to the edge of the mountains well beyond the airstrip. After a moment's hesitation I accept, he's really an exceptional man. It will also save well over an hour's laborious trekking across the very slippery ice field and will save me a lot of energy. Zen is explained as being effortless but requiring enormous effort and any way to conserve energy enables you to go that little bit further. Anyhow I enjoy being in Art's company as he never intrudes and is just there. You can talk to him or not, either way he's happy. He is so easy to be with he makes me keen to visit his Alaskan retreat. His own philosophy must imbue the place with a deep meaning and create a positive purpose which can only help one to understand that little bit more. That's really all most of us can or should ask for in life. The ski-doo trip takes just under 20 minutes. Art doesn't ever race and likes to feel the ice just below him and I am happy to go at his speed. He drops me at the beginning of the ice ridge, wishes me well, turns around and drives off immediately without a backward glance. The Antarctic quickly swallows him up as he crosses over a ridge and is soon out of sight.

I am alone. For a brief moment it is almost frightening. I feel as if I am the only man in the world, no one else left. It feels as if I could head off in any direction and never be seen again. Whatever the emotions I am experiencing I allow them to run over and through me. I may never be this alone again and I want to feel what that means. Being lost in the jungle, as I have been, is not the same. At least there you see and smell trees and plants, swaying and rustling and the sounds of other animals, whether welcome or not. Here there is nothing, no sense of smell, not the tiniest creature to be aware of. It feels beautiful, immensely so, but at the same time it is barren, desolate, abandoned even. What would it really be like to be the last man alive? I can remember the protest marches against the nuclear bomb; it was the fear of it causing the world to die that made so many people feel they must dedicate their lives to protesting against the manufacture of atomic weapons. Perhaps the world leaders should hold their disarmament conferences in Antarctica.

Whilst thinking these wild and rather gloomy thoughts, my legs have not stood still. They have taken me, almost of their own accord, up the first rock section. Now they are battling across a jagged shale field that causes me to slip and slide in all directions. I have to concentrate to stay upright and I force my mind to focus on the heavy work ahead. I use the ski stick to good advantage and manage to make good progress and fairly quickly reach the top of the first ridge. There are plenty to go but first I reward myself with a banana, folding the skin inside my pack to bring back. It proves impossible to wear my backpack over my very thick parka, so I carry the pack under my arm as I continue upwards.

Despite the initial intense coldness my exertions soon cause me to heat up and I have to stop and take off my jersey and warm shirt. To anyone watching it would certainly look very strange to see a man undressing on a mountainside in the Antarctic. There are alternate steep and easier sections and I have climbed some way before I need to stop for a breather. I'm still finding the shale areas difficult and head off diagonally to try and find more solid rock to climb. I hit an icy patch and start to slip backwards and only manage to arrest my slide by digging my fingers hard into the ice on the slope. I scramble higher over a section littered with large rocks and head for the next snow line.

It's tough climbing and I need to settle into my rhythm to maintain a regular pace. The way of the experienced climber is not to race upwards then continually pause, but to keep going steadily, even if only slowly. Previously I had told Art that I might be back at camp by about 4 p.m., but I am enjoying it so much that I want to keep climbing on further. I stop for another sandwich and drink some of the hot water. I had forgotten the tea bags but I'm happy with just the water. The thermos is big and heavy but it is worth the effort. In these temperatures water starts to cool down rapidly but it doesn't matter. In this rarefied atmosphere it still feels like I am feasting. I am isolated from any living soul and have only myself to worry about. I want to express my feelings and try a shout, then a burst of song but quickly quieten down as I remember the ice and snow could be unstable and a loud sound could trigger an avalanche. I think I could easily keep going for many more hours but realise I'd then have to travel all the way back. It's probably wiser to turn around, whilst I am still feeling fresh enough for it not to become a struggle. Also I mustn't risk the mists and winds suddenly whipping up, making it impossible to find my way.

I've made the right decision. Climbing down is not at all easy. My feet slip constantly and without the ski stick to balance me it would be much more difficult. I cannot see the camp at all as it has become quite misty but I remember the basic direction, although I am all too aware it would be all too easy to veer slightly off course and trek to either side and miss it altogether. This is a place where all ways lead north and a compass would not be of use. That's another reason why pilots out here will only fly when there is reasonable visibility and they don't have to rely on instruments even if the plane is equipped with the GPS system of navigation. It's another reason why the camp is situated in a broad plateau, so can be usually seen easily from the air, provided it's clear enough.

Trekking down into the ice field, it becomes extremely slippery and I have to slow considerably to maintain my balance. The winds are also building up dramatically and often I have to stop and push the ski stick in deeply to avoid being blown over. I am heading straight into the sun, so keep my head covered as much as possible and look down to avoid the intense rays.

Although the ice field seems to go on forever, eventually I see in the far distance the outlines of the three aircraft and then fairly soon afterwards the camp itself. I look back at the mountains but they seem much nearer than the camp and obviously I've still got far to go. I think about radioing for a pick-up but quickly decide against it. I don't want to cause anyone to think twice about letting me go off on my own another time. It's better if I show I can manage.

After trekking a while longer I see a moving shadow on the ice ahead, gradually becoming larger and it turns out to be a ski-doo. The amazing Art once again has come looking for me to see if I would like a lift. Would I! He brings me all the way in right to my tent. It is very lucky for me, as by now the wind has reached blizzard proportions and the whole camp is already half-buried. The sign with the name Byrd has completely vanished and I have almost to dig my way through to find the tent flap. In case they are starting to worry I use the radio to tell Duncan and Rachel that I've returned safely but naturally Art's already done so.

Resting only for a short while, I then go over to the cook tent, Robert Swan is there on his own and we can chat more quietly. He is an extraordinary character and has wonderful ideas and is also doing such a lot to help underprivileged children. He writes in my notebook, 'Excellent to see you South on 1 January on return from the Heart of Antarctica. I salute you. Robert Swan.' From one such as him that's a tribute indeed! He even agrees to sponsor me for my Red Cross fund-raising. I am feeling more than a little down however. The weather is so bad that it's looking even more doubtful there will be any chance of going to the Pole tomorrow and who knows when it might improve subsequently. In his inimitable fashion Robert bucks me up, we have some drinks to toast Britain and each other, and he explains that the weather can change in almost an instant. As Michael Palin of Monty Python fame (later to travel to the Antarctic himself) would say, 'Always look on the bright side of life.' They are both right of course and my own mood quickly brightens; it's definitely time for more music.

After another sumptuous dinner prepared by the inventive Fran and Ros (perhaps they could have a TV series called *Two Snow Women*), amazingly the weather suddenly improves and Max actually starts talking of the possibility of going tomorrow, 2 January. That would be 3 January, New Zealand time, at the Pole. I can hardly countenance it but I certainly don't intend to look a gift horse in the mouth and accept his change of attitude with alacrity. I spend the next hour with Max discussing the arrangements and what we can expect. Ian is not convinced and would prefer to wait for what the next day brings but I refuse to allow the possibility of not going to be discussed and I try to make it a fait accompli. Outside that is, inside I bury my own doubts into a deep, hidden recess.

Duncan Haigh gives me the visitors book to sign. I read the names of many explorers who have been here before me; including the versatile adventurer Ranulph Fiennes, the mountaineer Rob Hall who led me in Irian Jaya, the explorer David Hempleman-Adams, Norman Vaughan who signed it when he revisited the Antarctic in 1993. That last visit by Vaughan was when the DC6 crashed and all the huskies escaped. There are so many fascinating entries and signatures in this book but I tell Duncan that I would prefer to sign after I've reached the South Pole. He understands.

Chapter Thirteen

Throwing a Wobble

I sleep fitfully and half wake several times but try to fall asleep again. Suddenly I am wide awake, thinking I have overslept, it must be late and I might have missed my chance of trying to reach the Pole. My watch only shows 1 a.m., I guess the battery has failed because of the cold and therefore it could be any time. I dress in a great hurry and dash over to the cook tent. The large clock on the far wall also shows 1 a.m. and I feel relieved but more than a little foolish. Only Robert Swan, Duncan Haigh and Lorna Doone are still there and they have obviously been drinking steadily for several hours. Robert waves me over to join them but I make some excuse and beat a hasty retreat. Back to Byrd and bed again and this time I sleep soundly.

I'm up and dressed again at 8 a.m. and once more rush to the cook tent. This time it's full of people eating breakfast and I move to join them. Before I sit down someone quietly announces that Max has decided that the weather is good enough throughout the entire flying route to take-off. I hold down my strong to desire to scream out my excitement and try to appear nonchalant at the news. I nod in response, not able to find appropriate words. I have a quick breakfast, just in case it's the last food for a long time. Ian still hasn't showed and I rush round to his tent and tell him to get ready urgently. He's more cautious than myself and is not prepared to believe it without reservations. Leaving Ian to dress and pack I urge him to hurry whilst I set out to find Max.

Of course Max is with his beloved Cessna, making last minute checks and the necessary preparations. He is relaxed and cool but now very much the pilot, the man in charge. I help him fill the fuel tanks and he tells me to get all my gear together, including my sleeping bag. We must be prepared for any emergency and take everything we could possibly need in case we have to land suddenly and wait for a rescue. The total journey there is approximately 1,000 km. We will need to take all the necessary provisions for the journey itself and Max will organise the emergency equipment and rations in case of a forced landing. Max tells me we fly the first leg across some mountain ranges to the refuelling base of White Fields. It's necessary to fill up the tanks again as they are so small and can't get us much further. That's always the procedure; Patriot Hills to White Fields (85 °S), refuel, then final leg – White Fields to the Amundsen-Scott Base Station (90 °S). Just the name itself sends a thrill charging through me. I could almost have kissed Max I'm so happy, but that would have probably changed his mind and I don't let him see how excited I am.

I race round to the cook tent and find Ian eating an enormous and leisurely breakfast – he's not prepared himself in any way. I force him to finish quickly and go back to his tent to get his stuff together. Fran, bless her heart, is already preparing our food and drink for the journey in three separate packages and will have everything ready when it's needed. I zoom back to my tent and prepare my own backpack including my sleeping bag and anything else I might need. I don't forget to put in my lucky Kenyan safari hat (wearing it always reminds me of Slim Pickens in *Dr Strangelove*, when he's riding the atomic bomb after the mechanism fails and he's waving his cowboy hat and hollering crazily). I'm hoping I won't need to repeat that wild scenario as we descend to the South Pole but I can certainly feel the adrenalin already flowing. I round up Ian and the food packages and we rush over to the Cessna. I'm trying to get us off the ground before anything occurs that would prevent us from going. Steve, Ann, Lorna, Rachel and Art have come to see us off. But where is Max?

They guess he's at the Met tent checking finally on the weather and we all must wait, me very impatiently, until he returns. There's just no way of telling from his facial expression what his decision is. I raise an eyebrow as I can't trust my voice not to give me away and Max nods, 'Let's go.' He starts to load our backpacks and asks Ian why his is so light – Ian has forgotten to put in his sleeping bag. It's the first time I have ever seen Max angry, shouting out how every item is essential and this is not a picnic and we must prepare for the worst. He almost seems prepared to cancel the trip. Ian reacts just as angrily and it's a tense moment. I try to smooth everything down and run to Ian's tent and find his sleeping bag and hurry back with it and Max stuffs it impatiently into the back of the Cessna with our other packs.

The Cessna normally seats four, the pilot, the co-pilot and two passengers. However, as we are flying over such a desolate, barren wasteland we must carry on board a whole host of survival and other items. These include a 2/3 person tent, food for 18 days for each person, an ice saw and shovel, emergency locator beacon, several flares, portable radio, life vests, first aid kits, mats, and signal mirror. That's apart from our own extra clothing and our sleeping bags. Because of these emergency items one seat has been removed and Max will fly without a co-pilot. That seems a little precarious but at this stage I'm not going to comment on anything; Max is still looking a little frazzled and any query or criticism might be enough to cause him to cancel. Ian, as the biggest person by far, offers to sit in the rear with the equipment but I volunteer for the first leg and quickly scramble in.

We strap and buckle ourselves in and it's a tight fit. Max starts revving the engine and hands us ear cans to help muffle the heavy droning. The chocks are taken away, Max taxis the Cessna to the short runway and before I can even think about it we are airborne. It's 10.30 a.m. here and this would be 3.30 a.m. New Zealand time, actually the next day at the Pole. Max circles once round the camp, briefly flies around Patriot Hills and then we are heading deeper south, across hundreds of kilometres of ice and snow wastes towards our destination.

The plane has a GPS but Max feels it's not too accurate and needs adjusting. Anyhow he is confident he knows the fastest and most direct route. We fly around the Goodwood Mountains and pass three small peaks, jutting out of the snow like sails and naturally called The Three Sails. It's so thrilling that my heart is pumping; I am on the way to fulfilling the dream of my childhood! A triumphant song from the musical *Sweet Charity* comes into my mind, sung in the film by Shirley Maclaine, 'If they could see me now!' Max turns to give me a quizzical look and I wonder if perhaps I have started singing it out loud. I beam back and he gives me the thumbs up.

It's 1400 hours GMT and Max turns on the BBC World News. India has asked two US diplomats to leave Delhi, accused of spying; Pakistan has arrested one of Benazir's Bhutto's ministers; a bomb has exploded in Damascus resulting in heavy casualties; social benefits have been taken away from drug users in the US. We fly on and the weather is just perfect so we can see in all directions for kilometre after kilometre. Max checks the radio all the time to find out the weather conditions and warns us that it could still change for the worse. If that occurred we would be forced to abort the flight and turn back. I refuse to countenance that possibility, the longer we fly on the more likely it is that we will make it and go all the way. There are huge rock and stone formations and it's all too clear why Max needed to wait for very clear conditions and would have been worried to chance it otherwise. Without a co-pilot the total onus and responsibility is on him as both Ian and myself have no experience of flying small aircraft, although both of us have flown in Cessnas and Twin Otters before. We are flying pretty close to the ground, sometimes I think too close. However, Max has done this flight so many times that he knows exactly where and how to fly. All he needs are low winds, good visibility and he will fly us there safely. I begin finally to relax. I feel very confident in his hands and am begin enjoying myself immensely. I tap Ian on the shoulder to see if he is as happy and he gives me a big grin in response to mine. We fly over Mt. Goodwin. It's an incredible sight.

On the hour Max turns the news on again, 1500 hours GMT. The bomb in Syria has killed 15 and injured 30; Tanzania has arrested refugees from Rwanda and sent them to Zaire; Serbia's local elections have been cancelled; there's an EEC meeting in Vienna; a Russian oil tanker has broken up off coast of Japan; the father-in-law of Benazir Bhutto has been arrested in Karachi. It's surprising how, in so many ways, the news never seems to change, it could almost relate to any year of several decades as crisis after crisis continually recurs. If everyone had an opportunity to visit the polar regions, once in a lifetime, perhaps it would help to get more of a balance on things and everything would be more tolerable. It's another dream but one I'm prepared to hang on to.

Max tells us we are shortly coming in to land at White Fields and to be prepared. He asks me to look out of the right window at the ski attachment and to let him know whether I can see anything. I don't know what I'm meant to be looking for but it seems alright to me. Max then asks if the ski is wobbling but again I can't see anything amiss. I don't enquire why he is asking but continue to stare at the ski, wondering if perhaps it's suddenly going to drop off. I guess there must be some problem with the left ski attachment but think it prudent not to ask any questions. We are flying very low, practically skimming the ice and then with quite a bump, followed by a series of smaller ones, we touch down. The skis seem to have held and Max skilfully brings the aircraft to a standstill. It's 1.20 p.m., almost three hours since we left Patriot Hills and we've been flying straight south for 480 km.

We unbuckle and dismount quickly. It's so cold, the coldest I've ever known, and although we have everything on the bitter winds cut right through. I doubt we could survive very long here. Yet again I marvel at the strength of mind and body that polar explorers need to have in order to endure conditions of this extreme cold intensity. Max impresses on us how important it is to do everything very fast as the bitter cold can cause all sorts of problems, particularly affecting the engine. In fact the first thing we have to do is to drag from the hold a huge tarpaulin to cover the engine, to help prevent it freezing up.

Now we have to deal with the ski problem he had noticed. The left one has developed a wobble and he was worried it might have run askew when we landed. If that had happened the likelihood would have been that we couldn't take-off again and would have had to wait for a rescue flight to come for us. It doesn't sound too promising and I take a good look around at the White Fields refuelling base. I am not certain what I had been expecting, certainly not soft drink or Coca-Cola machines but at least some kind of hut or shelter. There is absolutely nothing. Just a vast expanse of absolute whiteness. Really just huge, white fields of snow and ice, with about thirty large drums, presumably filled with fuel.

Max has no time to indulge my reverie. He needs me to help him correct the wobble. His plan doesn't seem very scientific. He intends to reverse the ski and hope that this will sort out or at least lessen the wobble. He shows me the fitting. It's actually quite extraordinary but the attachment is only held on with a small, twisted, wire pin. Max will lift the ski off the ground to relieve the weight whilst I untwist the pin. We will then reverse the ski and I am to put the pin back through the tiny hole and fasten it again. The wire is so small that I have to take off my mittens and gloves to undo it, turn it and then organise the refastening. I am terrified I might drop it in the snow where it would vanish without trace. My hands are absolutely freezing but somehow I manage it and Max declares himself satisfied.

Now the three of us walk across the airstrip to the fuel drums, select a full one and push and pull it close to the Cessna. It's enormously heavy. The drums have been dropped previously, probably from a Hercules, for refuelling by the small aircraft that can't make a long flight without taking on board extra fuel. The cap of the drum is completely frozen solid and Max uses a hammer and chisel to break the top open. He takes a refuelling tube, attaches it to the drum and then clambers on top of the Cessna to insert the other end into the opening leading to the fuel tanks. Max has to stay there to make certain the tube doesn't jump out. Ian and I jointly or in turn pump the fuel through the tube. It's exhausting and laborious work and takes about half an hour. There are two main tanks that take 108 kg (240 lbs) each and two small auxiliary tanks of only 5.5 kg each for emergencies.

After Max closes the second tank, he climbs down and stores the refuelling tube in the hold. We then have to drag the mostly empty drum, although it feels just as heavy, away from the aircraft so we can safely take-off again. Hopefully. We remove the tarpaulin from the engine, hastily fold it into the hold and climb aboard. This time Ian sits at the back and I am in the co-pilot seat. We buckle up and Max turns the engine over. It fires immediately, huge sighs of relief escape from Ian and myself and within seconds we are again airborne and on our way. The South Pole awaits us!

Chapter Fourteen

Amundsen and Scott Stood Here

We are flying over really magnificent scenery and I am still amazed that there are mountains so far south. I had somehow imagined there were just vast expanses of ice in all directions, yet here there are mountain ridges and valleys, all kinds of shapes and wondrous colours. But above all it's a glorious, white world and it seems that we are the only ones in it. I look down at the rolling contours and can imagine the tiny teams of intrepid men and women who have striven to cross the Antarctic and find their way to the South Pole. Their courage was and is so immense that it is no wonder so many have dreamed of following in their heroic footsteps, yet so few have actually managed to. More than ever I acknowledge Robert Swan's tremendous efforts in becoming the first man to walk with his colleagues to both Poles; how supreme of Ranulph Fiennes together with Mike Stroud to walk for hundreds of kilometres across the Antarctic and how much they and the others have achieved.

Because of the clarity of the air the mountains seem nearer than they are and knowing this, Max has to concentrate all the time to make certain that he doesn't actually fly too close or in the wrong direction. Inside the plane it's not apparent how strong the winds are outside and they can gust with such strength that they could certainly force the small plane into the rocks. Needing to concentrate so intently it's difficult for Max to operate the radio as well as fly. He asks me to radio to Patriot Hills to ask for another weather report. I connect through and ask the operator who is manning the Met tent for the latest weather conditions and what's it like at the Pole. I hold my breath, almost praying that it won't be adverse news that could prevent us continuing. I give an almost audible sigh of relief as the answer is positive. I relay the messages but Max heard anyhow.

The minutes tick by and there's always something wonderful to observe; I'm in a constant pitch of excitement as we get nearer and nearer to our goal. We've flown over King Peak and have passed the Thiel Mountains. We're going to make it. There's no way we can turn back now. We are nearer the Pole than White Fields and even in any kind of emergency we will have to go on. If the aircraft develops an engine fault and we need to land for any reason the rescue team will have to, no matter how long it takes, come to find us from the Pole Base itself.

We can see it! It looks so tiny. Suddenly out of nowhere there is the completely isolated Amundsen-Scott Base camp. We, by the grace of Max Wenden, have reached it by flying the 500 km from White Fields, some 1,000 km in total from our base camp. A journey that on foot, using sledges, would have taken us up to two months. It's now about 4.30 p.m., 3 January by New Zealand dating, 2 January by Patriot Hills and United Kingdom dating. What a difference a day makes! Finally I'm arriving at the bottom of the world. My thoughts are immediately transported back to the time of my journey to the North Pole, nearly ten years earlier and the thrill of this moment doubles.

I look over at Max but he is concentrating on the landing. I refrain from shouting out my thanks and disturbing him but Ian taps me on my shoulder and I grasp his hand in solidarity. We are utterly happy to be sharing this unique moment. The ice is approaching fast, the aluminium dome of the camp has suddenly enlarged and it now looks massive. It glints in the reflected sunlight and is like something from a sci-fi comic or a space film. I almost expect to see space-suited people or robots walking stiffly around but at the moment everything outside appears completely deserted. Max, as I've learned to expect, makes a perfect landing, a little way from the camp. He then taxis us through to where there is a variety of many different aircraft, larger planes, DC6s, DC9s, Boeing 727s. He then continues to taxi down the marked runway and parks adroitly in a space, away from the other planes. He wants to make certain that we don't get hemmed in and can take-off without needing to ask anyone to help or to move another aircraft. He obviously knows the score around here and is anxious that we are not seen as a nuisance and requiring special treatment. He has to come back on many future occasions and doesn't want any of the Base managers to think he and future visitors will cause any problems. Once we were travellers of the future but now we are travellers into the past. We are visiting polar history. Max lets Ian and myself off to explore whilst he checks the Cessna and refuels for the return flight. He agrees to look for us and meet us inside the Base building later.

What to do first? There's no argument; we must stand where Roald Amundsen, the Norwegian stood first on 14 December 1911 and Robert Scott, the Englishman on 17 January 1912.

Although, unlike the North Pole, the South Pole is considered to be fixed at a constant point, set as it is on a solid land mass, in reality there is some slight movement each year. The actual, symbolic South Pole post has to be reset annually as the ice slips very slowly towards the ocean, approximately 10 metres each year. This means that the Amundsen-Scott Station is moving imperceptibly and implacably towards the Pole and for one historic year will be right on top of it. The annual marker has to be hammered into ice, which at the Pole is 2,740 metres thick. Of course a large plaque is sited permanently and exactly at the original place reached by both Amundsen and Scott, commemorating their incredible achievement and the amazing courage of these two men and their teams who battled to reach the Pole. Their stories are so legendary I must stand for several moments in absolute silence in acknowledgement of their bravery. I am convinced that their spirits surely must roam this place which I feel for evermore is theirs. I am incredibly conscious of the mindset that must have driven them beyond the limits of human endurance, to set foot here. These are precious moments and only the intensity of the wind and the cold forces me from my reverie. I must move on.

First, we take photographs of the exact place where Amundsen and Scott arrived all those many years ago. It sends shivers of emotion shooting through me. I try to imagine their very different feelings, one full of joy and triumph, the other of despair and defeat. Both such extraordinary men. Ian and I then photograph each other and the historic Amundsen-Scott plaque inscribed in their honour. Nearby, there is a small post with a mirrored globe on top, allowing the photographer to capture his or her own image in the reflection. It was left there by the first scientific director of the station, Dr Paul Siple. Then we go over to the thin, striped pole which commemorates the actual position of the Pole this year.

Now to enter the base itself. A structural feat of incredible engineering and design, against almost insurmountable odds. As we make our way across to it we pass one or two men or women, it's very hard to tell which, they are so muffled and overdressed and we wave greetings. They respond but do not stop. Naturally no one spends more time outside than they have to and they are hurrying to do whatever duties they must carry out, before returning inside. Actual time often has little bearing here, particularly when it is mostly permanent daylight. Sometimes though the mists descend and blot everything out of sight. Then only in absolute necessity does anyone venture outside and leave the gigantic mole-like burrow built into the bowels of the ice. It is still early in the morning and most people are in their rooms and probably haven't wandered out to eat or to deal with whatever their work duties are.

The Dome is constructed from geodesic aluminium, 50 metres in diameter at the base and approximately 17 metres high at its apex. The entrance is down a long, gloomy ramp, walking down it feels rather like entering into an underground dungeon or wandering through a set for a sci-fi film. We pass through several sets of doors and coverings designed to keep the cold out and the heat in. There are hot air blowers to provide continual heating. The system works well and soon we start to warm up and need to disrobe our outer garments. It seems almost impossible we are here, inside this structure that continually has to withstand the crushing forces of nature. A twentieth century wonder of the world.

Fortunately we are expected and Wayne Sukow the Base manager, a physicist by training, makes himself readily available to show us around. Previously I had heard that visitors to Antarctic bases were not generally welcome and were looked upon as something of a nuisance, causing too much interference in the daily routines. Often they were not allowed inside, even to use the basic facilities. Still Amundsen and Scott would have 'watered the ice' so anyone also doing the same would be in excellent company. Perhaps my work and connections with the Red Cross have helped, or more likely Max is well thought of as a pilot of grace and discretion. Whatever the reason, Sukow is welcoming and friendly and indeed asks his colleagues to support my fund-raising. Although he was born in the US his family were originally from Poland and again I take this further Polish connection as a sign that he will make a special effort for us and so it turns out. Sukow is very happy to answer all our questions and willing to show us anything we want to see. He tells us the scientists here are often referred to as 'beakers' and there is a whole Base vocabulary which those staying permanently need to learn and use. You can always tell someone who's been based here and is returning. He or she will say 'I'm going to the Ice,' meaning, returning to the Antarctic. 'Boondoggles', a wonderful word to conjure with, is used to indicate those much sought after occasional opportunities to get away from the base.

The Dome houses three two-storey structures which contain the living, dining, recreation and meeting areas, communications, laboratory and scientific facilities. There are all kinds of other rooms and depots containing power plants as well as fuel storage. The Amundsen-Scott Station is supplied entirely by aircraft from McMurdo Station, the largest in the Antarctic. Overall, the base is an amazing place, deeply constructed below the ice, it is an extraordinary feat of engineering and dedicated determination to build a research station at the most isolated spot in the world that it is possible to find. The elements are always threatening to reclaim it and Sukow explains that they need continual maintenance to keep everything operating. There are several back-up systems if one or two break down, as happens more often than one would imagine. Safety is of the utmost concern. One of the greatest dangers, strangely enough, is that of fire. There are fire prevention notices everywhere and constant fire drills. If a fire broke out underground and wasn't checked immediately the consequences could be devastating. In the single and communal living sections there are many notices 'Smoking in bed is not permitted'. I wonder how they keep a check on this! Everything always needs to be under constant supervision and the station is kept on a permanent state of alert.

Working in these ferocious conditions is constantly demanding and those underground most of the time need a great deal of personal freedom and the opportunity to relax. Now of course it is the Antarctic's summer period but in the winter months the weather can become very dire indeed. Sukow says that during the light months the number of people staying here is between 140 and 200 but this drops to 60 when it becomes permanently dark. It's much more difficult to withstand the enormous pressure, mentally as well as physically, for those that have to remain in this specially created sanctuary from the sub-zero conditions of winter that rage above ground. Particularly with the detailed rules and regulations everyone is instructed to follow.

Tempers can become very frayed when people are confined below the ice for weeks and months at a time and there have been numerous (so-called) accidents and injuries. In past years, chefs have been known to chase staff members, waving choppers and knives, if challenged about the state of the food and their cooking. When underground for such long periods it is very easy to lose one's temper or patience and the smallest incident can be blown up out of all normal proportion. Like the weather, nothing here under the ice is predictable or normal. It's all important to be aware of everyone else and to watch for any signs of abnormality. There is an intensity in living underground at the polar cap that is not like anything else on earth. Even with medical facilities readily available and several doctors, nurses and even psychologists on hand, anything can happen. Sometimes it's the doctors themselves who are the ones to crack, as they react against those who constantly come to them with minor or even imaginary problems. One Argentine doctor burned down his country's base to force an immediate evacuation.

At the Russian Base some years ago they even banned chess as being too inflammatory, after one Soviet scientist killed his opponent with an axe. I think surviving in the wilderness can actually be compared to playing chess. The game is mostly in the mind, you must be aware of the whole picture, you must anticipate, adapt, advance and overcome. Recent studies have shown that some expeditioners who have spent a year in the frozen continent display characteristics of returning prisoners of war. My old teacher, Mr Judge would have been able to cope by teaching everyone Latin.

We are led through so many different rooms and facilities that I quickly lose my bearings. I can only wonder at the tremendous size of these man-made underground caverns.

The work involved in maintaining them is obviously a feat of equal immensity. We are shown around one of the scientific research labs and talk to a few of the scientists there. Some of the station's programmes include auroral observation, study of cosmic ray intensity caused by solar activity, as well as continuing ionosphere and meteorological studies. The computer room, or at least the one we visit, is filled with state of the art equipment. Yet it is strangely silent as if the complexity of its machines is self-fulfilling and they need no human hand to guide them. The games room on the other hand is full and pool is the order of the day. They even allow me a few strikes, just so I can tell those more expert than myself that at least I've played at the South Pole. There are plenty of computer games and videos to watch or use in the privacy of one's own room. I am told the record for watching the same video is 90 times. There is also a well-equipped gymnasium, although few use it regularly after the initial burst of enthusiasm. The library has a scholarly presence of its own and there are rows of books relating to Antarctica and travel to other regions of every description. I offer one of my books *On Top Of Africa*, it's accepted graciously and recorded in their visitor records.

We are told that they will be arranging to open the base shop later that morning at 11 a.m. especially for us. This is really great news as we are particularly anxious to buy cards and stamps to send from the South Pole. An opportunity that we are unlikely to have again and therefore not on any account to be missed. Whilst waiting for the shop we are invited to eat in the dining hall, mostly referred to as the galley. This is a revelation. It's roomy with an open kitchen section, where you can have a variety of foods at most times of the day or night. It seems most people settle for junk foods, hamburgers, fries, Cokes, etc but as an healthy alternative there are all kinds of appetising food, including fish, steaks, varieties of vegetables. I am not very hungry but choose an apple pie and tea just to enjoy the experience of eating underground at the Pole. There are various labels everywhere stating DNF. It looks very officious but Wayne lets me in on the secret, it means 'Do Not Freeze'. I am not certain if it's an instruction regarding food or a friendly reminder to the scientists. It reminds me of Steve's, 'KW'. Most people had breakfast here earlier or in their rooms but many others still drift in and out all the time. It seems one of the pleasures is taking advantage of the round the clock facilities and the chefs seem willing enough to respond to whatever is requested.

Water, or the lack of it, plays the same importance here as at Patriot Hills. It still has to be produced by melting snow and therefore needs to be used carefully and rationed. Again there are instructional notices strategically placed. 'Showers should be taken no more than twice a week and are not to exceed two minutes of running water' (it's obviously important to shower wearing a waterproof watch). 'The water faucets (taps) are not to be left running while you are washing hands or brushing teeth.' One imagines secret cameras spying on those showering or cleaning their teeth and these rules must add to the strain of living here. The waste that arises is thrown into a large septic tank and then freeze-dried naturally. Eventually it has to be transported out to a waste treatment plant. That's why visitors are encouraged to show self-control and not to use the station's bathrooms and toilets. I guess it's either a matter of concentration or of constipation. Most people

I meet seem to be carrying more weight than is perhaps advisable. I guess that the routine of living the whole day in this very restricted place must impose tremendous personal strains, eating certainly would be one of the ways to ease the pressure. There are other ways of course and I enquire about the sleeping arrangements. There are a variety of bedrooms, some single, some double and others with communal bunks and beds, to suit every inclination. Sukow suddenly goes coy and switches the conversation. He explains that it's rare to spend more than two seasons out here. Everyone misses the freedom of living in a city or town where it's possible to catch a train, take a bus, or just go for a walk. Most people don't realise what it's going to be like living in such a relatively cramped environment and often become quite shocked after the first week or two. They start counting the days until their term finishes. Some can't take it and have to leave earlier.

Sukow mischievously asks whether we would ever consider joining the exclusive 300 club. It sounds rather like the Mile High Club and could be tempting but fortunately it's not really the season. During the summer period, half of November, all of December and January, and half of February, the temperature only gets up to -23 °C (-10 °F). In the winter when the temperature drops below -73 °C (-100 °F), some strip totally naked, step into the sauna heated to 93 °C (200 °F) and then race outside, still completely naked, to the South Pole marker. In fact, rather generously, you are allowed to keep your socks on to stop the ice sticking to your feet. Once at the Pole you can't afford to dally, otherwise you'd suffer more than a loss of pride. During the winter the temperature often gets down to -79 °C (-119 °F), but is the coldest after the sun has set in March. Fortunately at the very lowest temperatures the wind is almost non-existent. In the winter when the wind blows, the wind-chill factor becomes known as 'Don't even dare to venture outside; if you do you won't last more than a few minutes'. It has been said that Scott and his team may have encountered just such conditions in the March of 1912 which were a major factor in preventing them returning. Staff at the station usually find their way around on the outside by remembering which buildings and depots are where. Otherwise, as compasses are of no use, they might lock into the global positioning satellites (GPS) and work out the co-ordinates needed. Visibility can be reduced at times to perhaps a metre and it would be all too easy to lose one's bearings and get lost. Somewhat surprisingly, there are days during the summer when it is possible to work outside in shorts although it needs to be very sunny without any wind. The warmest temperature ever recorded at the Pole was -20.9 °C in December 1968. That still sounds pretty cold to me! The average temperature at the South Pole in July (usually the coldest month) is -59.9 °C.

Although there are no creatures that live at or near the South Pole, the skua bird has on occasion, been seen, having been blown off course by the fierce winds. It's a bird to beware of however, as it will dive bomb anything, human or otherwise in pursuit of food. The poor penguin chick stands no chance and is a favourite target. Though the reputation of the skua is somewhat maligned, its willingness to eat anything helps to keep the Antarctic clear of those creatures which have died and would otherwise rot and decay. Its full name is the McCormick skua. The skua has a powerful homing instinct. Five were taken to the South Pole, tagged and then released. They all made it back to their nests after a 1,290 kilometre journey over this fearsome and barren landscape. A rather confounding fact is that there is actually another South Pole station. The original one. Now it is buried under the ice and primarily inaccessible. Building commenced in late 1956 and was completed by February 1957. Although it was modified and extended over the years, it was soon realised that it was not large enough and needed too many continuing modifications to warrant keeping it. Construction of the new and existing station started in 1970. Work was mostly carried out in the summer seasons, when new materials and supplies could be relatively easily ferried in. It officially opened for business in February 1975 and the old one closed off forever. A modernisation programme of the station started in 1997 and is expected to be completed in 2005. It's rather an eerie feeling however, knowing that underneath the ice, just metres away, is a ghost station of laboratories, research and computer rooms, living and sleeping quarters, which are empty and vacant. All preserved within their own overwhelming bleakness.

Someone comes to tell us that the shop is open. It's really just a storeroom with many shelves filled with all kinds of items bearing Antarctic and South Pole designs and drawings, even specially labelled bottles of whisky and brandy. I buy some sweatshirts and T-shirts, baseball caps, mugs and toys and various smaller trinkets and gifts. Most of all, lots of postcards and the polar stamps so they can be sent out from here. We are allowed to use the many South Pole special ink stamps that were designed over a number of years. The evocative names include: Amundsen-Scott South Pole Station Antarctica, Antarctic Support Associates South Pole Station Antarctica, Global

Seismographic Network South Pole Antarctica, US
Geological Survey US Antarctic Program, USARP Gravity
Program. They are all interesting and illustrate the
tremendous variety of projects that have been and are being
carried out at the station. Mostly I use the more simple
stamp just with the words South Pole Station Antarctica.
Ian and I quickly start writing out our cards and the pile
grows steadily higher as we remember more friends and
family who should receive a special and unique greeting
from us. Wayne Sukow sees that we are happy to spend our
remaining time here and bids us farewell, as he needs to
get back to his office work. I thank him for his patience
and for giving us such a thorough tour of the base. He give
me his card with his US contact details and offers to respond
to any future queries I might have, especially if I do get
round to writing about my experiences. The store manager
is anxious to close up but we persuade her to stay open a
little longer as we continue to need more cards and stamps.

Max comes to find us and tells us we must plan to leave
now, as it will still take another six hours of flying before
we can arrive back at camp. Just to emphasise that we
shouldn't delay, he tells us that out here a flight which
departs but has to return, due to weather conditions or
mechanical problems is known as a boomerang. Max makes
a threatening circular movement with one hand and we
immediately get the message. Before the shop finally closes
I buy him a new sweatshirt to replace his torn one and a
bottle of malt whisky. He's absolutely delighted. I suspect
he will not wear the sweatshirt until he returns to New
Zealand at the end of the season, but will probably drink
the whisky as soon as we land back at Patriot Hills. I feel
he very much deserves it. We quickly scribble a last few

cards then hurry through the maze of corridors and find the ramp leading to the outside. We pull our parkas tightly around us as the cold air hits us with a huge icy blast. It feels very much colder. We must have got too used to the warm air circulating inside. It's extraordinary how protected everything and everyone is from the cold. The system of interlocking doors works so well to prevent the freezing air penetrating. No wonder everybody is so reluctant to go outside unless there is some essential work to do or repairs to carry out. Max is quite impatient now and almost pushes us towards the Cessna. It's nearly 12 a.m. local time although I've kept my watch on Patriot Hills time which is 17 hours behind Pole time so it shows 7 p.m. of the previous night. It's been at least 9 hours since we set out.

Some last photographs of the base and the evocative posts commemorating previous South Pole expeditions, then it's time to board. Ian is quite happy for me to sit in the front again. I suspect he wants to doze. Max starts to taxi and we are almost immediately airborne. All ways are pointing North, so again he can't use the plane's instrument compass and the GPS system is still playing up. Max is very confident he knows the way and I am quite happy to rely on his judgement. But he's looking tired and clearly we should have left earlier. It's been an extremely long day and he has already flown for well over six hours just to get here, as well as the time spent preparing the plane and fuelling it. He tells us that it will be faster returning as there's a strong tail wind but it means he has to be extra careful on controlling the plane and avoiding any sudden wind gusts. It's all systems go.

Chapter Fifteen

Return From the Bottom of the World

Flying back to White Fields, I keep up a barrage of comments, jokes and queries to help prevent Max nodding off. This time, with following winds, it only takes him just over two hours to reach it and we touch down gently and smoothly. Fortunately no ski wobble occurred this time. We follow exactly the same procedures as the first time; we whip out the tarpaulin to cover the engine, drag over a large fuel drum and Max breaks open the frozen cap with his chisel. Then he connects the fuel rod and climbs on top of the Cessna and inserts the rod that feeds into the fuel tanks whilst Ian and I pump furiously away transferring the fuel across. It's hot and hectic work but I can still feel the acute bitterness of the cold and can see it's also becoming much mistier.

After one tank is filled Max starts to fill the second but stops us after a short while. He tells us he is nervous about the worsening weather and wants to move off as quickly as possible. He thinks we have enough fuel to get us to Patriot Hills and now time is of the essence. He fastens the tank cap, throws down the fuelling rod and it snakes across the ice with a life of its own. I gather it up, roll it together, unclip it from the drum and help him stow it in the bottom compartment. After fastening the broken cap as best we can the three of us push and drag the half-empty drum back to where the others are still standing, almost like Easter Island sentinels. They are also waiting for visitors from the skies. This is not the time to philosophise, at least outwardly, but I can't help thinking about those that have come here before me and those yet to come. What really brings people to this uninhabited and far flung outpost of emptiness? What do they think of it and do they stare, as I do, at this vast white field which will always be, no matter whether anyone visits or not?

There's no more time to ponder about such questions, let alone come up with any answers. Max is in a great hurry and urges me to speed up, we must take off immediately. I pull the huge tarpaulin off the engine whilst he climbs in and turns it over. Fortunately with a sudden roar it instantly catches and starts revving with a healthy vibrancy. I quickly bundle the tarpaulin on top of the rod in the hold and fasten the two catches to close the flapped cover. Ian is already on board and I rush to climb in. Straightaway Max starts the plane moving down the almost invisible, almost flat, tiny runway. I am still scrambling to fix my straps and put on my cans when Max lifts the Cessna upwards and we are flying into the wide blue yonder. Only another 500 km and we'll have made it. I turn round to check on Ian and he is either asleep or giving a very good impression of it. I'm pretty sleepy myself so how very tired must Max be feeling?

I start an incessant chattering and surprisingly Max seems to enjoy the banter and even laughs out loud at my jokes. The mist has cleared and it is completely clear, we can see for many kilometres in all directions. The sky is azure blue with just tiny drifting cloud formations dotted haphazardly across the mountain tops. We are three men in a plane, a tiny Cessna aircraft, alone, flying somewhere within this incredible, vast continent. I peer down at the endless tracts of ice wilderness for any signs of other life but of course there aren't any. Apart from the few intrepid explorers and travellers who trek to reach their special goals, the scientists who research for occasional periods, the support teams and staff, this is a remote place, devoid of permanent human life.

Max again checks into the BBC World Service on the hour, now 2 a.m. The news is as sombre as always; Libya executes six people for treason, the President of Peru condemns the terrorist activity in his country, a bomb explosion in an Arab office in Washington; the Singapore ruling party wins with an overwhelming majority in elections with strike protests. It seems there is only bad or serious news, nothing to uplift a person's spirits. Then I think of myself here in Antarctica and my spirit immediately soars. Everyone should have the once in a lifetime chance to experience this solitude and emptiness that is like no other. The playwright, Samuel Beckett said, 'Nothing is more real than nothing.' I think Beckett and Franz Kafka both understood the Zen concept of nothingness.

I thrust myself back into the moment and watch Max for any signs of increasing fatigue. I look at the fuel gauges and see that one tank is completely empty and the other only about a quarter full. That gives me quite a jolt. Casually I mention this to Max but he does not react or seem perturbed. He states that provided the good weather holds up and there are no major winds driving us off course we have just enough to see us through. I don't ask Max what could happen should either of those situations occur and he doesn't volunteer the information. He radios ahead several times for weather clearance and to announce our position and expected arrival time. He still seems totally in control and I can only admire his strength and determination after so many hours flying. I ask about his photographic work back home in New Zealand and his future plans. He is adamant that above all he likes to stay loose, without being tied down and I guess that his girlfriend Ann will not be able to change his long-established way of life. He's one of the breed of men you often find in remote outposts around the world, men who prefer the isolated, often lonely existence, far away from a city with set times and all the rules and regulations to follow. To Max it will always be his plane first, his photography second and any personal relationship would follow away in third or lower place.

At long last we are finally approaching Patriot Hills, some 18 hours after we left the camp. Of course we have gained back the day we lost when arriving at the Pole Base. It again reminds me of Phineas Fogg in Jules Verne's *Around the World in 80 Days*, when, with his incomparable servant Passepartout, he almost loses the wager by forgetting they had crossed the international date line and gained back 24 hours. It's always possible to use the date line to gain or lose a whole day permanently, but only every 100 years or 1,000 years is it possible to make a major statement for the history books. Captain John Phillips, sailing the *Warrimoo*, on 30 December 1899 at midnight lay her exactly on the equator where it crossed the International Date Line; 31 December then never occurred as the date jumped immediately to 1 January 1900. By travelling the other way of course it's possible to celebrate two New Year's Eves. If a ship crosses the date line at the equator then the bow is in the Southern hemisphere where it is summer, while the stern is in the Northern hemisphere where it is winter. Choosing the right day it's therefore possible for a ship to be in two different seasons, on two different days, two different months, two different years and on 30 December 1999 it was possible to be in two different millennia, all at the same time.

I rouse Ian and we both start taking photographs of the Patriot Base and the surrounding mountains as Max does one or two laps of honour before taking us steadily down and making an absolutely perfect landing. We are back! We have been to the South Pole. Thanks to you Max Wenden. Although it's about 4 a.m., Patriot Hills time, several people have stayed up to await our return and to welcome us back. These include Steve, Duncan, Fran and the two Anns. They have champagne waiting to toast us both and have even prepared a hand-drawn sign, 'Congratulations to Neville and Ian'. Robert Swan comes rushing over and gives me a huge bear hug. I look for Max to thank him again but he has quietly disappeared with Ann.

Duncan Haigh again asks me to sign the visitor's book and this time I'm more than happy to do so. I want to write something quite special to record the high emotion I'm experiencing. Luckily the words almost seem to write themselves and after barely a moment's reflection I compose and jot down and sign the following poem (with apologies to Lloyd-Webber and Rice): 'Don't sigh for me, Antarctica. I'll always remember, I came in December. You were the wild one. Was I the mild one? So then goodbye, *au revoir*, *adiós*. You will always be the boss. You offered me all the thrills. One day I will return to Patriot Hills. Love Ever, Hurt Never.'

Chapter Sixteen

A Patriot's Goodbye

I feel supremely happy. I can hardly sleep at all, my brain is racing so. 'What a day it has been, what a rare mood I'm in.' Surprisingly my body dictates to my mind and I'm soon asleep. However, several times throughout the night I wake up, full of confusion, dreams and reality mingling, so I don't have any idea which is which. All I do know is that I have been to the South Pole and achieved one of my greatest ambitions. It was even more glorious than I could have ever dreamed it would be.

I try to sleep more but it proves impossible and I eventually get up around 11 a.m. I don't feel like a late breakfast but everyone is still eating so I take an early and light lunch with Steve and Robert. Of course we only talk about the South Pole and I can share in some small way their own experiences. Ian is still nowhere to be seen and I envy his ability to sleep wherever he is and for such lengthy periods. Robert has to get back to Punta as soon as possible to rejoin his UNICEF ship and is anxious to carry out further training sessions with the young children on board.

Another Hercules is expected in the afternoon, this time with a very full contingent of travellers, some to go to the South Pole, others to attempt Mount Vinson, some just along for the ride and to experience the magic of the Antarctic. All the tents will be needed and everyone will have to double up. Therefore the plan is that Robert, Ian and myself will take the Hercules back when it returns to Punta; Hans and Christian will stay on to have another crack at getting to Vinson and anyhow they have their own tent. There is, however, plenty of time as the Hercules hasn't left Punta yet and of course it will then take three hours to arrive. We should vacate our tents soon though so they can be tidied and prepared for the new arrivals.

I take a long stroll around the camp, sad that this is my last day here and I will be leaving soon. I then go over to wake Ian and suggest he gets something to eat and packs up. He's not so keen on leaving as he has no commitments to rush home for and his plans are flexible. He thinks he could travel through some of the South American countries and that cheers him up and he promises to get ready. I go back to Byrd, probably for the last time, and start to pack. With all my purchases at the South Pole store there's not enough room in my bags and I try to decide what to leave behind. I decide to donate my boots to the camp, to help any others who might want to ski but don't have ski boots with them. They are not perfect but will do for someone who just wants to have some fun. Also a few sweatshirts that might come in useful. The straps of my long, white bag have broken and I tie it with some cords and will have to replace it when we get to Punta.

I carry my two bags back to the cook tent, only to learn that the Hercules still hasn't left and as usual the weather is playing up. They don't know when or if it will take off today. It means we could be here for another day or more. I'm not certain how I feel as I have committed myself to leaving and it's unsettling not to know what's happening. I always feel the same on every expedition. When it's time to go, no matter how much I've enjoyed myself, no matter what I've learned and experienced, when it's time it's time.

Ian is eating something and is unperturbed, he still hasn't packed and is quite happy to stay on.

Originally the Hercules was meant to arrive here well before 4 p.m. but it reaches 1 p.m. and it still hasn't even taken off. That remains the position for the next two hours. It is looking more and more as if it won't fly out today. We sit around drinking endless cups of tea and coffee, discussing possible scenarios when the news suddenly comes through that it has taken off and will land at 7 p.m. There will need to be a fast turnaround so it can take off again at 9 p.m., otherwise, because of the situation at Punta, it might not be able to leave until the next day.

I urge Ian to pack everything and bring it across so they can get his tent ready for the newcomers. After yet another slice of toast and more tea his huge frame ambles off to do just that. Duncan and Lorna come in to announce that Lorna is also to return with us. Her eyes are red rimmed and I don't know whether it's just because she is leaving Duncan or for another reason. I had expected she would stay on longer and perhaps she had as well.

I know that when the Hercules arrives everyone will be very busy welcoming the new arrivals and sorting out their arrangements, so spend the next two hours saying goodbye and offering my thanks to all those who have made my stay so special and interesting and have been so helpful. I set out to look for Hans and Christian and find them, as ever, sunbathing. They don't seem any browner than when they first arrived. I wish them good climbing and they beam back and seem to be unconcerned at how long it's taking for them to get started. Then I seek out Max and perhaps it's his way of saying something but he's wearing the sweatshirt I bought him. He looks quite dashing in it. He's with his girlfriend Ann, and I wish them lots of luck together especially when they return to New Zealand. (Unfortunately my surmise that they wouldn't stay together is borne out when some time later I get a note from Max and he tells me Ann is back in England.)

I know the kitchen will soon be working flat out, so next I spend some time with Fran and Ros to thank them for feeding me so well and being so supportive. Finally it's time to thank Steve. He's more than 'quite a guy' and I hope we will stay in touch and meet up, although he has itchy feet and is likely to spend most of his time abroad. When he's back in England he lives in Cornwall and is a neighbour of David Cornwall, better known as John Le Carré, one of my favourite spy authors, my particular favourite is *Tinker, Tailor, Soldier, Spy*.

We can hear the Hercules approaching and now it's bang on time, 7 p.m. My luggage has already been taken out to the airstrip ready for immediate loading and I grab a lift on a ski-doo to see if I can help with unloading or anything else. It's certainly a big crowd coming in and I'm pleased for Annie Kershaw. The airstrip looks chaotic with drums and containers and sledges everywhere and huge piles of baggage. However they have it down to a fine art and as soon as the Hercules disgorges all the people and the final loads, everyone swings into action and our smaller luggage is taken systematically on board. I counted 25 people coming off. Annie is actually with them and tells me she has just come back from South Africa where she is starting up another travel company. She will also set up camp out here at McMurdo Sound, the biggest Antarctic base after the South Pole. Annie is a very nice but rather feisty, petite Scotswoman who I understand rarely has time to come to inspect the camp. I can't help but notice how everyone is very much on their toes when the boss is around.

I chat to some of the new arrivals and am able to give them a few pointers and explanations and tell them what a marvellous treat awaits them. They are so excited and I can enjoy their anticipation. It seems that most on this trip are going to attempt Vinson rather than try to get to the Pole and I feel I shouldn't tell them about the difficulties Hans and Christian have had. A few ask me to take photographs of them with the Hercules but mostly they are anxious to get into camp and set off trekking across the ice. One woman crashes over but is quickly on her feet and sets off again. It looks as if half at least are women and it's wonderful how climbing has become as equally interesting to women as men.

Final goodbye time and it's better to go quickly. It's painful leaving. One day I will return to the ice. Just a few more waves then Lorna, Robert, Ian and myself board. Lorna is now very tearful. Dr Ann Ward has followed us on board and I am surprised to see her as we'd already said goodbye. Unfortunately, it transpires that one of the women passengers is still on board as she's suffered some heart pains. However, she is adamant she wants to disembark, has pills to take and feels she will be alright shortly. It seems better than sending her back on a five or six hour flight so Ann agrees to take her off. It's not a great way to start a trip in Antarctica but hopefully she subsequently recovered well and the rest of her time was more enjoyable and less eventful than the way she arrived.

We take our last photographs before the back hatch is closed and the Hercules taxis down the ice runway and takes off with a great whoosh into the air. As when we came, the few of us are like peas in a giant pod and there's so much room we can all take a row each to stretch out. There are no announcements of safety instructions and it's up to us to use the seat belts or not.

The steward, if that's his title, brings round an enormous bar of chocolate so I break off a chunk and that's the in-flight service. As before there's a table at the back with cheese and tomatoes and bread. I bite into a tomato and the juice shoots out in a vivid stream. It creates its own fashion statement but I still have to remove it with some elbow grease. The artist Matisse was once asked by Gertrude Stein, the poet, whether when eating a tomato he looked at it the way an artist would. Matisse replied, 'No, when I eat a tomato I look at it the same way anyone else does. When I paint a tomato then I see it differently.' When I clean the tomato stain I see it differently as well.

Robert is as ebullient as always and we chat away about our past adventure activities and our future plans. Every so often he gives me a bear hug and shouts out at the top of his voice about my being at the North Pole, when he was trekking on his record breaking way there and now we've met in the Antarctic, after my journey to the South Pole. Perhaps it doesn't read as unique on the page but we are pretty hyped up by that point and it sounds very magical to us. Due to the engine noise we are all wearing earplugs so fortunately no one else seems to hear or is disturbed.

I remember every moment, falling on the ice, climbing up the mountain ridges, standing at the Pole. We gradually quieten down and the memory of being in Antarctica becomes everything. 'To a mind that is still, the whole world surrenders.' The lack of sleep starts to catch up with all of us and Ian is first to go, then Robert, then Lorna. First of all I want to take some photographs of my sleeping companions and some last ones of the Antarctic out of the portholes, then finally I also surrender.

Chapter Seventeen

Kissing the Big Toe

Landing is suddenly upon us and this time we are asked to fasten our seat belts. It's about 2 a.m., 4 January, South American dating. Fay and Sue are bravely waiting for us out on the tarmac and we quickly load our bags into the transit van they have brought to fetch us. First we drop Robert off at the Hotel Condor, he and I agree to meet tomorrow and then they take me to the original hotel I'd booked into at the beginning, Hotel Jose Noguiera. I say my goodbyes to Ian and Lorna who are staying separately at Hotel Cabo de Hornos and we promise we will keep in touch. It's now around 3.30 a.m. and at my hotel I quickly undress, fall into my roomy and very comfortable bed and snuggle between delicious, clean, white sheets. What absolute luxury!

I'm asleep in a moment and don't wake until 10 a.m. In his hotel I guess Ian will still be sleeping as he doesn't have to leave today as I do. I slowly shave, with gorgeous, instant hot water and shower for at least 20 minutes. I find the cleanest of my dirty clothes to wear and try to repack despite the fact that my white bag has totally collapsed. Somehow I cram everything into my hand luggage and the remaining large case although one wheel has broken off and one lock won't shut. Robert turns up to have lunch with me and I leave my baggage in the lobby as I'll have to take off for the airport immediately afterwards. We ask the reception manager for restaurant suggestions but fortunately he is interrupted by another guest, Cecilia

Fletcher, a beautiful Chilean woman living in New York, who recommends Solito's Bar on Calle O'Higgins. The Irish have the ability to get everywhere! Bernardo O'Higgins is honoured throughout Chile as someone who has contributed extensively to Chilean interests and many streets and places are named after him. There is even a special Order of Bernardo O'Higgins which is awarded to distinguished international personalities. Following the directions across town is like walking through a crazy nightmare. I'd forgotten how strong the winds were and that this is certainly the windiest city in the world. I am nearly blown over several times and sometimes I have to run to stay upright. The winds cut into us so sharply that it is incredibly painful. Everywhere you look people are struggling to move slowly forward. One lady is using sticks to help her walk and her husband is trying and only just succeeding in keeping her from falling over. You don't seem to see any old people in Punta Arenas as there is probably no way they would survive.

Eventually we make it into Solito's. At first it doesn't seem like much, but there is no way we are going to move from here without some food to give us strength to fight through the winds again. The waiters are courteous and old-worldly, dressed in dinner jackets and wearing black bow ties. Robert orders several gin and tonics but I stick to red wine although he joins me in helping to drink the whole bottle. We have an excellent meal, huge steaks, plenty of delicious fries and in the middle of the meal the lights suddenly go out due to the sheer force of the wind; it obviously happens here often. They bring us candles although the wind still reaches through and starts them spluttering. I'm worried the darting flames will catch the curtains that are also blowing loosely around us. We talk about children, he has one and I have three, and about the problems that so many young people around the world face without adequate facilities, education or resources. We both share a deep interest in trying to help children have better lives.

Somehow this leads me on to some stories told to me by Val Doonican, the British ballad singer. He told me these stories when we were both working in the BBC and he had one of the most successful weekly TV shows. Val had an alcoholic father and was part of a large, very poor Irish family. As a young child he had no shoes and eventually it came to his turn to be bought a pair. His mother, who had to control the family monies, gave an amount to his father and told him to take Val to the shoe shop in the High Street. His father took him to the shop and told the assistant to give him a pair of boots, one size larger than he needed, as was the custom in those hard times. He then told Val not to move and to wait there until he returned. He didn't return and eventually, when they were closing the shoe shop, Val was forced to leave. As he did, so he saw his father leaving the pub opposite, staggering blind drunk across the road without looking, then immediately being hit by a speeding car. There was blood everywhere and the young Val ran home as fast as he could and told his mother, 'I've just seen Dad being killed by a car.' She didn't respond in any way or do anything but made him sit down and eat his dinner. Val did as he was told while his mother continued with her ironing. Some hours later his father appeared, covered in blood, in a horrific condition. His mother didn't say a word but just put his dinner in front of him and he sat down to eat it. That was the very tough upbringing that in those days so many impoverished Irish families took for granted. These are stories that shouldn't be forgotten.

I follow that very sad story of his early family life by telling an even more painful one occurring just after Val had married, and he and his wife had just had a baby girl. He was still trying to achieve success as a singer and sang at any club in order to earn a small fee. Val was about to go out for a gig (a singing engagement) and, as always, went upstairs to kiss his daughter goodnight. To his absolute horror he discovered she had somehow suffocated in her cot and died. He just didn't know what to do but finally telephoned their doctor from the upstairs phone to come over immediately. His wife kept calling up to him to hurry or he'd be late and he kept calling out excuses saying he'd be down shortly. When the doctor arrived, together they told his wife the tragic news and, completely devastated, she collapsed with shock. Then, Val says to his shame and he thinks about it always, he left the doctor with his wife and went out to the club to continue to sing about romance and love, as they so desperately needed the money he earned there. I explain to Robert that those stories have always had a profound and lasting effect on me and have made me realise how tragedy can strike at any time to anyone. It's a torment that we all can suffer whatever luck and opportunities might come our way. Robert is obviously very moved. It makes him realise more than ever how important it is to understand the sufferings of others and to help children throughout the world. The lights go out twice more during the meal and each time the shadows caused by the flickering candlelight somehow illustrate the depth of the experiences we have both known and the lessons we all need to learn.

After dinner Robert takes me to Plaza de Armas, although generally known as Magellan's Square, where he shows me the impressive, huge, naked statue of Magellan sitting cross-legged on a stone plinth under the words, 'Tierra Del Fuego'. His naked right foot juts out and Robert tells me the legend that if anyone wants to come back safely from their journeys then he or she should kiss the big toe. Robert certainly did before his own epic struggle to the Pole. I make up for my lack of kissing it before I had set out, by kissing it several times, and for good measure all his other toes too. Just in case it was all a dream. We hug and take our leave of each other with tremendous affection; it's part of the icing on the Antarctic cake, to have spent time in Punta Arenas and also there in the white wilderness with Robert Swan, polar explorer extraordinaire.

Chapter Eighteen

Many Happy Returns

At the hotel I am met by Fay and Sue who are waiting to take me to the airport. Right to the very end, as befits an organisation that is operating at the bottom of the world, they are providing a service that is almost out of this world. They are both great and I appreciate their efforts so much. They give me my South Pole certificate and an Adventure International T-shirt and cap.

On the way to the airport we pick up Rebecca Johnston, a film screenwriter also travelling to Santiago. Another coincidence! Becky has written the screenplay for *Seven Years In Tibet*, the world famous epic book written by Heinrich Harrer. The film is being shot in Mendoza, Argentina, after suddenly being denied shooting rights in India. Becky had, one day previously, said *adiós* to her boyfriend who is climbing Mount Vinson; he would have been in the group that were arriving at Patriot Hills as I left. I mention my many contacts with Heinrich Harrer and that he has written a recommendation for my last book, *Zen Explorations in Remotest New Guinea*, printed on the back cover. Even more coincidences then arise; Becky used to work with Ridley and Tony Scott, two film directors with whom I work very closely. As we check in and before we say our warm goodbyes, Fay insists I acquire a Punta Arenas certificate which confirms I have journeyed through the Southernmost City of the World.

At the departure gate there are crowds of travellers waiting to board and it's a mêlée of chaos. There are in fact two flights to Santiago, both leaving from the same gate and within 15 minutes of each other. One is with Lan Chile the other with Ladeco. The people waiting for either aircraft are completely mixed up and there are no announcements on which flight is leaving first. Those without a little Spanish have no chance. They'll probably be there *mañana*. In fact Ladeco is scheduled to go first, then Lan Chile is ticketed before it and those who have their passes are taken on a coach to board. I'm sure that several miss their actual flight. I only work it out by constantly checking at the front desk and not accepting any information given without rechecking several times. Becky just follows my lead and when we are finally asked to board I call her over and make certain she gets on the coach to the aircraft. We have lots to talk about and spend most of our flights to Santiago huddled together sharing and exchanging stories.

We have a short stopover at Concepción and Becky immediately gets up to leave as she thinks it must already be Santiago. I go after her and pull her back and she's very relieved that I'm there. She easily could have got off and missed the continuing flight onwards. As a memento she gives me her special pass to the film set of *Seven Years In Tibet*. I don't have one of my books with me, so give her a Joseph Conrad book of adventure short stories. When we arrive at Santiago airport Juan my driver is waiting, we drop Becky off at her hotel and I continue on to mine. Then I discover I've left my precious McMurdo Antarctic hat on the plane. Hurriedly I phone Ladeco and they promise to find it and have it left for me at the BA check-in desk in the morning. After my earlier experiences I am doubtful, but there's nothing more to do.

The next morning there's luckily still a little time left to explore more of Santiago. I couldn't leave without visiting the Fundacion Pablo Neruda, Casa Museo Isla Negra, once the home of one of my favourite poets. The house was built facing the mountains and is called La Chascona in honour of Neruda's wife, Matilde Urrutia. At first he called it Medusa due to his infatuation with this Chilean beauty with reddish, curly hair, but eventually he decided a more Chilean expression would be more appropriate. Neruda wrote to Matilde, in the way only he could, 'I call you curly my tangler, my heart knows the doorways of your heart.' The bars of the windows have the head of Medusa, as well as the initials of Pablo Neruda and Matilde Urrutia, intertwined with breaking waves; the sea and the elements always moved him to poetic expressions of intense feeling. I pick up several of his books and a line jumps out from one of his many love poems, 'The moon lives in the lining of your skin.' I buy that book of love poems and several others and quickly take a number of photos. The atmosphere of this, his last home, is utterly entrancing but I daren't delay any longer. I'm lucky to find a taxi quickly and it's a rush to the airport to check in, just on time. It's unbelievable but my Antarctic hat is waiting for me at the BA counter. The only stopover is in Rio de Janeiro and to make certain I don't lose it again I decide to put it on. In the sultry heat of Brazil, it must look a little strange to be wearing something on my head proclaiming my connection to the coldest continent in the world.

But some like it cold.

Bibliography

Alexander, Caroline *The Endurance* (1999, Alfred A. Knopf)

Ashcroft, Frances Life at the Extremes (2000 Harper Collins)

Cherry-Garrard, Apsley *The Worst Journey in the World* (1922, Penguin)

Conefrey, Mick and Tim Jordan *Icemen* (1998, Macmillan)

Fiennes, Sir Ranulph *Mind Over Matter* (1993, Sinclair-Stevenson)

Fiennes, Sir Ranulph *To the Ends of the Earth* (1983, Hodder & Stoughton)

Goldsworthy, Andy *Rain Sun Snow Hail Mist Calm* (1985, Henry Moore Centre)

Goldsworthy, Andy *Time* (2000, Thames & Hudson)

Hempleman-Adams, David *Walking on Thin Ice* (1998, Orion)

Holland, Clive, ed. *Farthest North* (1994, Robinson Publishing)

Hooper, Meredith *A is for Antarctica* (1991, Pan Books)

Huntford, Roland *The Last Place on Earth* (1979, Hodder & Stoughton)

Imbert, Bertrand *North Pole, South Pole* (1992, Thames & Hudson)

Keneally, Thomas *Victim of the Aurora* (1977, William Collins)

Lucas, Mike *Antarctica* (1996, New Holland Publishers)

Mackenzie, Vicki *Cave in the Snow* (1998 Bloomsbury)

Mear, Roger and Robert Swan *In the Footsteps of Scott* (1987, Jonathan Cape)

Shackleton, Sir Ernest *South* (1919, William Heinemann)

Swan, Robert *Icewalk* (1990, Jonathan Cape)

Taylor, Barbara *Arctic & Antarctic* (1995, Dorling Kindersley)

Wheeler, Sara *Terra Incognita* (1996, Jonathan Cape)

Author Notes

Neville Shulman has undertaken expeditions to many remote and exotic parts of the world and is a fellow of the Royal Geographic Society as well as a member of the Explorer's Club, the Scientific Exploration Society and the Bhutan Society. He is a writer, author and journalist, specialising in travel, entertainment, philosophy and social issues. He is Vice-President of the NCH Action for Children and supports and works closely with the Red Cross and Kidsactive as well as many other charities.

He is director of the British International Theatre Institute, a member of the UK Unesco Culture Committee, an officer of the Theatres Advisory Council and Vice-President of the Drama Centre. He has written and produced for television, theatre and film and is an editor of Contemporary Theatre Review and a Director of Shepperton Film Studios.

His books include:
Non-fiction
Zen in the Art of Climbing Mountains
On Top of Africa
Zen Explorations in Remotest New Guinea

Fiction
Exit of a Dragonfly